Fault Lines

A Memoir by Meena Alexander

Revised and Expanded Edition

With a New Preface by Ngũgĩ wa Thiong'o

THE FEMINIST PRESS
AT THE CITY UNIVERSITY OF NEW YORK

Published by the Feminist Press at the City University of New York
The Graduate Center, Suite 5406, New York, NY 10016
feministpress.org

Library of Congress Cataloging-in-Publication Data

Alexander, Meena, 1951-
  Fault lines : a memoir / by Meena Alexander ; with a new preface by
Ngũgĩ wa Thiong'o.— Rev. and expanded ed.
    p. cm. — (The cross-cultural memoir series)
  ISBN 1-55861-454-0 (pbk. : alk. paper)
  1. Alexander, Meena, 1951- 2. East Indian Americans—New York (State)—
New York—Biography. 3. India—Social life and customs—20th century. 4.
Poets, American—20th century—Biography. 5. Poets, Indian—20th cen-
tury—Biography. 6. Women and literature—United States. 7. Women and
literature—India. 8. New York (N.Y.)—Biography. I. Title. II. Series.
  PR9499.3.A46Z466 2003
  811'.54—dc22   2003049504

State of the Arts
NYSCA

NATIONAL
ENDOWMENT
FOR THE ARTS

This publication is made possible, in part, by public funds from the New
York State Council on the Arts and the National Endowment for the Arts.
The Feminist Press would also like to thank Mariam K. Chamberlain,
Nancy Hoffman, Florence Howe, Joanne Markell, and Genevieve Vaughan
for their generosity.

Text design by Paula Martinac
Text composition by Dayna Navaro
Printed in the United States of America on acid-free paper by
McNaughton & Gunn

09 08 07 06 05 04 03   5 4 3 2 1

For appa and amma

Contents

Fault
Lines

Looking for Nadu

*I*t is difficult to find words with which to preface Meena Alexander's personal memories. As brilliantly captured in this new edition of *Fault Lines*, the memories are their own preface and introduction to a mesmerizing text culled from a life lived in fragments and migrations, a quest for *nadu* at home and in exile. So much of her life, she tells us, has been motion and flight, the tactics of self-evasion. But the memory is anything but self-evasive; it is more like facing the self. Hers is a life where the present and the past are simultaneous remembrances of each other. Her *here,* in India, Sudan, Europe, and the United States, is both everywhere and nowhere, a life of a ceaseless search for answers where the only certainty is the *qalam* she holds in her hand and with which she stitches together the fragments of her experience to make a healing wholeness. After all, as a writer, she asks, what does she have but the raw materials of her own life?

And what a life! Among the numerous global literary allusions that litter the pages of *Fault Lines* is the figure of Walt Whitman. Like him, she is a poet who contains multitudes and, not surprisingly, the word *multiple* is among the most potent of those that frequent these pages. Multiple religions—Christianity, Judaism, Buddhism, Hinduism—are part of her growing up. She dwells in multiple places she calls home, although quite often they are temporary abodes on her way to elsewhere, crossing borders of geography, culture, and language. India, Africa, Europe, and the United States are her home at different times, but they are also her places of exile from which she longs for home. But which home? Memories of the past and present mingle in her. They are memories of emotional, intellectual, and political awakening, memories of wonder, friendship, and trust but also, painfully, as we learn from this new edition's coda, "Book of Childhood," of betrayal from he who should have protected her.

It shocks the reader, it shocked me, the fact of something startling where one thought one was safest. But what most fascinates is Meena Alexander's response to these memories of betrayal. She is honest in confronting the memories, but there is also power and glory in her refusal to succumb to the negative. She has a friend and a guide in words and language, which give her the power to name the world, even when it is a world of violence, racism, divisions, and traditions that threaten the humanity in her, wanting to imprison her creativity behind barbed wires. Yes, Language is her refuge, but even here, there is no absolute certainty. She dwells in many languages, and which language shall she use to make sense of her many crossings? Malayalam, the language of her Kerala childhood? Arabic, the language of her home in Africa? French and English, the languages of colonial imposition?

She opts for English. But she wrestles with it, appropriating it rather than letting it appropriate her—and one feels, in reading this new edition of *Fault Lines,* that behind the mask of English she is always reaching out to the Malayalam she knows but cannot write. English is the chosen language of her self-expression, but Malayalam houses her being, the raw basis of her art and self-expression. In so doing, Meena Alexander creates a language of astonishing beauty and elegance of thought, which among her many other attributes, like her capacity to juxtapose experiences in times present and past, in locations here and there, is a compelling reason for reading *Fault Lines* over and over again. Beauty, in Meena Alexander, becomes a revolutionary ethic, an ally of unity over division, love over hatred, life over death, hope over despair.

Creative exploration of experience is her real nadu, and this new edition of *Fault Lines* is faultless in its determined refusal to compromise with the truth of experience—even when it startles one in areas that one thought one was safest.

Ngũgĩ wa Thiong'o
Distinguished Professor of English and Comparative Literature
Director, International Center for Writing and Translation
University of California, Irvine
2003

I. Fault Lines

When the time came for her to learn, all the knowledge
from her past lives returned to her, as wild geese in autumn
to the Ganga River.

Kalidasa, *Kumarasambhava* 1:30

To speak means to be in a position to use a certain syntax, to grasp
the morphology of this or that language, but it means above all to
assume a culture, to support the weight of a civilization.

Frantz Fanon, *Black Skin, White Masks*

1. Dark Mirror

What would it mean for one such as I to pick up a mirror and try to see her face in it?

Night after night, I asked myself that question. What might it mean to look at myself straight, see myself? How many different gazes would that need? And what to do with the crookedness of flesh, thrown back at the eyes? The more I thought about it, the less sense any of it seemed to make. My voice splintered in my ears into a cacophony: whispering cadences, shouts, moans, the quick delight of bodily pleasure, all rising up as if the condition of being fractured had freed the selves jammed into my skin, multiple beings locked into the journeys of one body.

And what of all the cities and small towns and villages I have lived in since birth: Allahabad, Tiruvella, Kozencheri, Pune, Delhi, Hyderabad, all within the boundaries of India; Khartoum in the Sudan; Nottingham in Britain; and now this island of Manhattan? How should I spell out these fragments of a broken geography?

And what of all the languages compacted in my brain: Malayalam, my mother tongue, the language of first speech; Hindi, which I learnt as a child; Arabic from my years in the Sudan—odd shards survive; French; English? How would I map all this in a book of days? After all, my life did not fall into the narratives I had been taught to honor, tales that closed back on themselves, as a snake might, swallowing its own ending: birth, an appropriate education—not too much, not too little—an arranged marriage to a man of suitable birth and background, somewhere within the boundaries of India.

Sometimes in my fantasies, the kind that hit you in broad daylight, riding the subway, I have imagined being a dutiful wife, my life perfect as a bud opening in the cool monsoon winds, then blossoming on its stalk on the gulmohar tree, petals dark red, falling onto rich soil outside my mother's house in Tiruvella. In the inner life coiled within me, I have sometimes longed to be a bud on a tree, blooming in due season, the tree trunk well rooted in a sweet, perpetual place. But everything I think of is filled with ghosts, even this longing. This imagined past—what never was— is a choke hold.

I sit here writing, for I know that time does not come fluid and whole into my trembling hands. All that is here comes piecemeal, though sometimes the joints have fallen into place miraculously, as if the heavens had opened and mango trees fruited in the rough asphalt of upper Broadway.

But questions persist: Where did I come from? How did I become what I am? How shall I start to write myself, configure my "I" as Other, image this life I lead, here, now, in America? What could I ever be but a mass of faults, a fault mass?

I looked it up in the *Oxford English Dictionary*. It went like this:

> Fault: Deficiency, lack, want of something . . . Default, fail-ing, neglect. A defect, imperfection, blameable quality or feature: a. in moral character, b. in physical or intellectual constitution, appearance, structure or workmanship. From geology or mining: a dislocation or break in the strata or vein. Examples: "Every coal field is . . . split asunder, and broken into tiny fragments by faults." (Anstead, *Ancient World*, 1847) "There are several kinds of fault e.g., faults of Dislocation; of Denudation; of Upheaval; etc." (Greasley, *Glossary of Terms in Coal Mining*, 1883) "Fragments of the adjoining rocks mashed and jumbled together, in some cases bound into a solid mass called fault-stuff or fault-rock." (Green, *Physical Geography*, 1877)

That's it, I thought. That's all I am, a woman cracked by multiple migrations. Uprooted so many times she can connect nothing with nothing. Her words are all askew. And so I tormented myself on summer nights, and in the chill wind of autumn, tossing back and forth, worrying myself sick. Till my mind slipped back to my mother—amma—she who gave birth to me, and to amma's amma, my veliammechi, grandmother Kunju, drawing me back into the darkness of the Tiruvella house with its cool bedrooms and coiled verandas: the shelter of memory. But the house of memory is fragile; made up in the mind's space. Even what I remember best, I am forced to admit, is what has flashed up for me in the face of present danger, at the tail end of the century, where everything is to be elaborated, spelt out, precariously reconstructed. And there is little sanctity, even in remembrance.

What I have forgotten is what I have written: a rag of words wrapped around a shard of recollection. A book with torn ends visible. Writing in search of a homeland.

"What are you writing about?" Roshni asked me just the other day. We were speaking on the phone as we so often do, sharing bits of our lives.

"About being born into a female body; about the difficulty of living in space."

"Space?" she asked quizzically.

"Really: living without fixed ground rules, moving about so much; giving birth, all that stuff," I replied shamelessly and laughed into the telephone. I could hear her breathing on the other end, all the way from Sonoma County, California; dear Roshni who has lived in Bombay, Karachi, Beirut, Oaxaca, and Boston. And then her gentle laughter.

Even what I remember best, I am forced to admit is what has flashed up for me in the face of present danger, at the tail end of the century, where everything is to be elaborated, spelt out, precariously reconstructed. And there is little sanctity, even in remembrance.

What I have forgotten is what I have written: a rag of words wrapped around the shard of recollection. A book with the torn ends visible. Writing in search of a homeland.

"What are you writing about?" Roshni asked me just the other day. We were speaking on the phone as we so often do, sharing bits of our lives.

"About being born into a female body; about the difficulty of living in space."

"Space?" she asked quizzically.

"Really: living without fixed ground rules, moving about so much; giving birth, all that stuff," I replied shamelessly and laughed into the telephone. I could hear her breathing on the other end, all the way from Sonoma County, California; dear Roshni who has lived in Bombay, Karachi, Beirut, Oaxaca, and Boston. And then her gentle laughter.

2. *Mirror of Ink*

*M*ultiple birth dates ripple, sing inside me, as if a long stretch of silk were passing through my fingers. I think of the lives I have known for forty years, the lives unknown, the shining geographies that feed into the substance of any possible story I might have. As I make up a katha, a story of my life, the lives before me, around me, weave into a net without which I would drop ceaselessly. They keep me within range of difficult truths, the exhilarating dangers of memory.

Kuruchiethu Kuruvilla Kuruvilla, my maternal grandfather, was born in 1881 in Eraviperoor in the princely state of Travancore in India. Three years later in 1884, in his father's ancestral home in Kozencheri just eight miles away, my paternal grandfather, my Kozencheri veliappechan, Kannadical Koruth Alexander was born. In 1892, in the town of Kottayam, twenty-six miles from Kozencheri, my grandmother Mariamma, Kannadical Mariamma was born. She was eight years younger than my Kozencheri veliappechan.

Grandmother Kunju, Elizabeth Kuruvilla, the youngest of my four grandparents, was born in 1894. That made her thirteen years younger than her husband K. K.Kuruvilla, my maternal grandfather, whom I called Ilya. As a small child my tongue could not get around the long syllables of veliappechan, which is grandfather in Malayalam, and the short name stuck. He was not a man overly fond of formalities and so remained Ilya to me.

Grandmother Kunju was the only one of my grandparents to be born outside the princely state of Travancore. She was born in Calicut, quite far to the north, where her father was working at the time. Calicut was in the old Madras presidency established by the British. As a child of seven I learnt that Calicut was where Vasco

5

da Gama first struck land in his quest for India, and that knowledge shimmered, shot through the awareness of where my missing grandmother was born. I call her missing, for she died a month short of her fiftieth birthday, three years before Indian independence, which was also the year of my parents' marriage, seven years before my birth.

Appa was born in 1921 in the ancestral home of Kozencheri. He was baptized George Alexander. In deference to the tug to Anglicize, his family name, Kannadical, was not officially used. Appa was the third child in a family of four children and the only son. Amma was born in 1927 in Tiruvella. She was the only child of her parents. A similar naming pattern held for her. She was baptized Mary and was first was known as Mary Kuruvilla and then after her marriage as Mary Alexander.

The first child of my parents, the eldest of three sisters, I was born in 1951 in Allahabad, in the north where my father was working, in a newly independent India. My sister Anna was born in 1956 and my sister Elsa in 1961. Amma returned to her home in Tiruvella each time to give birth.

In 1956 my father, who worked for the Indian government, had been "seconded" abroad to work in the newly independent Republic of the Sudan. My mother and I followed him in February of that year. I turned five on the Arabian Sea, my first ocean crossing. For the next thirteen years my childhood crisscrossed the continents. Amma would return to her home in Tiruvella, sometimes for six months of the year. The other six months were spent in Khartoum. In 1969, when I was eighteen, I graduated from Khartoum University and went to Britain as a student. I lived there for four years while I was completing my studies. In 1973 I returned to India to Delhi and Hyderabad. In 1979, just married, I left for the United States and have lived in New York City ever since.

My grandfather Kuruvilla was two months short of seventy when I was born. A century short of a single year separates his birth from that of my son, his namesake Adam Kuruvilla Lelyveld, who was born in New York City in 1980. My daughter Svati Mariam Lelyveld, whose middle name comes from that of her great-grandmother Mariamma, was born in New York City in 1986.

Ever since I can remember, amma and I have been raveled

together in net after net of time. What was pulled apart at my birth has tensed and knotted up. Without her, I would not be, not even in someone else's memory. I would be a stitch with no time, capless, gloveless, sans eyes sans nose sans the lot. Lacking her I cannot picture what I might be. It mists over, a mirror with no back where everything streams in : gooseberry bushes filled with sunlight, glossy branches of the mango tree, sharp blades of the green bamboo where serpents roost.

To enter that mist, I put out both hands as far as they will reach. My right hand reaches through the mirror with no back, into a ghostly past, a ceaseless atmosphere that shimmers in me even as I live and move. Within it I feel the warmth of the sun in Tiruvella. I smell the fragrance of new mango leaves.

But my left hand stretches into the present. With it I feel out a space for my living body. I touch rough bricks where the pigeon perched just an instant ago, on the wall at the corner of 113th Street and Broadway in Manhattan—Turtle Island as it once was in a sacred geography.

Moving west, both arms outstretched, I stand against the park wall, at Riverside Drive. The wind from the Hudson River whistles through my body. Thank God, I think, for two arms to bend and stretch, to make a try at living as what we are: crooked creatures that time blows through.

Tiruvella, where amma's house stands, is a small town in Kerala on the west coast of India. There one finds the old religious centers, seminary, graveyards, and churches of the Mar Thoma Syrian Church. Syrian Christian families have house names and Kuruchiethu is the house name amma was born into, my grandfather K. K. Kuruvilla's family name. The old lands are in Niranum where the Kuruchiethu clan, once so powerful, had established its own private church. My grandfather, who was born in 1881, settled, as a grown man, a little distance away in Tiruvella. Buying lands near his wife's paternal home, he built a house with a gracious courtyard and tiled roofs, whitewashed walls and ceilings set with beams of rosewood. The doors and windows of the house were cut in teak, quartered in the fashion of the Dutch who first came to the coast in the mid-century in search of pepper and other precious spices.

When I was a child, the scent of pepper filled my nostrils. When the green flesh around the seed turned crimson, I bit into the sweetness of thin flesh. My teeth grated on the fierce seed within. Yet

I found it strange that centuries ago Europeans had killed our people for this bitter prize. Still a child, I learnt of how the Portuguese—Vasco da Gama and his crew—set fire to an entire ship, all souls on board, as a sign to the Indian princes not to oppose them. Later, well established on shore, the Portuguese conducted an inquisition on the Syrian Christians, torturing believers because they thought them heretics, burning ancient church records inscribed on palmyra leaf, defacing the copper plates.

I learnt about the British and how, in order to consolidate their rule over India, they shot hundreds of unarmed men, women, and children who had congregated for a meeting in Jalianawalabagh; how finally they were forced to leave the country because of the massive nonviolent protests of Gandhi and his satyagrahis. Sometimes in my childhood dreams I saw the whole nation filled with men and women and even little girls and boys dressed in the colors of ripe pepper seeds, arms raised, singing

> Go away, go away Britishers
> or your lips will sting
> your tongues will ring with pain.
> No one can swallow us whole!

Under their red garments, some made of coarse cotton of the cheapest sort, others woven of fine, rich silks, how fierce the people were, just like hot peppers.

From the veranda of the Tiruvella house I had seen men pick the ripe peppers and toss them into baskets and then pour the harvest onto the sandy courtyard till it made a crimson carpet. In my dreams, it was as if that carpet had come alive, filled with people, raising their arms aloft, singing. And high above them was the clear blue of the Kerala sky.

I think of the Tiruvella house, the courtyard, the clear blue of the premonsoon sky, as filled with the spirit of my grandfather. It is where I trace my beginning. Even now, in New York City, I dream of the sparrow and the coil crying together in the guava tree, the blunt knocks of the woodpecker's beak on the day of my grandfather's death. I see the dry holes under the frangipani tree where the cobras crawled, seeking refuge from the terrible heat of noonday.

*

As a child growing up I knew that there were two spots where snakes loved to roost: in the dark welter of shoot and tender leaf at the base of the sixty-foot-high bamboo clump that stands at the back corner of the compound, and in the mound of earth under the frangipani tree whose thick clusters of white blossoms entice the new serpents out of their eggs as surely as music might, played on Lord Krishna's flute. The frangipani tree stands to the left of the compound, in front of the house, not far from the new railway line. The railway line is thirty-four years old but I still think of when it was being constructed, the metallic rails hoisted on the shoulders of working men, set over the wooden sleepers, secured across the fish plates.

I can see the first train that passed on the Tiruvella line. It was a clear, dry night and the stars made silvery tracks, maps of other worlds. I imagined another life, pierced by cold. Restless, gripped by excitement, I could not sleep. A train packed with passengers from Bangalore and Palghat seemed a metallic creature come from as distant a land as that of the stars. I knew the names of Mars and Venus, of the plow and the bear and Orion's belt, stars that my grandfather Ilya pointed out to me as he held me high on his shoulders in the cool night air.

At the first shrill hoot of the train whistle I leapt from under my covers, and grabbed Marya's hand. I pulled her out of the room with me, fretting in her grip till she was forced to free me from the woolly cardigan amma had insisted on, a protection for my chest from the cool night air.

There was a large group of us that night, amma, appa, assorted cousins and guests, servants, ayahs, and my tall, white-haired Ilya. The night before I had watched him shift his books around at the edge of his desk, rearranging a volume of Marx—was it published by the People's Publishing House in Moscow?—opening up his favorite chapter in Gandhi's *Autobiography*. Now he was ready in his khadi kurta and white dhoti, a shawl flung over his shoulders, set to race out with us. He held a palmyra torch straight in front of him and the sparks fell at his feet. Several of the sparks dashed into blackness, just a fraction of an inch away from my bare toes. One sizzled on the skin at my ankle and died away. I felt my hand held tight by Ilya as he ran. He was well over seventy but ran as a horse might in the king's army, or a giraffe, and I raced along with him, a young thing once removed from the original root, a heartbeat skipped. In the darkness he held onto my shoulders. I gripped the metal railings at the level crossing and watched the hot steel thing approach. It grunted and shoved forward and the sparks from the coal that belched in the dark funnel blew in fiery eddies that swirled into the sparks fleeing from our torches.

Chinna, my senior ayah, gasped with excitement. She sucked in her cheeks, blew out her breath. Aminey, her daughter, just my age, shivered in a thin dress next to the bars of the gate. Somewhere to my right, I thought I heard amma laugh, but it was just for an instant and then she fell silent. Thinking back I imagine her biting into her lower lip, pierced by a memory of grandmother Kunju's death.

A train took amma away when she was barely sixteen, to Madras to enter Women's Christian College. By the time another train brought her back, her mother, my grandmother Kunju, Ilya's beloved wife, was already dead.

Years later her cousin Susamma told me: "Your amma wept outside the door of the Tiruvella house, stood at the steps and wept, crying, 'No, I will not enter, will not enter a house where my mother lies dead.' When finally they persuaded her in, she was worn out with tears, shaking in her thin cotton sari."

I wondered how amma found the courage to open her eyes, to look at the bare floor, to look at the bed where her dead mother lay stretched out.

Grandmother Kunju: it's hard for me to think of her even now. To think, in the sense of setting out, clarifying, refining. I could say she is to me as a vein of sapphire buried in a strip of earth, or the shifting aureole of pollen on a champak flower that in another hour will have fallen to the ground. But to free my voice, tell my story, I need to say something else.

I never knew her. And that is the most brutal fact I have about her as she enters me, enters my life. But there are other facts that I have gleaned. She was born in 1894, into a Mar Thoma Syrian Christian family. She was baptized Eli—Elizabeth—the eldest daughter of four, third child in a family of seven children. Her father, George Zachariah of Marathotatil House, came from a family of feudal landlords. He entered the civil service and was named Rao Bahadhur by the British. Her mother, Anna, a spirited lady who was married off at the age of seven and managed a large household, never had any formal education. But great-grandmother had taught herself to read and write both Malayalam and English and in her forties, once childbearing was over, ran a small newspaper for housewives, filled with information about child care, hygiene, and cooking. Grandmother Kunju's three brothers were educated in the Western manner, and two of them were sent to Oxford while the third was groomed to manage the family property. It was different for her sisters. They were married off young, with large dowries, sight unseen, to young men of suitable family. Kunju, however, resisted getting married. She wanted to study further, to be of service, to make a difference. Her parents permitted her. Here now, over a century after her birth, I can only imagine what her struggles might have been like: tears, anger, overt rebellion, the slow, careful understanding her mother brought to bear on her husband's opposition to his gifted daughter's choices. Or was it the mustachioed Rao Bahadhur who said to her, "Go, daughter, go, if you must, be a Savitri, dedicate yourself—but not to a dead husband, rather to the living struggles of a people." Greatly influenced by certain Scottish spinster ladies, missionaries who encouraged her in her quest for independence, she persisted in her studies. She traveled to Madras, she studied further and gained an M.A. in English literature from Presidency College. She joined the YWCA, which was quite active in India in the early decades of the twentieth century. In her work for the YWCA she traveled all over the world, to Peking and London and other foreign places that melded in my head, in a long melodious string of place names.

I saw the photos of her in sari and shawl standing against the Great Wall and its bleached bricks, then, juxtaposed next to it, a photo of her by the Tower of London, smiling, mindless of all the terror that had gone on in there. And she was beautiful, that fact remained with me. All the portraits in the house testified to that: great luminous eyes, perfectly shaped chin and brow, smooth cheekbones, curly hair. When she finally married, having steadfastly refused an arranged ceremony, by Indian standards she was already quite old, twenty-eight, the age I was when I married. She chose a man who was a Nationalist already and a follower of Mahatma Gandhi.

I wonder how it was that she turned, my grandmother Kunju, from her youthful enthusiasm for Lord Chelmsford and his ilk—I recall my astonishment at opening up the album stashed in the spare room in the Tiruvella house and discovering a photo of Kunju demure, elegantly dressed, waiting to receive his lordship on his visit to Madras Presidency—how did she turn from that rough pupa cocooned by colonial ideologies into a full-blown winged thing, dreaming of national liberty? Was it a natural growth in one so sensitive to the needs of those around her, or was it more like an abrupt turn, a mental shock as of weighty waters turning, turning well, like a wheel already set in motion? Was grandmother Kunju's idealism, her belief in the need to serve the people, inculcated by pious Christian devotion, gathered in a fluent motion into the Nationalist enterprise? Was her growing admiration for the goals of the freedom movement and Mahatma Gandhi's calls for nonviolent resistance well knotted into her love for the man who was to be my grandfather?

After her marriage, Kunju's energy fanned out into work for the women's wing of the Mar Thoma Church, for children's education, for famine and flood relief. Her concern with women's education took her into the state capital at Trivandrum where she was nominated to the Travancore Legislative Assembly and became its first lady member. During the early years of the 1930s she was active in campaigns against the curse of untouchability. During the Vaikom satyagraha, the nonviolent action to allow all Hindus to enter the great temple at Vaikom, regardless of birth, regardless of the old curse of the pollution that so-called untouchables were thought to be born with, grandmother Kunju was active, collecting money for the movement, organizing men and women. When Gandhi visited my grandparents' home in Kottayam in 1934, he had spirited discussions with the Christian leaders gathered there, including Ilya and the younger bearded man who was to become Juhanon Mar Thoma, the fifth metropolitan of the church. They debated the rights of missionaries to convert—something to which Gandhi was quite opposed—as well as the need for the Kerala Christians to receive the Nationalist message. Grandmother sat quietly, joining in every now and then. And, when the wizened old leader opened out his hands, she handed him her frail six-year-old daughter.

As Ilya's youngest brother Alexander, old, freckled, and blind, tells it now, she stood there, the wind in her hair, holding out her only child to Gandhiji.

"The lantern shone in her eyes, I swear," my old great-uncle whispered to me. "And the child was laughing, laughing. Kunju seemed a little nervous though. Why? I wonder."

Amma does not recall meeting Gandhiji when she was six.

"Yes, yes, I knew he came to the house. But I was so young at the time. The house was filled with visitors. They poured in through all the doors and often flooded the courtyards too."

The following year when she turned seven, amma was sent off from the Kottayam house next to the old seminary where Ilya was the principal. She entered a boarding school run by two Scottish Presbyterian ladies who bore the surname Nicholson.

Once, when I was growing up in Khartoum and spent long hours preening myself in front of the mirror, amma placed her hand firmly on my shoulder, something she rarely did.

"Know something, mol?"

"What?" I paused, my pink comb in hand.

"Remember Nicholson where I went to school?"

"Uh-huh."

"Well, we never had a mirror in school. Not a single mirror. Can you imagine that? It was to prevent us girls from the sin of vanity." She was smiling a little as she spoke.

"No mirror, nothing?" I was dumbfounded. "Then how did you see your face? How?" I gripped her arm.

"We didn't really. Sometimes we looked into polished metal, or into a pool of water left by the rain. But there were no mirrors at school."

The school, designed for Syrian Christian girls, stands on a hill with flowering trees and well-tended playing fields, two miles from where the Tiruvella house was built. I imagined my eleven-year-old mother snooping around for pools of water in which to find her face, scouting out bits of polished metal in which she could fix her plaits. What would it be like to be in a boarding school where you could never see your face? I could not imagine. Even boarding school seemed hard to think about, but with grandmother Kunju so preoccupied with political work, it had seemed the only way.

Amma's education did not end there. After graduating from Nicholson High School, she left for Madras, for Women's Christian College. There she lived in the shelter of the high walls of the college, enjoying a strict regimen of studies and meals, sedate games of badminton and netball. College was seen as a completion of school, and amma's life in its dark fluid movement of girlhood growth found shelter in Christian institutions for young women.

School and college nurtured her but also cut her away from the daily routines of a parental home and its tight bonds of love. In her later years, in fierce reparation, as if the past might be done over again in the rearing of a daughter, amma brought me and my sisters up in the strict belief that women should stay at home.

"If you ever marry," she told me as I was growing up, "and if you have children, always remember that your role is to be there at their side, at home. It would be wrong for you to take a job. Remember that, Meena, a woman's place is at home, by her family." As she repeated the words over in her soft voice, almost as if she were teaching herself a difficult truth, I pondered the load of pain she had gathered into herself in her quest to live as a woman. And watching her stitch a torn hem, or stir a pot filled with dal, or outside, in the garden stooped in the shade of a neem tree, setting the fragile roots of a marigold into the flower bed, I learnt to love her, to love the slow persistence with which she had learnt how to live her life.

In my rebellion against my mother's advice, in those Khartoum years filled with teenage parties, the writing of explosive poetry, the harsh, addictive throb of desire, in odd moments when my rage against her strictures ebbed away, I tried to understand what it was that made her so stern about a woman's place in the world. Was it because grandmother Kunju's public life had offered her so little time with her only daughter?

Surely, it was amma's bitter longing for her own mother that made her this way. Grandmother Kunju had died an untimely death. She could never return from the grave, draw her lonely daughter to her side, sing to her, smooth her hair, set water to her dry lips as the first grandchild tore through the delicate skin of her daughter's vagina. Did the domestic world give my mother a feeling of safety that she craved? But whenever I have asked her about her own choice of a life, about her feelings for her dead mother, amma has brushed me aside. It was as if a second skin had grown over her mouth, barring her from speech.

I shut the door as tight as I can. Still the room fills with dust. Workmen are tearing up the wood in the hallway. Two weeks earlier a drain in the bathroom had burst, flooding the hallway with rust and corrosives. Dirty water rose several inches high, ruining the woodwork. Now the whole space is being torn up and fixed. I pick up a cushion and wedge it into the crack under the door. I do not need to inhale all the dust of Manhattan.

When I arrived in America in 1979, five months pregnant, newly married to David, whom I had met in Hyderabad, I felt torn from the India I had learnt to love. In those days I was struck by all the differences between Hyderabad and New York. I could not get over how little dust there seemed to be in Manhattan. Then why pack up the vegetables, celery, broccoli, cabbage, in plastic? My own soul seemed to me, then, a cabbagelike thing, closed tight in a plastic cover. My two worlds, present and past, were torn apart, and I was the fault line, the crack that marked the dislocation.

I was filled with longing for an ancestral figure who would allow my mouth to open, permit me to speak. I skipped a whole ring of life and made up a grandmother figure, part ghost, part flesh. She was drawn over what I had learnt of grandmother Kunju. I imaged her: a sensitive, cultured woman; a woman who had a tradition, and a history—precisely what I lacked; a woman who had lived to witness the birth pangs of a nation.

Now I think: what would it be like if grandmother Kunju were alive, intact in all her simplicity and elegance, and I, a dusty tattered thing, ran into her on 113th Street. How would we possibly recognize each other, we who have never met in the flesh? Or if we were to greet each other over tea and sweetmeats, what could we say? Would she be ashamed of me, a woman with no fixed place, a creature struggling to make herself up in a new world? Or would her grace extend to me, the granddaughter she has never seen, who has inherited her slim, slightly arthritic fingers, and labors at this electronic machine, typing out fitful amber letters. What would she say to me, a woman turned forty in the last decade of this century, writing of the world that comes to her in little bits and pieces?

Bits and pieces, I ponder the phrase. My mind moves to stones—broken and whole—pebbles, slabs of granite, pink boulders. Lines from the Egyptian Book of the Dead I first read in Khartoum repeat in my head. I had sought the book out after my visit to the Great Pyramid in Giza, a sullen, grotesque thing of sandstone, massive icon of gravity, crouched over its own inner darkness. I was frightened of the spirits of the dead who inhabited it, and had to be coaxed by appa to enter. Amma, who has always suffered from claustrophobia, waited outside with my little sister Anna. So I entered the pyramid with my father and the Egyptian guide, and let the darkness and the dank underground smell wash into my flesh. For weeks later that pyramid cut into my dreams. The huge stones seemed forged from human flesh, broiled by the desert sun into the melancholy gold of Egyptian sandstone. And out of the stones came voices crying out in Arabic, Syriac, Persian, the words babbling in my head.

In Manhattan the dream recurred and long-lost lines from the Papyrus of Ani repeated in my head. I stumbled over the words: "Be opened my mouth by Ptah, untied the bandages, twice which are upon my mouth by the god of my town...Be opened my mouth, be unclosed my mouth..."

Where was my town? If I could not invoke the god of my town, how would the bandages drop from my mouth? How would I be freed to speak? Far, far from Tiruvella and Kozencheri, Allahabad, Pune, Delhi, Khartoum, far even from Nottingham, on that lovely cold island, the words I had carried around for so long echoed in my inner ear. I wanted to be more than a tympanum, a pale, vibrating thing that marked out the boundaries between worlds. More than a mere line in the dry earth. I wanted to give voice to my flesh, to learn to live as a woman. To do that, I had to spit out the stones that were in my mouth. I had to become a ghost, enter my own flesh.

My earliest years flow back: skin, cotton, wall, mattress, and quilt. The old mattress mender with the blind blue of a cataract in his left eye, hand raised with the metal hook he threaded into the old cotton, puffing up the crushed stuff inside. It needed air, needed to tumble a little before being shut up in the striped ticking. I remember the clean scented mattresses of Allahabad; air so hot and dry it flayed my cheek; dirt, tons of it; the blue, blue glaze of heaven; moisture, sudden moisture.

How misty it all is, water vapor dashing against mirror and bed and bowl. We needed the water ritual to survive the Allahabad summers. Usually the maid did what was necessary, twice a day, as the heat rose from the Gangetic plains. But one night it was appa's job. He got up and fetched a metal bucket filled high with tap water, crossed into the middle of the room, tipped the water out. It hissed on the hot floor, spreading its wet film over the tiles. Bucket followed on bucket till the iridescent sheet of water petaled the stone floor, making lamplight gleam and flower, an unfinished paradise shifting till the whitewashed walls closed where they touched ground, making a pale bud, a vessel in water, rocking a little, a delicious safety, for I knew the light would subside and with it the motion of the water from the bucket. In its wake a heavenly coolness infiltrated the room, pouring through silks and pottery, metals and glass, and our human skin felt less like a hot tight helmet or body shield made out of copper as in those ancient etchings, and more like ordinary flesh should, smooth, vulnerable, the source of feeling.

There was no need for the water ritual in winter, or once the rains had come. So I lay curled up in a little ball, my toes poking through yards of muslin, willing to lie there the whole night, sleepless, or in that partial dream state I endured at night, fearful, edgy without amma, yet resolute in my own way, feeling fully able, when I needed, to knock over the earthen jar with cool drinking water in it and cry out shamelessly. I pretended the mist had come into my mouth, that it was wearing away the dark mahogany slats of the crib.

I remember one particular awakening, rude and clumsy. Amma came in mumbling something under her breath, housecoat all scrabbled up at the edges, the buttons askew. She rolled me up and carried me out, through one doorway after the other, crying and crying till we hit the cold night air and the dream, if that was what it was, dashed into rough earth.

She fell. She fell carrying me.

Appa ran over from the distance where he was, from the darkness, where the cracks ran in the earth. He had his big stick in his hand, the one he kept under his bed for snakes and dacoits. He ran over to help her.

But already she was picking herself up, clumsy, stepping on her long, lace-edged petticoat, lopsided with my weight, swaddling clothes all tangled. Behind us, on the veranda of the converted army barracks that served as our first home, the Gurkha in his heavy mailed boots was shouting something out. Everyone turned towards him. The bare bulb, lit all night to scare off hyenas and other night creatures, shone over his head. In one raised hand he held up the dead weight of a python, its head smashed in with his stick, body huge and green.

Time was, I want to write.

Time was, the tail trembled on the veranda floor.

In his left hand the Gurkha brandished a gun. Behind him, thrust onto the veranda from the safe niche in which it normally stood, was a heavy metal trunk in which appa kept all his documents, his M.Sc. from Imperial College London, his passport, shares to a rubber estate, my baptismal certificate signed by his Grace, Juhanon Mar Thoma, metropolitan of the Mar Thoma Syrian Christian Church. Attracted no doubt by the cool metal of the trunk, the python had rolled its heft of snakeflesh and smooth skin, coil after coil, through the drawing room window, through the dining room, into the main bedroom where the trunk was set.

The Gurkha, as he tramped around the barracks with his heavy nightstick, cracking up the small bodies of crickets in his fingers, whistling on his fine tin whistle, had caught a glint of the python's tail. Or claimed he had. For when appa, always a poor sleeper in the dry winter air, saw the light-colored shadow move, heavy and sluggish behind his metal chest, he sprang up crying out and it took the Gurkha quite a few minutes to get there.

Next the python hung from a beam on the veranda. Something dripped out of its mouth. Amma did not want to enter the house again. She walked with me, as appa led us, torch in hand, towards the cracks in the earth that ran beyond the Bambrali garden: fault lines, fine and feverish.

In dry weather an ocher powder, almost like the pollen of wild poppies, came out of them. It was dust really, hot Gangetic dust, but the color and pungent fragrance was like the pollen that fell off poppies. The small fault lines, fissures in the ground, were caused by the shifting of the underground plates that had caused even the Himalaya Mountains to form. In these northern plains those cracks were sharpened by drought and heat. But when the rains came and wildflowers bloomed in the spring season, they were scarcely visible.

Once I could run, amma or my ayah had to watch me all the time as I played in the garden, picking flowers, scrambling here and there, in case I stumbled and fell, hurting an ankle or heel. Worse, too, could happen. I learnt that children sometimes fell into cracks in the earth and vanished. Sometimes they jumped into wells or quarries full of water. It was never entirely clear to me why a child would ever want to do such a thing, but in my childhood dreams they seemed to be doing that much of the time.

*

Who says in dreams begin reponsibilities? In dreams begin craziness, the bitterness of shot silk in the mouth as your lover leaves and huddled on the subway you bite into your sari of pure kanjeevaram silk. Iron in the teeth as you grip the railings by the shuttle at Grand Central, and next to you the derelict stands, his entire assortment of possessions tucked into his sweatshirt, bits of paper, an old billfold, three cans of Sprite smashed flat that he can redeem for five cents apiece, and an undershirt someone cast off, somewhere, this side of the Hudson River.

You live three blocks from the Hudson River, on the island of Manhattan, three blocks away from wind and high water. There is the width of Riverside Park by 113th Street: rocks, a few trees stitched together, the glamour of sunlight streaking over old soil where grass prickles through in springtime. Further down, overlooking the river, is a rough square with concrete on it. People bike ride, or roller skate, or just hang out on the benches with their newspapers, books, or boom boxes mercifully shut off. Children race around on their tricycles, round and round in a madcap way. The stiff wind off the Hudson snarls their hair and stings their eyes.

The sunlight is so sharp in late springtime that it burns the child's eyes and she hugs herself to the handlebars of her tricycle, folds her body over, pummels hard, harder with her little legs. Her doll, made of plastic and nylon, bits of blue tinted cellophane where the eyes form, is tied on behind. It slips sideways with the sudden force of the wind. The cloth book with pictures of Miss Piggy and Kermit that the child had set over the doll like a quilt—"Its just like a quilt, mama, a quilt, isn't it? I think this book is a quilt"—flops onto concrete. The pink washcloth she had folded behind the doll to make it secure drops off too. The wind lifts it an inch, then another inch or two, threatening to blow it into the Hudson River.

We have a little house in the Hudson Valley, in Claverack, two hours by car along the Taconic Parkway, dead north of the city. In the bedroom that looks out onto sumac and wild rhubarb, there is a big wooden bed with ornate Spanish carvings, courtesy of Dorris. Dorris, in a fit of spring cleaning, got rid of much of her stuff from her Long Island house. She felt it was time for new furniture, new curtains, new mattresses, and all that. Toby, knowing our penurious state, bedless, mattressless, quiltless in the country, insisted on having her friend's castoff bed delivered to our doorstep. They carried it in, the old Spanish bedstead, three men who tumbled out of a truck as the neighbors stared. The tiny door at the back by the kitchen almost split open as the bedstead jammed and then the stove had to be shifted. The bed is fine as beds go but for some reason the sheet always slips off the corner of the mattress cover and has to be lodged in place with pins or hooks or whatever comes to hand. There is something so low-down, so thoroughly improvised about my housekeeping that any child visitor coming in can tell that my mind's been elsewhere, my thoughts surging out of the room in memories, dreams, reflections the mere walls will never tell, nor Spanish bedsteads catch.

Lying on that bed all alone one summer afternoon I had a dream that felt like a memory, a true happening evoked in the shot silk of time present, when sense fractures and real places shake themselves apart. I dreamt I was falling. I heard the wind whistle around me as I fell.

I fell and fell and there was no swing or helicopter, or trapdoor from heaven. I fell in a hot, unswerving motion that turned my body into fluid. There was mud at the sides of the quarry where I fell. Clearly it was a quarry. The kind of Kerala quarry from which sandstone is cut, pink-streaked sandstone. Little Svati was running across the steep-sided bottom, water up to her ankles. "Mami, mami" she cried as she used to do in those days. "Mami, mami." Time and again she slipped into the water, each time picking herself up again. By now her dress was splashed and torn. Watching her, I felt she was invincible.

Then something cramped inside me, right where the heart makes its strong, muscular beat. Exhausted, she bobbed up and down on the gray surface of water, brown hair bleached to the color of straw. I jumped in. I could not swim. I dragged her up as best I could and held her to my breasts. Her hair massed over my right shoulder, gained color as I held her there, my girl-child and I, both fallen. On the sides of the quarry, on stones marked with red veins, moss twisted and squirmed, making vowel shapes. The vowel shapes had serpent bodies, fish tails, glittering hooks, eyes. I heard a hoarse sound. Whose breath was it? Hers or mine? Or was it the blur of vowels in the quarry of flesh?

*

I was born out of my mother, and out of her mother before her, and her mother, and her mother, and hers. Womb blood and womb tissue flowing, gleaming, no stopping. I was born in Allahabad, in Uttar Pradesh, in the plains of northern India, the great city of God, where two rivers meet, the Ganga and the Jamuna. At the sangam, the holiest part of flowing water, ashes from the newly dead are set afloat. Elsewhere on the dung heaps, the bloodied tissue of abortions clots and festers. Pigeons, crows, vultures cluster in the air. The air is thick with cries.

Allahabad has many houses, built of sand, tin, mud, bricks, rocks, sandstone. The houses have walls, doors, windows. Some have beds, bedrolls, mats, cribs, sheets, rubber sheets, mattresses made of flecked stuff. From time to time the cotton in the mattresses needs to be puffed out, blown into the air by an old man who goes from house to house with his metal instruments, knocking at doors, crying:

"Ten paise, fifteen paise, two rupees. Who wants a mattress done? Who wants a razai done?"

He drags the old mattresses out into the cool sunlight, picks at the curled up cotton.

My eyes open. My cheek moist with milk rests on the newly furbished mattress. Amma brings me home from the hospital and lays me there. The mattress is covered in white muslin. There is a little stain under my cheek, where the milk dribbles down. I have enormous cheeks, all puffed up with sucking.

This is my first house: a military barrack left empty after the second world war and used now for junior civil servants in the newly formed Indian government. The barracks are long and spacious, but room runs on from room in a monotonous fashion. The narrow front veranda is divided up so that each family with its two or three bedrooms, living room, dining room, and so forth, has a fair share of the veranda. The land in front, cracked and dry in the summer season, is filled with wildflowers, poppies, sunflowers, and a few half-stunted mango trees. The small kitchen garden at the back is filled with tomato plants. As I grow older I race through that back garden, eyes shut, both palms extended, plucking as many of the sour green fruits as I can.

I pop them into my mouth as I rush. I try not to trip. Sometimes the little boy who lives next door joins me in this mad race, denuding the tomato plants. We grow noisy as we race, tagging each other through the soft leaves that scrape our necks. He shouts to me in Hindi. We are both three. Amma sipping tea at the kitchen window pretends not to see. For a whole eternity amma pretends not to see. She squints, she shuts her eyes, she screws her eyes up so tight not even the fierce winter sun can seep into her pupils.

Sometimes as I now toss and squinch in bed, I see amma as she was, frail and twenty-seven, black hair shining, her cotton sari tucked in at her waist, her eyes bright red with sunlight. She stands there at the kitchen window in Allahabad. Behind her is Motrilal the cook, making hot steaming chapatis. Amma has her back to him. She has absolutely no interest in chapatis. Never did. They always turn out like dried dosas when she cooks them, a south Indian unused to cooking with wheat. Rice was just right, wheat was too crude and raw. During the rice shortages in Kerala in the late sixties, hundreds of acres of paddy fields were devastated in the monsoon floods and wheat was sent down from the north. But who could eat it? Who could cook it? People waited patiently for hours for some rice gruel to fill their empty bellies while sacks of wheat grew damp in the godowns. When the shortages turned more acute the wheat was pulled out. Then ways had to be devised to cook it, make a palatable dough out of it, bake it, broil it.

But amma stands in my dream, her back to the wheat. Masses of it spinning out of the cook's immaculate hands. Wheat leaping its milky shapes onto the hot griddle, then turning just the right shade of golden brown, tiny bubbles of heat bursting so the black spots smoke and fall apart on the fine cooked surface, giving just that burnt savor to the chapati. I loved to poke my tongue into the burnt holes of the chapatis. Amma would pour ghee over the chapati and when I poked my tongue in, the warm ghee dribbled out.

But as I watch her now she touches nothing. She has her back turned to all the cooking business. On and on Motrilal goes with his task as if she weren't there at all. But I know he knows she is there and she knows too. For her palms are clenched on the windowsill and her eyes shut tight are bright red and dry. I can see through her lids. Her eyes are red like fish eyes pulled from the living stream. Sharp red with all that sunlight burning her.

Though I was born there, Allahabad is not my home. It is far from Tiruvella, about a thousand miles due north. *Nadu* is the

Malayalam word for home, for homeland. Tiruvella, where my mother's home, Kuruchiethu House, stands, and Kozencheri, where appa's home, Kannadical House, stands, together compose my nadu, the dark soil of self. I was taught that what I am is bound up always with a particular ancestral site. Perhaps I will return there to be buried, my cells poured back into the soil from which they sprung. How tight the bonds are, how narrow the passage from birth to death.

But for a woman, marriage makes a gash. It tears you from your original home. Though you may return to give birth, once married you are part and parcel of the husband's household. You enter those doors wearing the rich mathrakodi sari his mother draped over your head at the marriage ceremony. When you finally leave in a simple rosewood casket, the same sari becomes your shroud. Hence the song I heard as a child and repeat now in my own head:

> Glistening silk
> the color of milk
> decking the bride!
> Who'll bind up the shroud?
> Amma, amma I'll come
> for the ride!

Amma was married into the Kannadical family. She followed appa north to Allahabad and gave birth to me in Kamala Nehru Hospital sometime around nine o'clock on a winter's morning, on the seventeenth of February 1951. No one will tell me the exact time of my birth, perhaps no one knows.

Kozencheri veliappechan, my paternal grandfather, had a horoscope made for me, based, he claimed, on the precise instant of my birth. He would never show it to me. It was locked away with his files and ayurvedic potions, somewhere in a teak cabinet in the large white house he built for himself, high on a hill on ancestral property in Kozencheri. Kozencheri is only twelve miles away from Tiruvella, but in my mind's eye it is a lifetime away; more archaic, more backward, bent to the darkness of blood feuds and feudal torments. The white house, fitted with electricity, was built after veliappechan tore down the house of teak and mahogany that had stood for four hundred years in the lower garden at the edge of the sugarcane fields. Together with the granary and sacred relics, clothes and books and rosewood furniture, together with my grandmother Mariamma's carved chests that once bore her dowry of muslins and silks, the horoscope was carried to the upper garden, to the drawing room of the new house and locked away. I never got to see it. Perhaps I never will. For many years, though, I wondered whether his refusal was based on some fault in me that the learned astrologer had foretold. A dosham, a grievous wrong.

Something like, whoever marries her is fated to death. Or fated to her infidelity. Or fated to her constant flitting back and forth. Or even worse: she will never marry and will remain like a ram in a thicket, a pigeon in a fence spike, throat caught in the paternal house of origin.

When I asked amma for the time of my birth, she said she was so weak and exhausted that she couldn't possibly have asked for the time. It was a difficult birth, she confided to me later, and quite frightening really.

"There was no one to tell me what to do, child. Afterwards, I never wanted to wear the tight wrap around my belly they told me to. Nor could I stop drinking water. I was so thirsty! Allahabad was hot and dry! So my belly never became tight and slim again."

Amma always had a large belly and her children snuggled up against it, first me, then Anna, then Elsa. It was time itself, the first home. It housed us, growing slack as she aged and its old uses failed. When she gave birth to me amma was twenty-four, sixteen years younger than I am now. Grandmother Kunju had died seven years before that. One night in Women's Christian College in Madras, where she lived in the hostel, amma had a dream. In my mind that dream is colored blue, flashing and fitful, a bird's feather, a vanishing covered over by darkness.

She dreamt her mother had died, that she was waving goodbye to her. Waving and waving across a gulf. She knew it was a gulf, for no sounds came. The next morning the telegram arrived. Grandmother Kunju had died. A gold injection had killed her. There was a new English doctor at the Mission Hospital in Tiruvella, a man called Churchwarden, supposedly very bright. He knew of a cure for arthritis. Grandmother's fingers were racked with arthritis. She played her piano early each morning, then arranged the new tiger lilies in the vases along the window, so the light would catch the soft petals and open them. Later in the day her fingers grew worse.

First the gold injection made her skin itch. As the itch grew worse her skin started to peel off in layers. The poison rose in her blood, making her hot and feverish. Her whole body burnt with an invisible fire, its heat so great that forty-eight hours after the injection she fell into a coma and slipped away. Ilya never recovered. Nor did amma, though it has taken me all this time to realize it.

As soon as she had graduated from college, amma's marriage was arranged. It was done in an unusual way, for the boy's side did the searching. Kozencheri veliappechan, having heard that amma was ready for marriage, made the proposal. He called on Ilya in the Tiruvella home, accompanied by the go-between, a relative on both sides. The go-between carried appa's M.Sc. answer papers, in which appa had a perfect score of 100. Since amma came from a distinguished family, veliappechan wanted his future relatives by marriage to know his only son's worth.

Years later, grandmother Mariamma told me, ''You know we arranged the marriage because we saw your grandmother Kunju from a distance and all sang a song to her: 'Welcome, welcome Mrs. Kuruvilla, M.A. kum!' '' Kum was just a suffix, a little lilt at the end of the song that the children in Saint Mary's School, Kozencheri, had made up to welcome grandmother Kunju. She was coming to open the new school building. Appa in those days was just a boy, a rather naughty boy who ran wild in the paddy fields and raced straight at white bulls so that his oldest sister screamed out in fear. He saw nothing of all this. But my grandmother Mariamma came out of her proud seclusion and stood by the granite gates watching as this other woman, young as she was, dark and beautiful, her curly hair bound back in a tight bun, stepped out of the car to the claps of the children and the songs of the elders.

Did grandmother Kunju bear scissors in her hand, glinting silver scissors with which to cut the pink ribbons strung across the new school rooms? Did she feel the sunlight on her hair and blink her eyes at the light? Had she any sense at all that her only daughter would be married into the family whose ancestral lands lay all around the schoolhouse on the hill? She smiled at the children, she stepped forward on her small feet, she folded her palms and bent forward in greeting. She was tired of all the traveling. But she held her mind clear and free.

After her mother's sudden death, after her college graduation, amma served tea and sweets to the young man who came to visit.

She saw him just once, her sari drawn over her head, her eyes peeping through the fine cotton. He wanted to return, to see her again, but his mother prevented him.

"It would be quite improper, what would people say?" I giggled as amma explained this to me when I was thirteen. I could not imagine what the world was like then.

I turned to appa. "But why didn't you insist?"

"How could I? She was my mother."

I think I understood him. Grandmother Mariamma, though quite reclusive, was the power in the Kozencheri house. Appa would never raise his voice in her presence. Nor would he ever let her see him smoke. Like a small boy, stealing away, he would go to immense lengths to light his cigarettes in the shelter of the lime trees that rose in abundance around the side of the house. He strolled back and forth in the darkness, only the tips of his lighted cigarettes showing, quickly stubbing them out if his mother chanced out in search of air. The scent of my father's imported cigarettes, Players, Winston, Camel, pervades the night air where the lime trees bloom, on a hillside in Kerala. On the other side of the hill is the school where the grandmother I never saw with ordinary sight strode up briskly, silver scissors in hand.

I do not know who cut my umbilical cord. Or how it was cut. Did he or she use scissors? Perhaps it was a harassed doctor. Perhaps a nurse held me, all slippery and mussed, my head a purplish cone with the pressure of entry. Perhaps by this time amma was too worn out with tears to care. But she put me to her breasts as soon as they let her and set the sweet milk flowing.

I know she loved me. I also know that she was broken up, not quite ready for the difficulties of the world, when I popped out. The normal custom was to return to one's mother's home to give birth. While marriage is a parting, an exile from the maternal home, giving birth is a time to return, to celebrate, to feast on rich nutty sweets, to imbibe life-giving proteins, to have your body, numb after childbirth, rubbed over with hot oils and unguents steeped in herbs.

But with grandmother dead, amma had nowhere to return. The closest was her mother's sister, my great-aunt Sara. She lived in Burhanpur where her husband had retired from Simla. Their house was filled with crystal and cigar smoke. Appa went by train to fetch her and brought her back to the little house on the empty field filled with wild flowers that was our first home. She spent her time in

Allahabad, preparing muslins and baby woolens, waiting for me to arrive. After my arrival she stayed for a few weeks, then left. Great-aunt Sara was the closest amma could get to home. I know she wept bitterly, missing her own mother at the season of my birth. She felt very far from home. In five years she was to travel even further, again following appa, but this time across the boundaries of a new India, across the Indian Ocean and the Red Sea, further, much further than Allahabad.

Sometimes I think that the journey across the ocean was like a death to her. Or perhaps I should say that it made for an entirely different life for her. As for me, just turned five, my days changed utterly and I became a child of a different sort. My life shattered into little bits and pieces. In my dreams, I am haunted by thoughts of a homeland I will never find. So I have tuned my lines to a different aesthetic, one that I build up out of all the stuff around me, improvising as I go along. I am surrounded by jetsam. It is what I am, the marks of my being: old, overboiled baby bottles, half-used tubes of A and D ointment, applications for visas to here and there, an American green card with my face printed on so dark you can scarcely make out the flesh from the black hair floating around, a diaphragm I no longer use, a wedding ring I cannot wear for my finger has grown plumper, scraps of scribbled paper, a fragment of silk from my grandmother Kunju's wedding sari that I have preserved in a silver box with intricate patterns of mango leaf and the wings of dancing herons that belonged to my mother's mother's mother's mother and is set now on a bookshelf in my bedroom in the Manhattan apartment where I live.

3. *Katha*

*S*ometimes I am torn apart by two sorts of memories, two opposing ways of being towards the past. The first makes whorls of skin and flesh, coruscating shells, glittering in moonlight. A life embedded in a life, and that in another life, another and another. Rooms within rooms, each filled with its own scent: rosehips, neem leaves, dried hibiscus leaves that hold a cure, cow dung, human excrement, dried gobs of blood.

I come from there. That conch shell, that seashore, those bellies, that dung, those dried leaves holding a cure for the aching mind, all know me. The rooms, enfolded each within the other, the distant houses all have held me.

I see amma, her hands bent into brown shell shapes for the wind to whistle through. She holds up her hands in sunlight, in moonlight. She stoops to pick me up. I am two, perhaps two and a half. She lifts me high into the wind. I see appa's hands, the veins rising on them. He is almost seventy now, his hair combed back on his head, streaked with silver, that handsome face whittled from within by a blood disease, time and sickness consuming the flesh that just about sustains him. He stretches out his hands to me. I want to dissolve, become a ghost myself so I can race to my father, into his outstretched hands.

Behind him, my mother stands in the doorway. She too has grown older, the laugh lines deepen on her face, the curly hair blown loose from her bun is gray, shot through with black. Now I see her in the half-darkness, the sari drawn over her head. They are utterly quiet, for there is nothing that needs to be said. They wait for me in the Tiruvella house with a sandy courtyard where the ancient mulberry tree blossoms in sunlight.

But the rooms of the house are filled with darkness. I am in that house, somewhere in between my parents, hovering as a ghost might. I cannot escape. This is the house of my blood, the whorl of flesh I am. It is all already written, already made.

Another memory invades me: flat, filled with the burning present, cut by existential choices. Composed of bits and pieces of the present, it renders the past suspect, cowardly, baseless. Place names litter it: Allahabad, Tiruvella, Kozencheri, Pune, Khartoum, Cairo, Beirut, Jerusalem, Dubai, London, New York, Minneapolis, Saint Paul, New Delhi, Trivandrum. Sometimes I think I could lift these scraps of space and much as an indigent dressmaker, cut them into shape. Stitch my days into a patchwork garment fit to wear.

But when she approaches me, this Other who I am, dressed in her bits-and-pieces clothing, the scraps cobbled together to cover her nakedness, I see quite clearly what I had only guessed at earlier: she has no home, no fixed address, no shelter. Sure, everything else looks fine. She has two hands, two feet, a head of long black hair, a belly, breasts. But it is clear she is a nowhere creature.

She babbles in a multitude of tongues: Malayalam, Hindi, Tamil, Arabic, English, French. Desert sands fill her eyes. Bombers spit fire down on her. She crouches right where she is, at the edge of the subway platform that runs under Broadway: uptown local, at 110th Street. She listens to the youth cry out through his harmonica, lisp out of the side of his mouth for a few dimes, the odd quarter: ''She is a material girl, and she knows what she is, she is a material baby, she is an American girl, huh, huh,'' he cries, pitching his voice as high as he can. Now the metal body of the train grinds in, people press bellies, thighs, elbows, fists shoving in the haste to enter. Thrust against a white ceramic pillar she crouches low, witnessing it all. As the train doors smash shut, she sucks in her breath. I am here she thinks. No elsewhere. Here, now, in New York City.

What does it mean to be born, to live in houses, to be held by the hands of mothers? What answer is there except to say, this is what shapes the fluid stuff of desire, warms it, till the very bedposts cry out for us to return and the past rises, fragrant, spiked with the bitterness of a nostalgia that can never be eased. Pothos, a homesickness that is never sated. When I think of homesickness, the Tiruvella house where Ilya lived rises up for me. Those corridors wind through my blood. But in dreams that house becomes one with the other great house of my childhood, the Kozencheri house that belongs to my father and his father before him. But neither was my first home literally, for I was born in Allahabad.

The literal is always discrepant, a sharp otherness to what the imagination conjures up as it blends time, emotions, heartbeats. In imagination I put out my hands and as a blind woman might, I enter the hospital room where my father lies. I breathe in the sharp scent of antiseptics, alcohol, the metallic stuff around the oxygen cylinder. I lean forward. I touch my father's cheek. His eyes are open, worn with fatigue from fighting for his breath. He does not see me. I shall be as the warm air that billows you, the soft scent of your dead mother's sari, I whisper. Become a ghost now, let me be as air, as water washing over your flesh.

Sometimes a katha is recited in a deep singsong voice, in a formal standing position. Sometimes it is told simply, with a child on one's knee. Ilya had brought me up on recitations of the katha he made up for me. He was a learned man, and when he turned away from the Bible or the Mahabharata or stories of the Buddha to make up his own tales with a special girl, Susikali, playing the heroine, I was delighted.

Susikali had a knack for finding trouble. She raced through paddy fields in pursuit of rakshasis, those demon ladies with long black hair. Sometimes she stole food, or plucked the ripest mangoes in someone else's orchard and black birds chased her all the way up the Nilgiris. Sometimes she witnessed fearful things. She saw a man of God from Patananthita, a priest of great faith, pick up his cassock, tuck it in at his waist, and chase after her. Or so it seemed at first. He had long iron nails held firmly in his hand. He swung a wooden mallet.

"Aaiou," she screamed in delight as he slipped into a ditch full of fish. It was monsoon time and his face was as filthy as a water buffalo's, all streaked with mud. But he hoisted himself out. He caught up with the rakshasi. Long hair making jagged spikes in sunlight, wilder than the thornbush by the well, the rakshasi raced just behind Susikali, like a mad shadow. Huffing and puffing the priest edged closer, stuck his hand into that matted hair. Not a moment too soon. In another half minute the rakshasi would have bolted three-quarters of the way up the great Parvatam Mountain.

Susikali crouched behind a tree. The man of God flung himself on the rakshasi, banged her head against the jamun tree, the fruit shook dark and bloody. Susikali trembled in excitement. With his right hand he raised up the first nail. He tugged at the dry, jet black hair. He banged the nail into her head. Her skull was not human. It was dried up turtle shell. He banged another nail and another and another into her. Her eyes grew dull. Her ugly eyelids fluttered. Susikali felt she wanted to cry. She leapt from her hiding place and ran and ran. She ran all the way down the lower mountains down the plains, all the two thousand miles back home to the front veranda and the steps where Ilya sat on a rosewood chair telling the katha.

In Ilya's katha, after the rakshasi was subdued, Susikali had to get on with the next adventure. I made up the ending about her running like the monsoon wind, all confused. She didn't like the look on the face of the man of God. That much was clear. She was me. I was she, Susikali, exact replica of my four-and-a-half-year-old self granted the boon of magical powers. But I was also the rakshasi. I loved the fierce glitter of that mad woman, the power that let her leap over the rice fields swollen with water, bolt up the highest Indian mountain.

And of course the man of God had to do his bit with his iron nails. I hated it. Quickly he shut his eyes. Oh so quickly, his thick finger moistened with spittle, he made the sign of the cross on his own forehead. In a trice, before you could say "Aaaiou, potho" or even "Ende Yesue," an iron nail flashed in his fist. He banged it into her smooth brow. Her brow was made of turtle shell, or so it seemed, polished, squared out with the lines of persistence.

A turtle holds up the elephants that hold up the earth. I knew that. And her head was made of turtle shell. So how could she bleed?

She didn't bleed, not Sarama the demon lady. Down, down went the nail. Deeper and deeper. As if the Vindhya Mountains were in her skull and the Indian Ocean too and the Bay of Bengal and the Arabian Sea.

Sweating now, his cassock hitched over his thighs, he banged harder. He had a flint in his hand. Sarama was laid against rock and thistle. Her mad eyes rolled. "O bitch demoness," he swore, "I'll get you now if it's the last thing I do."

"I do, I do, I do," he stuttered, all his prayers on the steel pin. It came from the edge of the wall that held up the granary. Filled with shining rice, the granary was carved and bolted in finest teak.

No iron touched it. But the wall that held it up needed iron joints, hinges, nails. Surely all the gods had blessed that nail, all the saints in heaven, all the ancestors.

Down, down went the nail. Two inches longer than her skull, but it never emerged. How can a nail come out of the turtle shell that holds up the earth? Out of her mouth, from her long red tongue came a sigh, a little wind. That was it. Kaput. Katham. Finis.

Susikali was watching all this. She was hidden by the gooseberry tree. I saw the tree. I made it up in my head. I saw the shower of light that fell from the gooseberry tree. I saw the nail, its metal glint, and then the long red tongue of the demon lady. A rakshasi with the nail going down, down into her skull as out of her mouth came short sharp sighs. But Sarama refused to die.

Ilya's voice was going on and on, about the Buddha. But I wasn't in the mood for it. I considered creeping into amma's arms but she was so thin, her upper body fitted into exquisitely tailored blouses. She wouldn't have understood. I considered racing away through the long grasses that grew behind the well to climb the love apple tree. I loved swinging from the black branches that swung as low as the ground. Or perhaps I would crouch in the dust at Ilya's feet right where I stood and watch the minute kuriaana with their ridged backs make circle after circle of dirt till they fell into their own holes utterly satisfied, fat bodies and dirty tails wiggling with delight.

His voice was hesitant, gentle in my ear. He had almost reached the Buddha's conception, Maya's dream of the white elephant as she stood there, clutching the sala tree. A great white beast with six horns entered her womb. I tugged at his dhoti, I prodded his feet with my toes. My toes were filthy, oozing mud from the garden. I shook my head so hard, my hair blew into my mouth. He laughed. He knew I wanted out. Anyway there were visitors at the front gate. They held black umbrellas in their hands, umbrellas with fine sculptures of horn at the handles. Our visitors were well shielded from the sun. Ilya rose, preparing to greet them. I couldn't bear to stay and be courteous. They would surely notice my muddy legs and scratched knees, my mussed-up hair. And amma would be fearfully embarrassed. Quickly I pressed myself against Ilya's knees then raced to the kitchen.

The cooks, the maids, and the ayahs were outside under the palm trees, in a clear area of sand. One of the cooks, Verghese, a young man who wore his checked shirt open and sported bright red lungis on his days off, was slitting a large swordfish for our dinner. Marya adored him. Whenever she could she brushed herself against his shoulder or his hairy arm. He was enamored of her milky white complexion. "Like a Kashmiri maiden," I heard him whispering to the old man Sankaran, the chief cook. I watched them through the kitchen window and knew they could not see me.

I pulled up a wooden stool. Tucking my skirts in between my legs so the soot from the stoves wouldn't get me, I stood on tiptoes and stuck my fingers into a big ceramic pot. My fingers touched the roughness of crystallized cane syrup. I eased a little bit out, rubbing it back and forth against the inside of the jar to break it off. I lifted its moist crumbling stuff and set it to my lips. As laughter floated in through the windows of the kitchen, and footsteps pounded closer, I screwed my eyes tight. I tasted the sweet glittering brown on my lips and tongue, it coursed through my blood all the way down to my muddy toes. I imagined myself turning as dark as that lump of gur so no one could find me till I was ready.

Suddenly I heard a voice through the kitchen window, saw Ilya beckoning me. "Come Kochumol," he said almost gruffly, "let's see how Susheela cow is getting on." I ran towards him, wondering how in the world he had managed to escape our visitors. Susheela had given birth and it gave us both a great deal of pleasure to watch her lick her thin freckled calf as it inched forward on spindly legs to suck at Susheela's speckled teats.

The cow shed was built of wood and brick with the plaster painted white on two sides to keep it cool. For the same purpose the wooden roof was raised on its high beam. It was just a few nights ago that, hearing cries in the darkness, Ilya had awakened, flung on his woolen shawl, and picked me up in his arms. He had promised to take me to see Susheela's calf arrive. For days Susheela had ambled around hot and heavy, hardly able to summon the energy to drive the flies off her back with her stiff tail. The cool winds that blew in at night from the Indian Ocean did little to comfort her. "Her time is almost here," Bhaskaran the cowherd would mutter with a worried little frown as he set about his tasks of tugging down fresh hay from the haystack that was high as three men, pouring fresh water into the cow's drinking vessels, cleaning out the cow dung with a hard broom, then pouring out bucketfuls of water till the stuff ran rich and putrid into the ditch nearby.

Bhaskaran had a very personal interest in the matter. It was on his recommendation that they had brought in a white bull several months earlier. The bull was so fierce it came with two men to hold it down, one fitting his bare hands to its hot hump, the other tugging at the nose strings as the creature snorted and reared on its legs. The bull, which belonged to the Brahmin Govinda who lived on the other side of the bridge, had been led in with due ceremony and tethered to the tree behind the cow shed. Susheela, traipsing at the end of a nice long rope, was led out. He raced towards her, then halted, stomping around her, pawing and hissing. She made little mewing sounds such as I had never heard before and let her hooves fly. I stared from behind the tapioca bushes as long as I could. I had to keep still in case Chinna pulled me away. A grasshopper settled in my hair, ants crawled up my thighs as I squatted, staring at the curious pageant, the brown cow rock still while the bull humped her. The dirt from his hooves rose in puffs, his front legs butted at her shoulders. Afterwards her eyes were even more moist than before, and she let the cats and crows edge towards her almost as if she did not notice. Then as she lay on the straw, she made circular whisks with her tail, jutted her ears till they stood at perfect right angles to her head. I could smell the sweat on her and knew something had changed. The scent excited me.

Later, held in Ilya's arms, in the circle of lanterns and the flare from torches lit with palm leaves, I saw the bloodied stuff that came from her, her great brown belly heaving. And out of the dark hole in her popped a head slippery with mucus. A grown man helped it out with his hands, for Susheela was having trouble. Finally it slithered out, all knees and hooves and huge black eyes moist like the mother's. It lay there that night in the circle of her legs as she licked it with her tongue.

Now in broad daylight, Ilya and I stood by the sheaf of hay and watched the little thing tug at its mother's teats. "See, Meena, that's how we all were. Look carefully. Someday you will make this into a katha." He smiled at me gently, scooping me into his arms so I could see the nest a bulbul had made in the mango tree just behind us, a gulmohar leaf freckled with pink.

And so he led me from sound to sound, from sight to sight, the moving surfaces of the garden exerting a pressure on his brain, a relentless consonance of sense, a shimmering thing that wrapped us both. It only struck me later, after he had died, that my childhood, coming so late in his life, must have seemed a rare gift to him.

As for me, I could not conceive of life without Ilya. I drew nourishment from him, as a young thing might from an older being already gnarled with time. Even now as a grown woman, almost three decades after his death, I can touch a wall or a tree in the Tiruvella garden where we spent many hours together, and a stream of feeling will flood me. Sometimes in my dreams I cry out his name and wake up confused at so much longing welling up out of a grown woman.

Through his life he drew me back into an India that could only be history to me, a life of struggle and yearning, travels and disasters in foreign lands, a restless idealism that really believed the earth could be transformed.

In some ways, though, he died in the nick of time. Else we would have quarreled terribly I now feel, my own desires for freedom, for a fresh life, tugging me away from the gnarled roots that made his. And I was a female child, three-quarters of a century younger. The blood that skipped in me had another pulse. So I learnt early that the deepest loves bear a dissonance within them, a measure of the earth we are bedded in, where everything is fractured, plural, multiple. Else even the fluids that make up the vitality of our bodily substances would get thinned out, drying as the flesh does, in fanaticism, that unpleasant quality I sensed in the gaunt evangelical man who came up to visit us on his bicycle every third day, swallowing his bile, unable to tolerate Ilya's high church creeds.

I was party to their disputes, having been inculcated very early in the finer points of the Nicene Creed as well as the various heresies. Within the hearing of the evangelical man, a member of the dissident Pathyam group, I sung out as if it were a nursery rhyme:

Who is the Lord Almighty?
Is He one substance or three?
He is only one.
What about me?

And in reply to the last, quite forgetting his theological colleague, Ilya would pick me up and point out the shining gooseberries in their halo of green, the silken threads in the love apple flower. "You are all that, my child, and an immortal soul too." "What about the leper?" "The leper too. We are all God's children, as far and wide as the eye can see or heart hear." I laughed, my mind moving away from the poor leper who had squatted by the kitchen for his food, his metal dish in his stumpy hands, his feet bound up in rough cloth. I laughed at the thought that the heart could hear. "Yes, yes." Ilya patted his chest "Most certainly sure!" Even the listening Pathyam man was mollified. Who could deny a child?

The Mar Thoma Church, in which Ilya had been ordained as a priest in his younger days, was going through a great crisis. Someone in the Pathyam group had shut the door on a visiting bishop from the Mar Thoma Seminary in Tiruvella. The slammed door reverberated in our house. There were all-night discussions about the finer points of ancient theology inherited from the beginnings of the church, from the days two thousand years ago when Saint Thomas the Doubter had come to Kerala, and, after him, the church fathers had followed the rough overland trail from Antioch and Babylon, bringing the liturgy, the details of the Syriac sacrament. What could the future hold in a church split and torn? How could the old heritage be maintained? Already I knew that the reformer Abraham Malpan was Ilya's great-great-great-grandfather from his mother's ancestral side. The Malpan was shocked by the lack of godliness in his congregations. They were far more concerned with lighting candles for saints, worshipping images of the Virgin, and counting up roosters with their heads torn off, fit material for a blood sacrifice, than in intuitions of a Godhead one might never see, *nirguna,* a Being without Qualities. Abraham Malpan had organized a protest movement two hundred and fifty years before to cleanse the church of idolatry. Then, too, a kinswoman had shut the door on the Jacoba Bishop, helped the Malpan tear down the ancient icons and cast them into the waters of the Pamba River. The reformation movement tore apart the centuries old Syrian Church of Malabar, dividing it into the older, Orthodox Jacoba Church and the reformed branch, the Mar Thoma Church.

When it came to my time, I was forced to stare at the beautiful white walls in the ancient churches of Kerala, with nothing but dull spaces where the treasured icons had hung. And gazing on that blankness, I felt as if I were in a perpetual hangover. I would have quarreled with the Malpan, but the Mar Thoma Church was part of my early life. I was baptized into the church in infancy and I was brought up by Ilya, one of its great theologians. And I took the theological disputes that surrounded my childhood all in my stride—the intense concern with substances and properties, the sparring between Sathyam and Pathyam groups about the precise symbolic nature of the Triune Deity or the status of the Malayalam liturgy as opposed to the ancient Syriac one.

Had Ilya lived longer I might have outgrown that world, like a skin that no longer fit, like a garment that was too tight. But as it was, the torment of his death plunged us into grief and rage. I think neither amma nor I have ever gotten over it. With the death duties and loss of the cardamom and rubber estates, our lives changed. A whole world shivered and cracked. The hoarse sounds of his last breathing, the rattle in his throat as he died, filled my ears.

It took me a while to realize that Ilya must have been a lonely man. I sensed that there had been a companionship between Ilya and his dead wife that appa and amma knotted together in an arranged marriage did not have. I saw my grandmother Kunju's face through Ilya's eyes and loved her. I knew she was beautiful. There was a large portrait of her in the drawing room, under the elegant teak ceilings that rose to a high point. Under those ceilings, in the profuse gardens edged by mango and bamboo and the clusters of gulmohar and laburnam blossoms, my childhood was free. I did what I wanted to and what I wanted to I did or so it seems now, harking back. While in Pune I had a mother and a father and was accountable to them. I knew I could not race out into the busy thoroughfare of Deccan Gymkhana without courting death. In Tiruvella I could run as fast as I wanted, eyes closed, heart thudding and no one would stop me. I felt I had no need of parents. In the large house in which Ilya lived, there were visiting relatives and cousins coming to call, servants and older aunts, multifarious visitors all bound together in the loose yet formalized functions of the family. There were crevices and gaps for me, places I could hide in and find myself again, utterly transformed in the magic of childhood, so that a bush laden with green berries or a goose flapping its wings could make me into that and I raced around crying, "Athe, athe—That, that," as if that I was. "Tat Tvam Asi," it says in the Upanishads and in my childhood I realized its truth. And surely the "I am that I am" of Hebraic religions is much akin and realizes in the child of mud and blood and skin an irremediable joy, the closest we get to any possible paradise.

4. *Kerala Childhood*

When the frangipani blossoms, the thick sweet scent draws the cobras out and for this reason the trees with their gnarled trunks and thick shining leaves are set at a good distance from the Tiruvella house, near the edge of the kayala—a low mound of earth that divides the compound from the dirt road that runs towards the railway tracks. All during the summer I stood by the fence and watched groups of men with their turbans bound in red work away at the edge of the scarred run of earth where the tracks were laid.

Sometimes I stood close to Marya the maid, watching as the men worked, pickaxes raised. I stared as metal hit harder rock and gneiss, as fragments of quartz broke loose into the sunlight. Sometimes as the laterite soil of central Travancore tore free, I saw bits of granite once embedded underground, splintering, or laid plain for any child to see, a fault mass of reddish sandstone, the stone cracked by underground pressure, yet welded into a whole whose fissured surfaces made the water stream and drip.

The men rested to drink some water, or chew on a beedi drawn from the turban or the knotted waistband of a lungi. The beedi smoked for an instant before the burning tip dissolved into light and the men raised their voices high, in a ribald, bantering way. Sometimes they crowded into excited knots. Were they quarreling, sharing a joke? Who could tell from the middle distance where words split open as they fell, sense dissolving into the hot air with silk cotton seeds, whose soft stuff shimmered overhead, then vanished into the blue. Only the inchoate syllables remained, and over by the tracks, the hot, gleaming bodies of men, mouths open, laughing. Something in me wanted to slip under the fence made of fresh laburnam shoots, race forward till I was inside that knot of men, able to hear what they were saying, able to touch my cheek to a sweaty shoulder muscle, or the flat of my palm to a heavy metal rail they lifted up to the singsong chants of labor. But Marya gripped me tight and try as I might I could not work my fingers free of her milky clasp.

After the earth was smoothed out and the large wooden planks that were brought in all the way from Kayankulam were laid out, end to end, the metalwork began. Lorries lumbered in from the other side of the red welt of earth. Metal bodies shook with the burden of nuts and bolts and fish plates. Noon after noon they came in on the bridge over the Pamba River. The grove of rubber trees by Aswathy's house burst open, smoking with the exhaust fumes of the lorries. Smoke from the back of the lorries mingled with the scent of the frangipani blossoms.

"The cobras love the smoke from the lorries," Marya whispered as she held my hand, watching the work intently. "No, don't be nervous, the footsteps of a child are enough to make them docile. But quick, move out of that rat hole." Her movements were all quick and lithe. She was aware of the men watching her out of the corners of their eyes as she pushed my feet away from the squishy earth near a rat hole. I was standing there barefoot as I always did in Tiruvella, gripping Marya's hand. She was a new, junior ayah, brought in to help out Chedthi and Chinna now that I was to have a little sister or brother. Marya had flashing amber eyes, and large breasts that tilted upwards under her tight chatta. Her hair was long and black and hung in a single plait down below her waist. It swished over her ample hips as she walked.

When Marya came out of the servants' bathhouse at the edge of the five acres my grandfather had fenced around his home, her hair knotted high over her shapely head, the towel wound tight around her middle, men might have crawled out of holes to see her, as they do in the Malayalam film where the heroine slips in and out of river water, clad only in the sheerest of towels and hosts of men leap out of the rocky cracks in the ground by the river, wave their hands and fists in a loud male chorus of "Zindabad" at her beauty. And so quickly she becomes the Goddess of Liberty as the distant Delacroix had imaged it, and so quickly she shoots out four arms as Parvati did when Shiva, smitten by her beauty, bent low for her and raised her footsole and kissed it.

But no cobra ever came forward, hood raised, to kiss Marya.

It may have been the heaviness in her milky white feet, for Marya
had the coloring of a Kashmiri film goddess, or perhaps it was her
eyes as smoky as a cat's—puchakane they are called in Malayalam—
light eyes streaked with amber or onyx or pearly gray, rare indeed,
given the norm of black eyes that the poets have praised for centuries. Whether it was her eyes or not, no cobra was ever sighted in
her vicinity. Whereas when old, wrinkled Chedthi approached to
greet the schoolmistress who wanted to take a shortcut through the
rubber grove, or when she hobbled out, bent almost double, stick
in hand, to yell at Beshir the fishman for an indifferent parrot fish
he had palmed off on us, the very soil shook with the little puffs
of air let out by the cobras as they poked their heads out, or aired
their flashing tails. Once I saw a whole forest of cobras surround
Chedthi and the light was smoky vermillion with the power of their
eyes. And out of their forked tongues they spat syllables, soft curling
vowel sounds, the aa—ee—oo, au—um, ahas, I was being taught
by the Malayalam tutor. And the syllables started slipping and sliding till they seemed to be English, Hindi, Arabic, anything, any
speech at all. But when I mentioned this to amma the next morning, just after breakfast, just before she took out the black bound
Book of Common Prayer to read aloud in her soft singsong voice, I
could not raise her interest in the matter.

"You must have dreamt it, Meenamol," she said, not unkindly, "a dream, that's all."

"Where does it come from, amma? And how does Chedthi have
that power?" I insisted. But before she could figure out a reply, I
leapt away from her, suddenly anxious that she might summon me
to sit at her knees and listen to the prayer of supplication to the Lamb
of God, who alone takes away the sins of the world.

Did Marya's flesh have a voice that Malayalam or Hindi couldn't
quite match? Was her flesh sin that the Lamb of God would have
to take away? Surely no one believed that, given all the delight it
aroused. Yet there was something in the black book with its prayers and ritual supplications that made me nervous.

And I knew about the power of the sarpam. I had listened to
Ilya read out the Genesis story in his pure Malayalam diction, and
sometimes for fun he read it out in the Hindi translation, since Hindi was our national language and I was having tuition with Vaariar
saar from the local college in my Hindi syllables and sentences. And
a sarpam—who really was Shaitan—had taken the apple and given

it to Awa who gave it to Aadam and he ate it since it came from her sweet hand.

And how sweet her hand was. It was the hand of his beloved holding out the apple, but as he bit into the sweetness all hell broke loose. And thinking of the hand of Awa, I thought too of Shakuntala, Kalidasa's heroine, whose sweet hand had touched her lover in the forest. But when the ring he gave her slipped off, he forgot all about her, and her flesh lost its fragrance, and he could not recall who she was, and she meanwhile had borne him a son. And it was only when the belly of the fish that swallowed her ring of remembrance was slit open, that King Dusyanta saw and recalled their nights in the forest. Meanwhile how terribly she suffered, Shakuntala, her tears falling into the eyes of her beloved doe that followed her everywhere. And how Awa must have suffered with the weight of all that sin, forced to bear her children in terrible, gut-splitting pain. And how Shakuntala suffered, blocked out from the gaze of her beloved.

And sitting here in New York City, at my writing table in a room filled with dust, I recall my childhood fears about what it might mean to be born into a female body. Quite early I was taught how the sexual body enticed men and then was crossed out in the interests of a higher truth. Women had to bear the burden of all that sin, all that forgetfulness. Of course at the very end of Kalidasa's play, Shakuntala was borne sky-high in the chariot and apsaras sang to her and the peacocks at the edge of mountain slopes spread out their fans and danced for her. But none of that took place till her lover King Dusyanta remembered, at the very end. I wondered how poor Shakuntala had borne the weight of memory, the terror of erasure.

Perhaps with Marya and the snakes, it was something altogether simpler. Perhaps it was just that the snakes sensed her deep disinclination to see them dance in sunlight. Her flesh was altogether too bound up with the burden of the human to be mindful of snakes or moles or rats or mongooses. That sort of fear washed over Marya with the bright red Sunlight Soap she used on her footsoles and the rough skin on her elbows as she squatted by the well side, giggling at the cowherd who stood staring at her quite helplessly, jiggling the long rope that was meant for the brown freckled cow. What Marya was concerned with was the line of working men, the loud laughter that came now from the fresh row of tracks. I think she might even have caught some of the words they chanted out as she stood there open mouthed while I tried once again to work my fingers free of her grip. Suddenly we heard a gruff voice. Someone, terribly thin with scrawny hair pulled back, a common towel draped over one shoulder in place of a proper cavuni, was yelling: ''Maryaee, keke, Mole kondu va. Ipum tirichu va!''

It was Narayani, freed from her task of sweeping the ashes into the ash room, who was sent out to summon us. Tea would be ready shortly and amma wanted me washed and clean, hair combed and tied back with a bow, for visitors from Kozencheri were expected. It was thought that grandmother Mariamma might come too, and she was always most particular about my appearance. After all, looking the way I did, my dress stained with tree sap and my footsoles all dusty, my hair uncombed and blowing about my face, not even a single clip in it, who could tell me apart from Chinna's child, or Gomati's child, or Bhaskaran's niece. Indeed there was no way at all of telling me apart from any servant child, or the child of any Sudra who lived within a fifteen-mile radius of the Tiruvella house. Looking the way I did, I would bring nothing but shame to the family.

The Kozencheri family, appa's side, was most particular about appearances. They were also very strict about crossing lines. Playing with a woodcutter's child, or a milkman's child as I did in Tiruvella, would never be permitted in the Kozencheri house. My Kozencheri veliappechan had large holdings of land that he inherited from his paternal side, sugarcane, paddy, rubber, and coconut groves. He had middlemen and overseers working for him, supervising the labor of large groups of peasants who plowed the rice fields, transplanted paddy, and worked with the rubber sap as, still warm, it poured out of the cut bark into the little coconut cups and then, after being bound into round, stringy balls, was transported to the rubber factory where they turned it into the ridged mats that smelt like vomit a day old, laid out in the sun to dry.

After the day's work the laborers would come up to the house and squat outside on the sand as the middlemen stood by watching. With his legs outstretched veliappechan sat on the rosewood and rattan chair with the immense arms that he had bought from the British Resident well before the British were forced to leave India. In one hand he held the wad of chewing tobacco that he had pulled out of his leather pouch. In the other he held the wad of money that was to be distributed to the laborers for the day's work. Watching him from the doorway, or shutting my ears with both my hands as he raised his voice, shouting in reply to one of the women laborers who'd shot her mouth off: "Hey, you owe us more than that" or "There were twelve bushels not ten there." Then hearing him shout back in his deep throated voice, or spit, in a perfect arc of tobacco and betel nut juice, past the woman's bent knee, where the spittle landed in a little bubbling mass, forcing her to move forward, I hid my face in shock and embarrassment. Already I was starting to glimpse the curse of property, the lines of power that held us all in.

Later at night as we gathered for prayers around his bedside kneeling, singing out the portions of the Syriac liturgy veliappechan had chosen, I watched the same man weep out loud as he recited the prayers for the salvation of the soul. Then in the impromptu prayers added on, he called upon the Lord to save all of us, entire and whole for the kingdom to come, called upon the Father in Heaven to rescue us from the Communists whose powers were growing. Surely the Almighty knew they had murdered a tax collector in the mountains to the north and three landowners in the east. And now they were threatening him too. We would all breathe loudly, in chorus, after the "Amen" that followed, while behind my shut eyes, my gaze doubly shielded by my clasped palms, I imagined young men and women with their hair tied up in red bandanas sweeping down at night into the Kozencheri property. I always shivered after these thoughts and moved a little closer to my grandmother Mariamma, and she, quite gently, would pull her silken cloak over me for protection. I knew she scarcely spoke to veliappechan and maintained a staunch silence in his presence. Surely the Communists would spare her.

It is in me still, her voice, her bearing: Kozencheri veliammechi, grandmother Mariamma, my appa's mother who loved to scold me for running around in the sun as I did in Tiruvella.

"Only boys do that." She raised herself magisterially on her carved stool. "Only male children; and the other thing," she stopped, sniffing a little into her muslin handkerchief. She had a large, rather dashing wart at the tip of her strong boned nose, a bumpy grayish thing. She refused to have it removed surgically and gave a reason that made perfect sense to me, the logic of instant recognition.

"They'll know me wherever I go," said my grandmother, who never set foot outside her own compound. "They'll know who I am when they come searching for me in the other world, 'There's Mariamma,' he'll say, your veliappechan, 'there she is!'"

As she explained this, seated at the edge of her bed, gazing into the mirror I held up for her while she combed out her long gray hair, I had visions of her, upright, unbowed, her eyes looking straight at the Tree of Life I had learnt of from the biblical Book of Revelations. But the tree was almost hidden by the curvaceous apsaras, long-nailed rakshasis, rosy-cheeked angels with wings jutting out of their shoulders. These creatures who were part of the local population tumbled over and over each other, pouncing, tussling in the mud-colored stuff that filled the long tunnel between heaven and earth. Grandmother did not flinch as she stood there. Through the tunnel wafted the scents of lemon blossom and cigarette smoke, appa's secret vice that she supposedly never knew about.

Try as I might, I could not hear veliappechan's voice, crying out, "Mariamma, Mariamma," as he sometimes did from the lower garden as he stood there with his overseer and the servant who held the black umbrella over his head. Then, wiping his chin with his handkerchief, he would mutter a little and send off one of the servants with a message for her. His voice calling her in the other world was reserved for her ears alone. Perhaps it is the privilege of lovers, who, imagining death in the very act of sex, set up echoes and doubling sounds, curves of sight, even cruel mirages so that the senses, playing at their own deceit can better accommodate the perishing surfaces of the body, sole sites of delight. Surely grandmother Mariamma had made love to no one else. She was a second wife though, for veliappechan's first wife had died in childbirth, and the male child the first wife gave birth to had also died. It was then that the marriage with my grandmother Mariamma was arranged.

Her father was the celebrated Wilson Master of Kottayam. A philosopher and scholar of Sanskrit, he narrowly missed being censured by the church for having publicized his atheism, and was cursed, it was said, with seven daughters. My grandmother came somewhere in the middle of that long line of unwanted women.

"You know she married beneath her, you know that, don't you? If Wilson Master hadn't had his head so filled with papers, he would have taken more trouble with finding your grandmother a husband.

She could at least have been the first wife then, instead of marrying a widower.''

Was that amma's voice? Surely it was. She was explaining to me the circumstances of grandmother Mariamma's life, a conversation we first had when I was approaching puberty, far away from Kozencheri, in Khartoum. Was it always the fate of a woman to marry beneath her? I did not wonder this aloud for I felt amma might be touchy here, since this would certainly seem to be the way she felt about her own life.

In Kozencheri amma tried hard to be the perfect daughter-in-law. She got up as soon as her mother-in-law entered the room and in her father-in-law's presence she always had her head covered. Indeed she rarely entered the same room in which he sat, preferring rather to hover in the doorway. I have a memory of my mother, her head covered in her katau sari with the pink flowers printed in sprays over the border, her head covered, half-hiding her face in the doorway as the great man with his legs raised on the railway-station-waiting-room style of chair questioned her from a great distance. Isn't that where the voice of God the Father is supposed to come from? From a great distance?

But there was no blue sky between them, and veliappechan was certainly not lodged in heaven, on a high rock at the foothills of Mount Meru. There he sat on the massive square veranda of the new house he had built for himself high on the hill. He chewed tobacco, he inclined his head as the servant who boiled his bath-water and rubbed him down with herbal oils, stood at attention, palmyra fan in hand.

''So, what does the letter say? Everything fine, fine?''

Amma said nothing. Veliappechan raised his voice.

''What did you say? Why don't you speak up?''

How timorous she was. I leapt off my perch on the parapet and ran to her, to give her some courage. After all, the letter was from my father, from Khartoum. And it was only because of my appa that she was here, in the in-laws' house.

''Yes, appachen,'' she called out, stung to words by my insouciant behavior. I was making quite a nuisance of myself, pretending to crawl under her sari, and amma wanted to keep all quiet and decorous. ''He's fine.''

A little over two decades later, it was amma who had to speak louder again, for veliappechan was on his deathbed, and had almost lost his hearing. Just before he died, he lost control of his bowels and excrement poured out of him. With the help of Annokochu, who was the only other person there at the time, amma wiped him up and laid out his wasted limbs in fresh muslin.

"His lips trembled, Meena. He was singing Pathiravil, his favorite hymn. But no sounds came. I knew it was over then."

Amma confided this as we sat side by side on the Tiruvella parapet.

"What could we do, or anyone, then? He had held out till his only son, your father, returned from Africa. After that he was too weak to hold on."

She sighed, she looked down at her hands, at the left one with the heavy gold wedding ring on it, the ring she has never removed since the hour it went on.

"Not even when my fingers grew swollen with the last stages of pregnancy, it was Elsa then, remember, I was pregnant with and they feared I had toxemia. Not even then, though it marked the skin so deep, would I take it off."

I looked at her hands. She was fifty-five then, and her hands, the same color as my own, had shrunk a little. The large vein was visible running forward from the wrist to the depth beneath the fingers. Blood raced through her body, as it did through mine.

"You don't wear it much, do you?" She was curious, that was all. It was a moment of peace between us.

"Well, I like to do different things." I held up my hands, the finger nails painted dark red, the latest Lakme color available on the main street in Tiruvella. No rings were visible.

"But David, I notice, always wears his."

"Yes, well, it's different for men, I think, don't you?"

But she wouldn't rise to the bait and rose hastily, to make sure the chicken was marinating in its black earthenware pot and to make sure that the fishman wasn't calling from over the hillside.

"It was the fishman, do you think?" she asked anxiously. How different she was from her mother-in-law, grandmother Mariamma, who never showed her anxiety, who always sat like a queen, mundu laid out straight in pleats down her knees, elbows elegantly crooked, neck straight, even in those days when she moved her stool to the edge of the kitchen to listen to the chatter of the milkmaids and cooks, a basket of tiny blood-red onions in her lap for her to peel.

It was growing harder for grandmother Mariamma to see. In

those last days I watched her as she kept peeling the onion and only stopped when the narrow-bladed knife nicked her flesh. She held up her index finger and off from it, almost as if it were a strip of human skin, rolled the pale, translucent bands of onion flesh.

The summer after I turned five, amma and I were in Tiruvella waiting for my sister Anna to grow to her full nine months in her nice warm lodgings under our mother's belly button. Suddenly, veliammechi and veliappechan arrived for tea. In the bathroom, shivering under the cold water Marya slapped on my cheeks, I heard the car grind to a halt. When the door of the black Ambassador car opened, how carefully grandmother Mariamma put her foot down on the gravel. My Kozencheri grandparents made their way to the drawing room where Ilya was waiting for them. Veliammechi asked for me, her only son's child. Anna, whom they all hoped would be male, was still three months away from birth.

I squirmed free of Marya, who was trying to clean me up. She was forced to rush into the garden, waving her arms. I hid in the love apple tree, the same hiding place I chose when I fled the arrival of the Malayalam tutor. The great green globe the tree made with its branches swooping down was the perfect haunt for a child. The thick leaves with pointed tips were interspersed with milky flowers whose petals were so light and feathery that if you set your tongue there and licked, your whole body would tickle, ever so sweetly. The bark of that tree was perfect too—smooth, not rough and cracked like the bark of the mango or jackfruit trees. I hung in the upper branches, parting the leaves to catch a glimpse of the car that stood in front of the porch with the pointed archway at the entrance to the Tiruvella house. Somehow Marya knew I was there. She stood below in the shade, peering upwards. I could see her breasts through the pointed vee of her chatta. "Meena, Meenamol," she whispered, pleading with me. "Come down, Veliammechi wants you."

Finally I took pity on Marya. I shinned down the tree like a monkey and allowed her to lead me off. Swiftly Marya rubbed the towel once again over my knees and cheeks and straightened my dress. There was no time to do my hair properly. She patted it down with her hands and pushed me forward till all of a sudden I stood in front of veliammechi, who had left the drawing room and made her way to the dining room with the huge teak table, over which Chinna had set the damask tablecloth.

Veliammechi seated herself quite precisely so that her cotton and silk blended into the pointed tip of the tablecloth. Catching sight of me, she sat up even more stiffly. She caught hold of me by the hand and looked me up and down. There was an instant when her voice quavered, an affection, a pity for me, something like that. But she needed to remind me of who I was and then prepare me for my future.

"Child, come here now." She made me stand up close to her, looking straight at the wart on her nose.

"First, never forget the pure blood that flows in your veins, from the Kaitheyil kudumam and the Sankaramangalam kudumam."

She deliberately omitted her husband's family from the accounting of pure bloods. I did not let on I had noticed her lapse.

"Never forget that pure blood. Come here, child, don't shuffle off." She gripped me by the elbow, kinder now, having to break the sore thing to me, a child without beauty, a plump dark-skinned thing.

"The point is you are so dark. You take after your mother's side in that."

Veliammechi had no compunction in saying this. She would have said it even if amma were listening. How straight she sat with her immaculate form, her starched garments drawn upright as if a pin descended her spine, much as they taught me in elocution class years later. "Walk as if a pin were dropped through your spine and an invisible wire held you up to the ceiling." Those words that came out of the Australian mistress's mouth in Unity High School, Khartoum, might have been inspired by veliammechi's gleaming posture.

My grandmother Mariamma was so fair skinned, I imagined all her blood coming from the Syrian side of the family. Her great-grandfather, sent to Antioch for spiritual training in the Orthodox doctrines, had married a Syrian woman and brought her back to Kerala, and many of his descendents had the pale skin and light eyes of the Syrians, or so it was rumored. But indeed there were many servants and others of lower status who were as fair as veliammechi.

She drew me close to her so that I could tell, young as I was, that by her side I seemed a different race altogether, and the whole

of beauty lay with her. She drew me so close I could smell the
fragrance of the herbs she boiled into her bathwater and the
rosewater that was sprinkled over her silken cloak before she pinned
it into place.

"Look child, you are dark enough as it is. How will you ever
find a husband if you race around in the sun? Now it's time to stop
and do a little embroidery and let one of the maids plait your hair
properly. See how terribly dry it is? Let her braid those velvet ribbons into it." She placed two dark velvet ribbons in my hand. I trembled with pleasure, in sheer surprise.

Her words never left me. She spoke so little that those sentences
constituted a grand speech and I could not forget them. Nor could
I ever forget the confusion her words created in me. Already by virtue of what I was, dark like my mother, I was a cut below her and
beauty was impossible. And I knew it was only because of the fine
ancestral lines and the landholdings that she had permitted her son
to marry such a woman. Then, because appa had gone to work in
Africa, there was always the danger that I would become a jungli
of sorts, ill-kempt, barbarous, impossible to tame. Furthermore, it
was clear that amma, having been used to ayahs and maids all her
life, had absolutely no idea of how to raise a girl-child properly.

Still, and this only added to my confusion, I was left with the
sense that, if I tried hard enough, behaved well enough, I might
overcome these faults, so grievous in me. In time I might even marry a handsome man with large properties. But decorous behavior,
embroidery, and some musical skills were essential and what was
I doing in that direction? What was I doing to overcome my defi-
ciencies? In my grandmother's eyes, I had to try very hard. I had
to learn how to grow up as a woman. I had to learn my feminine
skills, labor hard to grab hold of what beauty I could.

I comforted myself with the knowledge that in two hours the
black car would have left for Kozencheri with my grandparents inside and I could return to my barefoot pleasures, tree climbing, hiding out in the ash pit or rabbit hutch, mango picking, tapioca tasting.
On rainy days, in Tiruvella, with no one telling me what to do, I
could amuse myself in Ilya's study, pulling down heavy volumes
of the Bible and its various concordances and translations, the lighter
volumes of Marx and Engels and Gandhi and Niebuhr and Tillich.
I could make them into an unwieldy pyramid of words and dance
around them, pretending I was a rakshasi come down from the

Vindhya Mountains or an apsara who had suddenly lost her wings and was forced to seek shelter in a human home.

In my early childhood in Tiruvella I could play with the children of the servants or watch the workmen sweating with the effort of laying the railway line, and remain ignorant of the labor unrest or the large-scale organization of workers that the Communist Party of India had brought about in Kerala in the mid-fifties. If over breakfast I heard Ilya read from the newspapers that five men had been killed near Kayankulam in a labor dispute or that twenty striking workers had been imprisoned, what did it mean to me, a small child, held firmly in her five-acre garden. The worried huddle of servants in the kitchen courtyard, words whispered about a fisherman who was too vocal in his demand for a fair price and had his tongue cut out, or of a whole family murdered by local goondas, meant more. There was fear then, in the air, some possibility too, of the wretched poverty in which so many lived being alleviated. But those words vanished in the security of tea and dinner and the order of silver plates laid out on the damask tablecloth grandmother Kunju had brought back from Ireland many years ago.

Ilya believed in the social gospel and the uplift of the poor. He had many friends who were Communists, including the great leader E.M.S. Nambudiripad who used to come when I was a child and take tea on the front veranda with Ilya. But Ilya was a staunch member of the Congress Party, which seemed to him, as the party Gandhi had founded, the best means to any truly Indian version of social justice. In any case he never questioned his own class basis. He came from an old feudal family with extensive lands in Niranum, and while land could be given away, as he and grandmother Kunju did during the years of the Nationalist struggle so that some landless peasants could be resettled, he never questioned the condition of his birth. Still, rather than live a traditional life, he went out, beyond its borders, in search of knowledge and truth. But at home there were always the house and garden and the estates of cardamom in the hills, the basis of property from which the new nationalism could emerge, what Gandhi had spoken of as ''trusteeship.''

The thoughts about nationalism and the social gospel of Christ were those that Ilya forged in the company of other intellectuals of his time, in response to the pressing needs of the new nation. I must have been only five when he first described one of his journeys to me. As a young man, he had traveled to the United States, to Trinity College in Hartford to study for his divinity degree. Returning to India in 1913, he filled packing crates with his theology books and shipped them separately. It was 1913 and the height of the tensions preceding World War I. The ship that carried his books was torpedoed and all his student belongings sunk to the bottom of the sea. Ilya, who had traveled on another ship, was stranded in Britain. He made his way to Ireland and spent time with the Irish Nationalists there. In London in 1914 he met Gandhi as well as the poet Sarojini Naidu. By now Ilya was part of the Indian student groups pressing the claims of self-governance. On his return home, he threw himself into work for the Nationalist movement.

Almost seventy by the time I was born, he was well established as an intellectual and community leader, a spokesman for the Mar Thoma Syrian Christians of Kerala. From all those who came to call on him and from the numerous public speeches he gave, I learnt to accept his place in the world around him, his public power. I loved him more than I have ever loved anyone in my life—in that intensity that childhood brings, severing us from ordinary light, the daily bread of routine and orderliness. Still, I sensed that the very things he taught me about—love and equality and the sameness of all human beings in God's sight—were what our lives in Tiruvella did not have and could not brook.

5. *Crossing Borders*

When I think back through earliest childhood, the houses I lived in, the real, solid places I knew shine out for me, various, multiple, bound together by the landmass of India, an accustomed geography. The constancies of my life, the hands I held onto, the rooms or gardens I played in, ripple in memory, and sometimes it is as if the forgotten earth returns. I remember little things, a window ledge with white paint, the fragrance of wildflowers, appa's bicycle.

In Allahabad appa had a black bicycle he rode to work each day. It suited him well. Sometimes the path that led to our house was so bumpy and he rode so fast that the tires jerked up a halo of dust. Appa was full of verve and loved to travel. We lived in Bambrali, near the Civil Aviation Training Centre where appa taught pilots the basics of meteorology, how to tell an oncoming storm, how to navigate their planes through rough weather. The buzz of aircraft filled my infancy.

When we moved to Khartoum, again we lived near an airport and the whine and splutter of low-flying craft, the low drone of the larger flying machines made a constant brown sound against which I lived and moved. My first lines when I made poems as a child were etched in my own head against the metallic sibilance of aircraft. How frail the words seemed when set against the constant reminder of flight, the skies crisscrossed by thundering silver birds.

In 1947, after his marriage to amma, appa set off for further studies in England. With a master's degree in physics from Madras University, he had trained to be a meteorologist in the Indian government service. Now he was going abroad to study further. It was customary that a young man, before setting off abroad, be fitted out with a bride, an anchor, a calling card in reverse. There would be no danger then from temptations in London: liquor, white women, or whatever might befall a handsome, earnest young fellow determined to do well in his life. Returning two years later, in grand style, his M.Sc. from Imperial College in hand, two garden parties at Buckingham Palace behind him, appa picked up amma who had been waiting all this while and took her off to Allahabad, his first posting after Indian independence.

Amma was frail and beautiful. She was quite unsuited to life as the wife of a junior civil servant, which was what appa was in those days. He had to show her how to make tea and how to prepare a meat curry, his one culinary accomplishment. He never forgot that he had to borrow money from her father to hire a cook, Motrilal, an elderly man in clean white kurta-pyjama whose arts made for a precarious peace in the family. Motrilal prepared the delicious chapatis, flat whole-wheat pancakes. Rolled out and fried, they puffed up slightly. Massed on a piece of muslin, one on top of the other, basted with ghee, they melted in the mouth.

Sometimes amma would fill a hot chapati with jam and roll it up for me. She would let me stand on the front veranda of the Allahabad house, rolled up chapati in hand, warm jam dribbling down my lips. I amused myself by staring at the crows that pecked the overripe melons. Sometimes the crows circled very close to me, but they never actually touched me with their crinkled wings. Once as I stood on the Allahabad veranda, a cur approached. It had dirty matted fur from the ditches in which it slept, brown and white patches on its thin body, and held its tail erect. It approached me, wagging its tail. I inched back into a rattan armchair. It pounced at the chapati. Later that day amma and appa in a panic carried me into the clinic and I had seven injections in my upper thigh. Seven milk injections. I was fairly sure that nothing but the saliva of the dog had touched me. But their fear was acute and real. Had that scrawny creature been rabid, I might have been at risk. There were cases in the neighborhood of children dying terrible deaths, moaning and shaking and pulling out their own hair.

I lived with my parents in Allahabad till just before I turned four. Each year before the hot season started, amma, with an appropriate female traveling companion, a servant who could help with my things, set off with a four-day supply of food and fresh water. We entered the first-class compartment of the train, with its plush padded seats and shiny electric fans. The train could take us home, all the way to Kottayam. On the first journey, when I was four months old, Appa helped amma and the ayah into the train and the porter lowered his red turban, unloading a huge slab of ice. The ice was covered in sawdust and rough sacking. It had the odor of crushed jasmine, a rich, slightly overripe scent. With the fans turned on and the ice secure underfoot, we were kept reasonably cool for the long overland journey. The temperatures outside, as the train sped though the northern dry lands, could rise as high as 114 degrees.

The food and the drink were all secured in thermos flasks and stainless steel containers, piled into the baskets with two handles especially equipped for carrying. There were rolls of mattresses and pillows and piles of little diapers with separate safety pins. There was a pair of scissors too, lest a food parcel need to be slit open, or someone's hair—this was my worst fear as I grew older—caught in one of the fans in the train and the long tug to death began.

I was taught very early that I should never stand with my head close to a whirling fan. Throughout childhood, in addition to ceiling fans, there were fans set on tabletops and pedestal fans that stood on the ground with their long silver stalks, capable of being adjusted for the maximum circulation of air. Girls were especially at risk. In a trice their long hair, pink ribbons and all, could be sucked up into the death machine.

That had happened to Graciemol, my uncle's daughter. She was a grown woman, a surgeon with an FRCS, a brilliant woman with a fondness for red silk saris. She had lovely long hair down to her knees. One afternoon, while combing her hair after her bath—like all Kerala women she had a fondness for oiling her long hair and washing it twice a day—she stood by the fan. There was only an aged servant woman in the room with her. Graciemol's hair started to tangle and knot as the fan whirled tighter and harder. The electric shocks passed into her poor twitching body and all that brilliance shivered into a heap of red silk. The old woman was too panic-stricken to touch her and so saved her own life. My uncle Patros, a man so proud of his English accent that he hardly knew what to say in that tongue, never revealed his pain. But each time I looked at him I wondered about it.

He was marked in my mind. He had lost a daughter to electric shocks. Yama, the God of Death, in the form of an electric Usha fan had carried her off. Even when his fine, aristocratic mouth rounded out English syllables that sounded so odd in the shade of the lime trees where the doves perched, or by the tethered goats, I could never forget the fate that had befallen his daughter. Indeed there was always a slight suspicion, fostered in me by amma, that it was Graciemol's brilliance, surely somewhat unbalancing for anyone, let alone a woman, that led to her absent-mindedness that monsoon morning. And surely her love for red silks could not have helped. It too was distracting.

There was always something unnatural in the exceptionally gifted—fate strung them down into darkness, held them on a hook, sometimes even sprung them into death too soon. Like Sheemon, grandmother Mariamma's cousin. I had seen his face in the photos of the *Kudumacharitram*, the family history book. He had a tight face, with high cheekbones, thin lips. A student at Presidency College, Calcutta, he favored the winged collars and dark Edwardian suits of the day. Just before he was to set off to Oxford, he suffered a terrible brain fever and died in Bengal. It was said that he could quote the whole of *The Ancient Mariner* by Coleridge without a single pause. No intake of breath, nothing. I marveled at his grace. I wondered what this terrible, exotic poem could be. I never reconciled myself to it even when finally I read it. With its palpable torment, its high seas and albatross, it seemed part of a fatal excess to me. Its author's opium addiction and periodic craziness, when I learnt of them later, framed the brain fever my grandmother's cousin had suffered.

Back and forth, forth and back, I went as a child. The train rides did not cease. They persisted right through my childhood. Once I saw a mad soldier tied up in knots. It was in Pune Station. Appa, amma, and I were waiting for a train. At the other side of the wide platform, curiously deserted for that time of day, was a group of soldiers. One soldier, a strongly built man, was stooped over, all contorted. Abruptly he jerked himself down, sideways onto the platform floor. I could not take my eyes off him. As he straightened up, his arms shot out at odd angles. Three others closed in on him. I kept staring at him though amma turned away. The muscles in his face grew swollen as his comrades approached. They were dressed in regulation khaki. They pummeled him to the ground. He struggled, a bullock with cramps in its gut. They tossed a tough net over him. Foam spilled from his mouth as he struggled and leapt, dragging the net tighter over his limbs and head. So knotted up and raging, he was pulled off to a reserved compartment of a train that had just drawn in. The net was so tight it seemed like a second skin within which, helpless and kicking, he was throttled.

In 1955 appa was transferred to the Meteorological Office in Pune, in the foothills of the Deccan. In Pune, I started a few mornings of school at Saint Mary's, a convent school run by Protestant nuns. Each morning, a van with a driver picked me up. I was helped in and sat by the window, next to another little girl. I was stiff, uncomfortable at first in the dark navy uniform with white blouse that hurt my shoulders with the heaviness of starched cotton. I was proud, though, of my leather belt and little bag. The nuns were kind. They checked our fingernails before class and, in deference to four-year-old needs, laid out mats at noon each day for our naps.

I recall the great balconies of the school and the banyan tree with vines twisted over its trunk. The French windows on the second floor were open as we lay on the mats and the tree was so close, its upper trunk almost flush with the mosaic floor. When I squinted as I lay on my side, the mosaic bits came closer, splitting and moving in their patterns of maroon and black and white, making a figuration of roses, dancing roses that I kept behind my eyelids as I watched the trees. I was held in a bowl of stalk and leaf and vine that revived my Kerala summers. Bird song entered my ears, persisted as the noisy streets came closer, rough and bumpy as we rode back home. Amma was waiting for me at the red painted door of the house. I could not have conceived of returning home without her.

In summer there was the ritual return to Kerala, to Ilya's home in Tiruvella. Amma traveled south when the heat grew too heady, when the green painted screens could not be flung any lower, nor mango juices cool the senses. However hot the season, the Kerala seacoast prevented terrible excesses of temperature. After a few months we returned to Pune. And so my life, though filled with motion, was stable. My childhood had a clear form: parents and then displacing them for part of each year my Ilya, the grandfather I loved so dearly.

*

In Pune, we lived in a little house with a large garden next to Deccan Gymkhana Road. "Deccan Gymkhana ki galli me hai," amma made me learn the address in Hindi, a language that was native to me given my earliest years in Allahabad, but one which I have never acquired again with the delight that should surely be incumbent upon using an early tongue. I can read Devanagari script, though, if slowly and with great care, and the memory of learning those letters in Pune returns to me.

Behind the Pune house was a tangled garden with sunflowers that amma cultivated, their heavy black seed heads lit by the early morning sun as it rose over the hedge and flooded us. On the other side of the hedge was the home of the erstwhile actress of the Marathi stage, Mistress Snehaprabha.

She called on us very late one night with her hair marcelled in waves, in the manner of certain ladies of the stage and screen. She wore a red brocade blouse cut very low and her forehead was clean and pale. I think appa was rather charmed by her. He was young and handsome and had an eye for female beauty, though I knew his religious fervor, bred in the Syrian Orthodox churches of his childhood and then overlaid with the Anglicanism of his years in London as a young man, effectively prevented any effusion of passion. So Snehaprabha called on us that night, accepted the cardamom tea amma offered her, and called me to sit on her lap. I did so, feeling the shiny silk that covered her thighs. How white her face was with all that powder. And what was her story? I was fascinated by her, a single woman living across the hedge, quite independent it would seem, though one never knew if she had a protector in town: quite desirable, flaunting herself in that way, rather than being a wife. Amma was a wife, Snehaprabha was not. It seemed to me that all the benefits lay on the other side of the tamarind hedge where the sun rose in the morning: the profusion of chocolates she gave me on feast days, the expensive cars with gentlemen in them that landed on her side of the road, the clowns and even the bear-toting vagabonds, or men with dancing monkeys she befriended, calling me over in a loud voice, her cheeks dimpled with the effort, "Hurry, hurry before the bear stops dancing." So I raced over, barefoot, my dress covered with dust, and watched the heavy footed bear tread on her daisies, its long sad shambles rewarded by shakes of the tambourine the thin man held, his loose arm hugging the drum as the bear danced, faster and harder, and the dust rose in a sheen.

It was Snehaprabha who explained to us the significance of the round concrete pit, three feet deep, large as a good-sized swimming pool, that lay in the back garden:

"Godavaran's circus. All those young things from Tamil Nadu used to pitch their tents here. Those were the days! With my rehearsals at the theater all day, the acting at night, what a storm of applause we used to raise. And then at night, returning past the main road, the tents flickering with lights. Sometimes they set up flares in metal hooks, at the sides of the tents as the trapeze artists swung."

She patted me on the arm as she said this and I was filled with expectations. I wanted to be a trapeze artist. I was convinced of the merit of my decision and told Ilya when I saw him that summer. He did not say much. So I whispered it all to Susikali, the mad magical little girl Ilya had made up for me. In the large southern bedroom in the Tiruvella house I crouched under one of the desks where the books lay in heaps, and paper shone with ink markings—Ilya was revising his *History of the Mar Thoma Church*. I crouched, making up tents and flying bodies, the shining suits of the trapeze children bulging from the dark underside of the teak desk on which grandmother's initials, E. K., were marked. Why, I asked amma, why did grandmother Kunju want her initials on the furniture? Several of the fine wood pieces had the same letters.

"That was so that, if Ilya were in prison and the British came to take away the furniture, it would have her initials and she could hold onto it. The pieces marked with her name could not be impounded." Amma was quite serious. There was something in her tone that made me stop, a vein of hardness, of facing up to things that it took me years to appreciate. So under grandmother's desk, tucked behind the white khadi dhoti that Ilya always wore, his legs shielding me from the world outside, I dreamt up the fliers in red silk, their bodies hoisted and framed by the threads that ran glittering through Godavaran's circus tent that had once stood in our Pune backyard.

In 1956, just before I turned five, I left India in amma's company. In 1956 when the Sudan gained independence, Azhari, the president, turned to Nehru for help. Rather than have the British send technical aid, he wanted assistance from other Third World countries. Appa was thirty-five at the time; amma was twenty-eight, my age when I made the journey to America. A position for a meteorologist had been advertised in the *Government Gazette*, and full-time members of the Indian Service could apply. He applied for the position and was chosen to work "under secondment" from the Indian government. When I was four and a half, he left Pune for his new job. It was five years since his return from London after his studies at Imperial College.

I have often felt that my father was a Royalist at heart. Something in the pomp and circumstance of British rule appealed to him. He was devoted to the secular ideals of the new Indian government, but the British sense of order, of stilling the "native" chaos in the colonies struck a chord with my father. Perhaps that had to do with the tumult of the feudal family he came from and his constant efforts to keep his own emotions under firm dominion. Years later he told me he believed in Newton's conceptions of the universe, the order and clarity presumed in the universe. The instabilities of the winds and waters, of the monsoon and the haboob (that dark desert wind he had to forecast in the Sudanese summers) coexisted in his mind with the geometric precisions of a physics that could refigure all things in a divinity without division.

The photographs of the time show a handsome young man, slender, with strong shoulders, even-featured, with dark wavy hair. His eyes are tender with happiness. Amma by his side is slight, her hair pulled back in a low, tight bun. Her face is delicately molded, the cheekbones high, the forehead wide and handsome. There is something quiet, even reticent about my mother in the photograph. She looks down, away from the photographer to the little child in a smock dress, whose curly hair is pinned to one side. I am there, at four, skipping between my parents, one hand in each of theirs. I am wearing shiny shoes that catch the light and deflect the image. We are standing in the back courtyard of the Tiruvella house where the roof points down in two triangles for the rain water to fall onto granite slabs. We are close to the mulberry tree, a bit of a blur in the photo. Like my Kozencheri grandfather before him, my father has strong shoulders. In the photo I see a small child swinging in the air, between her parents. Like the clot of blood the Koran speaks of. The rest abyssal.

*

In Ilya's study there was an old atlas with shiny oil cloth covers. The rivers of all the world were drawn in blue-green. Ilya showed me the map of Africa. He explained that amma and I were going to live in a place called Khartoum. It was colored yellow like the rest of the Sudan. What a curious country it made in the atlas, with the straight lines that marked out the boundaries to the top and sides, as if someone had taken a ruler and drawn it all out. Ilya ran his fingers over the green lines of the Nile, that met and held in a great fork. He pointed out the twin arms of the Red Sea. Just south of it Meroë hung like a pool of great water, an ancient Christian civilization. "It was an extraordinary civilization," Ilya explained to me, "with many connections to our own." His voice seemed to come from very far away. Sometimes I thought it was because he was so much older than I; sometimes I reasoned it was because of his great height, six feet, one inch. I tugged at his hand and he bent a little closer and hugged me. I sensed some intense emotion in him, something that churned inside, of which he could not free himself. I raced away into the bedroom where amma slept and I bumped straight into my great-aunt from Chenangeri, a tiny woman swathed in a white silk cloak, who was supervising the elaborate packing.

For many weeks on the cool stone floor of the two central bedrooms in the Tiruvella house, trunks and suitcases, portmanteaus and traveling bags had stood with their mouths yawning open. Women sat on the low rattan modas, packing and unpacking all that we might need. Almost as much was taken out as was put back in. Pickles, for instance, the delicious tiny mangoes stewed in spices and coconut oil, wedged in with the tiny green chillies that grew on the bush by the kitchen window. Great-aunt from Chenangeri had insisted they be packed, so Marya without thinking too carefully wedged them in next to amma's silk saris. Never mind that the mango bottles had their cocoon of wax paper and stitched cloth all over them, or that they were wrapped up yet again in newspaper. When great aunt saw them she tugged them out with a loud yell and placed them upside down on amma's embroidered pillowcases. The old lady had an odd sense of humor. "Like decapitated fishes, won't they bleed!" she cackled. Little tears of joy ran down the edges of her eyes. I thought her special, not quite of our time or place, a dark red stitch that held us to the past.

She and Ilya's oldest sister Mallapallileamachi were the only women in our immediate family whose ears had been stitched with those heavy gold ornaments, studs of ruby and diamond and fret-work so intricate that the inner cubicles of gold were never visible to the eye, only the jeweler's awl had reached them. I wondered at the delicacy of the hidden tympanum of gold, never visible to us, hidden in the burden of metal and precious stone that was so weighty it had to be pinned into the hair and suspended with gold chains over the head lest it tear the cartilage in the woman's ear. But the earlobe grew and grew with its burden, flapping its long oval form till the flesh reached great-aunt's humped shoulder and its drape of white silk.

"Hurry, hurry," Chenagerileamachi cried. She was dancing a crooked dance of joy, "before the cut fishes bleed!" She loved to watch people prepare for travel, watch people leave. No one thought of her as crazy, for, in an instant, an inner sorrow shut her up and her eyes misted over. Her mother had died when she was just a baby and the loss had confounded her forever. Married early to a man with large holdings of property in one of the more waterlogged districts of Central Travancore, she had lived out her days as the mistress of the house, overseeing the long boats as they bore in their cargoes of pepper and coconuts, and watching out of the carved wooden windows as dusk fell over waters that in monsoon time rose so close to the house that the cows had to be moved into a makeshift stable just outside the kitchen and the whole brood of chickens with their cackling and filthy droppings accommodated in what had been her clean pantry.

It was then that the Chenangeri chickens took to laying eggs everywhere, in little nooks where brass vessels were kept, under the shrine where the candles were lit so the image of Jesus would have light under it, in the ash in the warmth of the old-fashioned earthern stoves. Having seen the Chenangeri chickens in action, I tried fruitlessly to persuade the Tiruvella chickens to do the same. But at the slightest scratch of chicken claw in the clean stone kitch-en, Chinna rushed out with her broom in hand, crying *"Shoo-Kori-Shoo,"* glaring at me as I imitated her gesture. Now I was happy to see that it was a tearful Chinna who presided over the packing for our departure. There were blouses and saris and petticoats to fold, books and toys and a boxful of beads, sweets boiled in sticky gur, almonds pressed into jackfruit, brocades and silks and muslin frocks with matching underskirts. I had special clothes laid out for the trip, the first leg of which took us to Madras.

Ilya accompanied us as far as Madras. As we left for Bombay, I saw his tall figure dressed in white dhoti and juba, and clung nervously to amma's hand. As the train started up, metal wheels biting into tracks, I felt for an instant as if I had metamorphosed, become another thing. Looking back, I feel as if in that instant my life split, then doubled itself, in a terrible concupiscence. That moment of parting from Ilya, repeated time and again as we returned to Tiruvella, only to leave again, became my trope of loss. Even now, I see his tall figure standing in the sunlight at the edge of the runway in Cochin airport, or in the station at Madras. Just before the sun blinded me, I saw the tears on his face. "Unless the eye were soliform, it could not see the sun," Coleridge wrote, quoting Plotinus, in explanation of our bond to divinity. For me that bond comes from radical loss, the light pouring into the place where Ilya stood as the train that was carrying me moved its metal body into the future.

On the train to Bombay, I remember the cool air wafting from the fans in the first-class compartment, but in my excitement I found it hard to sleep. I clutched my picture book, given me by Ilya, a book of Bible stories. I loved the pictures of Joseph best because of his many-colored coat, but could not bear him trapped in a pit like a wild beast. I felt that not all the years in the Pharaoh's favor in the courts of Egypt could restore the grace he was robbed of by that first betrayal. So when I came to the Joseph story, as the train rattled north and amma flipped through her *Eve's Weekly* magazine or stared listlessly out of the window at the brown dusty landscape that turned cows and horses into the same color, I shut the pages of the coloring book with a quick snap. I shut my eyes and tried to imagine the Tiruvella garden, the freckled green leaves on the mango tree by the cow shed, the chickens that might finally have tricked Chinna and managed to lay their eggs in the ash pile, cackling and dancing in their triumph. For an instant I thought of Ilya, who was probably approaching the empty house now. How would he live without me? What would he do? I could not bear the thought and pushed it aside. Then lulled by the jogging train, I fell asleep in my soft cotton holdall.

In Bombay amma and I spent an afternoon by the sea in the elaborate stone house that the Pisharotis lived in. Dr. Pisharoti was appa's friend and he was to take us to the SS *Jehangir,* in which amma and I would set sail. It was at Bombay that I got my first taste of the middle stretches of the Arabian Sea. Not that I hadn't seen the sea before. From Tiruvella we were quite close to the southern seas and I had made lots of trips in the black car with a driver to Kanyakumari, home of the virgin goddess Meenakshi. I felt a kinship with the eponymous goddess but could not understand why she needed to remain virginal. I knew that Kanika Mariam was a virgin too, Marya the mother of Jesus after whom I was baptized. Why were they both virgins? I had asked Chinna once, but with her eyes fixed on the elaborate fish stew she was cooking at the time, ladling in the fresh grated coconut, adding a dash of turmeric, heaps of chopped coriander, she refused a real answer. ''They had nothing better to do child, except keep themselves that way. Though for the Holy Marya who can say? Perhaps that was the commandment.'' Behind her, Marya the maid, buxom, pink cheeked, a veritable siren by the waters of the Pamba where she was learning how to swim, started giggling.

I wanted to be back in Tiruvella, but as best I could I threw myself into the afternoon with the Pisharoti girls and the picnic they had arranged by the waters of the Arabian Sea in Bombay. We were just a stone's throw away from their veranda in Colaba and the mothers could watch us.

I had never seen seawater like this. It lacked the blueness of the ocean on the Kerala coast, or the ruddiness in monsoon time when the undertow loosened the laterite that bled into the sands at the shoreline. Here where the seawater washed onto humped rocks, it was gray, lashed with white; I thought I saw darting fish. The foam washed in almost as far as the balcony where we all sat drinking tea and eating the most perfect dahi vadais. The sweet dahi dripped onto my wrist. I licked it up.

There were seven Pisharoti children, and Jaya, thin and birdlike, closest to me in age, drew me as far down to the water's edge as I would venture. The foam hissed and blubbered. Now there was no one else in sight, a few spindly palm trees, black rocks, and the purring foam. I felt my feet slipping forward. But the grains of sand underneath, hard and prickly, saved me from that old croaking sound. Round the curve of the veranda amma and Mrs. Pisharoti were laughing, their voices rippling out towards us, weightless. I was glad amma could not see me now, my legs smeared with salt water, leaping as I clutched one of Jaya's incredibly long plaits, woven up and looped with shining black ribbon. Both of us were dressed in the long pavade, ankle-length skirts that South Indian girl-children wear. Mine was fastened up around my waist, tucked into my bloomers that hung around my thighs in bagged swirls. Jaya's was pinned up to her little blouse. She was most enterprising and kept a safety pin tucked into her bodice for precisely such exigencies. I was glad she was there with me. I did not like the cold, slippery water and the pale bleached sand underfoot, dirty-white colored like tired, unbleached garments worn by the very poor.

That first ocean crossing obsesses me. I think of it as a figuration of death. Losing sense, being blotted out, thrown irretrievably across a border. But it also provokes the imaginary. I am forced to fabricate, trust to the maquillage of words, weave tales. A five-year-old child, I stood still by amma's side on deck watching the dark coil of waves. She wasn't dragging me off in a net. Could I have stopped her? My mind moved to the mad soldier dragged off in a net at Pune Station. What would they have done if I had rolled myself into a ball, then flung out, kicking, biting Chinna's hand, tearing Marya's blouse, crying, "No, no, I don't want to go." I felt I hated my mother for taking me away. I let go of her hand. I stared at the thick dark waves. Even now, in memory, they unfold like cut tongues.

Lying in bed, dreaming of that crossing, I am invaded by the fragrance of burning water. How can water burn, you might ask? What fragrance can it have, this burning water?

In a white painted steamer of the Mogul Lines, the SS *Jehangir*, amma and I sailed from Bombay to Port Sudan. On deck with the shining glass beads that our neighbor from Tiruvella had wrapped up in tissue paper for my birthday, I sat mute, wordless. In spite of amma, sitting in her Kashmir silk sari in a deck chair in the shade, I felt I had no name, no nature. The water was flat and blue and endless. That night, out of the porthole, I saw an oil tanker sailing towards Iraq.

We sat at the captain's table. Amma had tried to school me in how to use my spoon correctly, how to adjust the white napkin on my lap. I felt uncomfortable. A Parsi lady sat next to me. She kept picking at her fishbones with a silver toothpick. "Sweeti, sweeti," she cooed at me. Once, after a glass of too much of something, she leant over and kissed me several times on the cheek. Instinctively I lifted my right hand and did what I did with my great-aunts who were given to the same mischief. With great deliberation I wiped her wetness off my cheek, first with the outside of my hand, then with the palm. Then I glared at her with my rakshasi gaze. I imagined my eyes smoking red as Shiva's did in his rage, or as the rakshasi's when the priest from Patananthita approached her with his hammer and nail to capture her.

Out of the corner of my eye I saw amma gulp down her glass of water. She shifted uncomfortably in her chair. As if from a great distance I saw her trying to placate Mrs. Bootliwalla. I kept my eyes on the lady's large bosom where a red rose, cut and crimped from stiff Bazaar lace, bobbed uncomfortably.

There were no other children among the regular passengers. There were old retired civil service men, a few diplomats nodding in the shade, several wives, and some unattached ladies. There were also those who traveled in the hold, though I had nothing to do with them. I could hear them when we sat on the lower deck with parasols over our heads, amma and I. My legs were thin and long already and covered at the ankles with little white socks, their rims turned down. If I dropped a book or a ball of thread from something I was stitching, I could peer down through the angle of my legs, past the little white socks, blurred now with my haste. In that way I could see the figures in the hold behind us, through the part of the metal covering that was raised.

A blur of figures, mothers, children, old grandparents, all knotted into each other. I heard a babble of tongues, watched rice bubbling in a blackened cooking pot, parts of life I recognized, the poverty, the desperate energy of making do, the enervation. All the while amma and I sat quietly, cut out like two paper figures in our well-ironed clothes. I was drawn towards the figures in the hold, frightened too by the darkness there. I knew that, when the rains came, the passengers would have to huddle under the huge canvas pilings tossed now to the side of the metal bulwarks. And sea storms were sudden. In the rising heat that always overcame the rain on the Indian Ocean, the hold people would hang out their bedding and wet clothes, boil up the lentils, or play cards. The children, in little groups, chattered and raced. I heard their stamping feet.

I was tempted once to stand by the side of the hold and peer right in, but amma would not let me. She would not even let me look directly at them, so I was forced to drop my ball of wool or the book I was glancing at in order to gaze through my knees, my hair swinging low, touching the wooden deck. The blood rushed to my face. I felt the winds, with the scent of salt in them as I hung there. Bit by bit I learnt from amma a shyness in the face of the world, a fear of looking straight at the lives of others. I did not want to be seen. I did not want to intrude. What would they make of me? But that reticence, even as it has held me back, has served me. For I learnt from her too the art of withdrawal, of thinking inwards so that no one could look and tell from a woman's face what her heart might hold.

When amma tucked me into my berth at night, I asked about the tanker I had seen in the distance, as we sat on deck.

"Sometimes those tankers burn on the water and there is no way to stop them. So it's best not to go too close," amma told me. "Captain Irani is very careful." I shut my eyes tight. I imagined the braid on Captain Irani's immaculate coat catching fire. The golden threads shot out as fireworks might and played in the night air over the tanker bound for Iraq. Flames trickled from the tanker, first in little sprays, then sharper forms, arrows or stars as might have adorned an excessively ornate captain's uniform, then fierce plumes, cascades that tumbled from the chariot in which her faithless lover descended into Shakuntala's garden, quite forgetting the pain he had caused her by failing to recognize his true beloved.

Finally I fell asleep, but in the middle of the night I dreamt of a sheet of burning substance such as I had never conceived of before, a covering of immaculate heat, impossible for wood, flesh, or metal to bear. It coated the steamer and the water too, till darkness boiled over into flames and flames burned into waves and danced over the vessel filled with crude oil. But there was no substantial vessel there. No skeletal thing even. Only a ghostly spume upheld by the burning.

I woke up sweating, crying a little, so that amma, sleeping above me, woke too. She came down from her bunk and held my hand and gave me a glass of water to drink from the carafe the steward had brought in. Icy cold water. As I held the glass in my hand, I peeped over her head at the darkness where no flames were. Amma had become a dark silhouette framed by the porthole.

Staring into that black, inky mirror, night water cut by a gray line where water ends and sky begins, I saw my mother. She was poised out of time, a girl again. I saw her as I see her now in my mind's eye, freed from the constraints of this perishing flesh. I saw her as if for the first and last time. I do not know if I knew then what I know now, or perhaps I sensed it dimly in my child's way, taking the knowledge whole into myself where it settled into a place no words could reach: amma and I, mother and child, were crossing into another life.

A week later she was sick with chicken pox and confined herself to the small but well-appointed cabin. All our meals were delivered to our cabin and I never ventured beyond the door. Sometimes I caught a quick glimpse of waves at the edge of the deck, or returned the greetings of the friendly Mrs. Srinivasan who was sailing to Port Said to join her diplomat husband. "Amma is ill," I told her in my very bad Tamil, slipping into Malayalam. And since her own mother was from Palghat, that border region where people speak a mixture of the two tongues, she understood me perfectly.

But amma did not want her in our cabin lest the chicken pox spread, so Mrs. Srinivasan was reduced to keeping a benign if distant gaze on me as she sat like a plump Parvati on her mountainous deck chair, piles of unread Kalki and Anandaviketan spread out around her. In the middle distance the dark waters of the Indian Ocean broke into waves that could not touch her.

Arriving at Port Sudan in March 1956, I laughed and wept all together, freed onto dry earth, freed from those ocean tongues. I rushed into appa's arms, forgetting about amma who walked with her head modestly covered, her cheeks with the chicken pox scars shaded by her silk sari.

Over and over again in the days that followed, as we ate supper in the cool shade of the Red Sea Hotel, or as we crossed the desert in a railway train to Khartoum and I saw the rough glittering sands on either side, I made appa repeat the tale of recognition. I think it gave him real pleasure to tell the story to me, though sometimes he had to be prodded a little till he fell into the rhythm of it.

The narrative repeated made an entry for me into a new life, affixing a running stitch of child and father, appa and I. Without his words, those inklings of the actual, where would I be? Stuck somewhere on the docks at Port Sudan, in between the huge bales of cotton tamped down with metal. I watched fifteen, twenty men with huge heads of hair sticking up high over their shoulders, their muscles working in sweat and sea heat, straining to lift the bales up to the cranes that waited with metal hooks dangling in place. Cotton, grown in the fields of Gezira and Atbara, was packed into bales and loaded onto ships bound for Lisbon, Manchester, Newcastle.

Lacking my father's recognition as I raced up the pier, shorn of the tale he repeated over and over again for me, I might still be held in the darkened cabin of the SS *Jehangir*, still haunted by an oil tanker bound for Iraq, its hull fit to burst into flames.

On the train journey through the desert, from Port Sudan to Khartoum, I recall the polished wood of the table in the Sudan Railways dining car where we had our meals. There were lamps with hooked brass necks built into the side of the carriage, whose green shades cast double images in the bright wood, and thick glass windows and beige curtains to shield the travelers from desert glare. I saw date palms, clumps of them out of the window. Then a wave of speckled sand blew forward, covering them up.

In Kerala the sunlight was always filtered through the green of a vigorous tropical growth, leaves, coconut palms, new paddy fields, acres of intricately bordered fruit trees, while here in the sub-Saharan desert it glinted off the sameness of one earthly substance—sand in all its forms, sliding, shifting over the surfaces of perception. Sometimes I saw a single lorry in the distance, jousting with its own reflection. Sometimes a camel and its hooded rider and then four or five others in a caravan appeared in the moving window, upended, reflected in imaginary water. It took me years to reflect on mirages, consider what is involved in sighting water where there is none, bitter, mimic doublings that dazzle, deflecting gravity, shattering all coordinates.

Reflecting back on that train ride, I am struck by a dry pleasure, a sensation almost aesthetic in the lack of comfort. The desert remains for me a place of austerity, a site where skins are stripped away, where words dance with their illusory doubles.

I enjoyed that train ride immensely. Appa was handsome and well trimmed and I loved to sit next to him, lapping up all his attention. After the efforts of her journey and her recent sickness, amma looked pale, even nauseous. She spoke little. Perhaps she felt that my father, in his pin-striped shirt, was well able to take charge in this strange land to which he had brought us. Over the glass of fresh lemon juice and the cakes the bearer brought in, appa began the story for the third time.

"What did I do? I went up to the top of the Red Sea Hotel. The very top, mind you. And from there I looked out to sea. There it came, slowly up the waterway, the white steamer. And who should I see on the deck?"

Shifting on my seat, I hugged myself in delight, in anticipation.

"I saw Meenamol. Meenamol herself, with two plaits and this very same dress."

I almost knocked over the glass of lemon juice. Now even amma was smiling. By this time all three of us had forgotten the patently fictive nature of this detail.

"Did you see me, appa, did you see me on the ship? Really?"

"Of course, my dear. What do you think? Of course I saw you, right on deck." So on he went with the tale.

"Then I knew it was the right ship. So I rushed down the stairs and jumped into the taxi. The taxi raced the ship to the dock. We were racing neck to neck, my taxi and the SS *Jehangir!*"

I sighed. I was happy now, at peace. I almost didn't need his last words.

"And then you ran down the gangplank, ran and ran into my arms and I lifted you up, up, so high in the air!"

He raised his strong arms above me as he spoke and I felt the air whirl and the mirage outside the window seemed to enter with all its glittering force, till we were lifted, appa and I, in a warm gush of air and we levitated without moving, while amma, so long my guardian, was left behind, a frail, pensive figure seated by the window in a silk sari marked with patterns of mango leaf and bird wing, the very same figures that were etched into the silver box that belonged to her great-great-grandmother, which she was carrying with her in the trunk safely stowed away in our sleeper.

Having left India, on the brink of turning five, I spent the following years of childhood partly in Khartoum, partly in Kerala. Each summer, till Ilya's death in 1962, amma returned with her children to Tiruvella. My sister Anna, who has inherited our grandmother Kunju's lovely heart-shaped face and curly hair, was born in the Mission Hospital in Tiruvella in 1956. My little sister Elsa, who like me has inherited our grandmother Mariamma's lean cheekbones and straight hair, was born there in 1961. Often, for several months after appa returned to Khartoum at the end of each summer, my mother, my sisters, and I remained in the Tiruvella house. My attachment to Kerala deepened. Retained in memory, my affections grew closer, adding layer upon layer to the soil of my imagination. In Khartoum I lived with my parents just south of the ancient cities of Nubia, broken, buried under rubble and sand. The music of oud, zither, and lute, the dark elongated faces of men, women, and angels bristled in me. They formed a spiral in my thoughts with the virgins and saints of my native Kerala.

Khartoum was as parched as a shed snakeskin. I learnt to love the shifting dunes with their spare versions of color, beige, nut brown in the shade, blackness where the sand dipped into invisibility and then a pouring silvery whiteness, almost like the stuff that came off the wings of the cabbage butterflies I trapped in between the rocks of Kozencheri. Freeing the wings, I found my fingers coated in the silvery stuff and afterwards imagined the wings of a human soul composed of that stuff, which seemed to me as rare as the atoms of Democritus, less accessible to touch and taste than the most refined delights of sensuality, akin finally to the spirit the sage Yajnavalkya had dreamt of.

The sands of the Sahara swept into Khartoum. In the stiff winds the sands tore into the heart of the city, into the palace General Gordon had built, into the golden tomb where the Mahdi was buried. The winds were as harsh as coir on the face and hot as spilt ash. Sometimes in dreams I saw them turn and, in a sudden metamorphic twist, dissolve into the finest of silks, torn up, particled, drifting like the powder on a Kerala butterfly's wing.

But dreams, images, cannot annul the shock of transition. The child gulping her vomit down as the plane soars and then drops precipitously through the clouds above the Red Sea; the green fields of Kerala fallen into the brutal heat of the desert.

In the desert, rocks jut out at odd angles and the traveler gazing out of the window of the train or car in the empty regions south of Port Sudan catches a sudden glimpse of mimic water, where trucks painted ocher and dull green drive with their mirror images laced to them, where camels hobble, hooves nailed to other hooves, humps doubled, the lonely riders in gelabia and turban, buckled knee and thigh into imaginary water.

First catching sight of a mirage in the Sudanese desert, a child of five, I found myself clutching the window ledge of the train in sheer excitement. In my mind's eye, the waters of the Tiruvella well, the cool depths of the Pamba River that turns past my Kozencheri grandfather's paddy fields, even the gray welter of the Arabian Sea, all began flowing into this sheer kingdom of doubling, murderous site of vision.

From Ilya I had heard of how a traveler, parched and fit to perish, would stumble to the pool of water under a date palm, sink his mouth into it, and end up bruised. I understood early how the hollowness of the actual can hurt. One mirage too many and one could lose all one's energy and end up too tired even to crawl towards the real source of water.

Twelve years later, at the age of seventeen, that season of excess, I gladly accepted the hyperbole of passion when a man whispered, ''No mirage, you are my oasis.'' I tried hard to contain the ache in my soul when he left to return to Prague. That was in the spring of 1968, and our meetings in a small flat left empty by an acquaintance of his, in a white room by the Nile, were filled with tales of excitement in Wenceslaus Square, of how the Vltava was lit at night by the songs of young people, newly liberated, pouring out poems, plays, stout ideas for reform. He read out the poems of Pushkin to me in the original and the shining lyrics of Pasternak. In between sips of mint tea he described a train ride he had made from Moscow to Vladivostok passing by Siberia. I could only imagine such a cold landscape and I curled into his arms. From down below the cries of the seller of melons and the seller of fresh-caught pigeons rose up from the avenue that wound past the Blue Nile.

In his halting English my friend said, ''You must understand, Meena, if you want to be a poet, there is no stopping place. We poets go on and on. Stations. Small stops. Sometimes an oasis. That's it, on and on and on.'' In speaking to each other we made do with fragments of English and French. For I knew neither Czech nor German, and he had no Malayalam, no Hindi, no Arabic, languages that had served me well. When he left, I longed to follow him, across multiple borders, leaving all my skins behind me.

Quite early in childhood though, I had been forced to accept the burden of flesh, the impossibility of leaping out of my own skin in the direction of desire. There was no way to evade the sheer distance in miles between Khartoum and Kerala. To get from one to the other, I was dependent on the metal bodies of trains, boats, planes. So I danced in my dreams, the imaginary burning up space. "If you can't walk, dance!" runs a Nubian proverb, and for years it haunted me. Sometimes, though, I wonder if such mimic motion rivaling that of the angels and apsaras, covering continents held in a child's soul, hasn't left me with a fear of walking, of covering ground. I think of it as a feminine fear, because, had I been a male child, brought up between two lands, surely I would have been able to read maps, figure out the crossroads of the world.

But I was a Kerala girl-child brought up abroad and one of my feet was bound to the raised wooden threshold of my ancestral home. I often tripped trying to walk out. At times I have sighted water where there was none. Occasionally I have been overpowered by maps that covered whole territories so completely that the earth beneath vanished and I spent all my energies shutting out buried cries from rubble.

But the rubble is what I am.

Sometimes I think of the English language as a pale skin that has covered up my flesh, the broken parts of my world. In order to free my face, in order to appear, I have had to use my teeth and nails, I have had to tear that fine skin, to speak out my discrepant otherness.

Sometimes I think I have to write myself into being. Write in order not to be erased. What should I write with? Milk, blood, feces, spittle, stumps of bone, torn flesh? Is this mutilation? Surely milk is not torn out of a female body, nor blood: each might be a perfect blossoming. Sometimes I think I write to evade the names they have given me. "Mary Elizabeth" I was baptized, the names of my two grandmothers strung together, anglicized from Mariamma and Eli as befit our existence in the aftermath of a colonial era when English was all powerful. Fifteen years old in Khartoum, I changed my name to Meena, what everyone knew me as, but just as important to me, the name under which I had started to write poems. On all my papers at the university, I put Meena, crossing out Mary Elizabeth. Appa was dismayed: you will get irretrievably confused in the public records, no one will know who you are, he insisted.

And as long as I lived under his protection, I was Mary Elizabeth in my passport. Then I added an alias: Meena. I felt I had changed my name to what I already was, some truer self, stripped free of the colonial burden. The name means fish in Sanskrit, enamel work or jeweling in Urdu, port in Arabic. It is also the home name my parents had chosen for me at birth. It is the name under which I wished to appear.

What does it mean to appear, to be allowed to appear, or to be wiped out, to be wiped off the slates of publicity? Audre Lorde's voice rings in my ears. June 1990. I am standing with her in the Barbizon Hotel. Together we look at the program for the Fourth International Interdisciplinary Congress of Women that is being held at Hunter College. The three names—Kamala Das, Claribel Alegria, Audre Lorde—are missing from the entry for the poetry reading I had planned as an evening's highlight. I had invited three poets I admired: Audre Lorde from the United States, Kamala Das from India, Claribel Alegria from Nicaragua. But from the general program—not the glossy brochure—the three Third World poets were missing. Now Audre was in front of me, in the hotel room in the Barbizon where she was staying:

"I came because you asked me, Meena, I respect you, otherwise I would not have come, all the way from Berlin after the cancer treatment. There are no white women on the program you have put together. What the hell is it all about? They want to suppress our names, Meena, they want to scrub us out."

Her pain, her rage entered me, her delicacy too. I was filled with admiration for her passionate being. When I first entered the room at the Barbizon, she had pointed out the tree outside her window, its branches spare in the summer sunlight. A poet needs a tree, I had said to her, always.

"Audre," I replied, looking at the tree, "I feel devastated that the names are not on the program. I feel so ashamed. What can I do?"

"They cannot bear us, Meena," she said, "those women of color who talk out."

"We are living here," I said to her, "in this city, in the shadow of the skyscrapers, inside the skyscrapers. See the driveway outside where the tree stands. If I lie in that driveway and put kerosene on my sari and burn my body, what would that do? It would not even make the newspapers. What would they say? That a woman of color had immolated herself? Would they even know that? What skin would be left to know the color by?'' For an instant, standing next to Audre, I imagine the words in the local paper: ''Woman of Color from the Edge of Harlem Discovered Burnt, Wrapped in Long Oriental Garment.'' I open my eyes again, and looking at Audre's lovely strong face, I try to shake myself loose of the craziness. I thank her once again for coming to the city.

She has many admirers here and the news of her reading spreads by word of mouth, through little leaflets the women students pass out, and two nights later the auditorium in the old Hunter building is crammed full of people, waiting to hear the three poets read. I introduce each poet, speak briefly of how poetry brings us news of the world. Kamala, her hair flowing, glorious in a red silk sari, goes first. I feel a rush of blood, a thrill in me as she reads out, slowly and clearly—using a borrowed flashlight, for the stage lights are defective—the long slow syllables of her poem ''Blood.'' How early that poem had entered into me and remained: a Kerala woman's tracing of her bloodlines. I think that poem was within me when I looked backwards to my grandmothers, forward to my son and daughter. Claribel reads next, in Spanish and in English, the delicate passionate lines that tell of terror and love, and the clarity of the image upheld in the glass of time. Then Audre reads and her power and her anger mingle in the words, sometimes sung, sometimes spat out in rage. Her voice seems an instrument for her daring, ravaged spirit, nothing more, nothing less. The applause after the reading is thunderous. It reminds me of a mushaira in India, or a kavi sammelan, the listeners entering into the rhythm of the lines, hearing their own longings voiced, transfigured, in the syllables of poetry. How essential poetry seems, placed in the ordinary world in which we live and move and have our being.

6. *Stone-Eating Girl*

When I was seven, my cousin Koshy gave me a pile of Bata shoe boxes. I do not know where he got them from—perhaps the shoe store in Kottayam; or perhaps he had brought them from as far away as Bangalore where he went to boarding school. Koshy's mother was my appa's second sister and so we had the Kozencheri house and our Kannadical grandparents in common. Each summer when I returned from Khartoum for my Kerala season, three to six months of each year, Koshy and I would meet. He taught me how to prick holes in the shoe boxes and set sprigs of lily leaf inside. Then he showed me how to cradle the fat pupae he helped me pick off leaf and stone and place them inside the shoe box.

I loved butterflies and even after Koshy returned to Bangalore, I would often spend my afternoons in Kozencheri picking the ugly, shapeless pupae off the leaves of white lilies and sequestering them in the shoe boxes. When the wings seeped out, frail and wet, I would set the creatures free. I stared hard as they rose in the air, trying to fix in my mind the first fluttering motions that held the living creatures vibrating in blue air, in sunlight that bathed the low hills of Kozencheri.

A child of seven, crouched on a rock by the well side, I tried to figure out what it might mean to be a dark incipient thing. Struggling now to recapture what I felt then, I set the imprecision of these words to a child's fluid thoughts. Did the ugly pupa know it would become a butterfly? Where did the butterfly part exist, when the plump thing clung to a leaf in the darkness of a shoe box? Was there some secret that sustained it? Where did my Khartoum life go when I was in Kozencheri or Tiruvella? And what of this life of rock and stone, under the thick green leaves of Kerala, when I was living in a desert land so far away? Where was I at any one time? What was I? I was transported from Tiruvella to Khartoum and back again each year. Cupped in the silver capsule of a DC-7 Air India plane, I crossed the rough winds and covered more space than a freed butterfly could. But if the part of me from Tiruvella were not already there, in invisible incipience in Khartoum, how could I be me? What was I when I was not quite in one place, nor in another, just in midstream? Was I like that ugly pupa, unfit to see?

I dropped the thoughts in confusion, picked up a tiny round pebble, wiped it on my sleeve, and set it to my tongue. Then, giving a little gulp, I swallowed hard. Fortunately my guts didn't hurt. Swallowing that stone gave me a sense of comfort, of power even. I felt I was a child who could accomplish certain feats, sustain something hard and solid inside her. It was a month later that summer, when I went to amma's house in Tiruvella, that I first saw the stone-eating girl.

She was sitting quietly underneath a tree, in the way that people do, doing nothing much, not fiddling or anything with her sari pallu. An ordinary-looking chit of a thing, one might have said, except for the unnatural pallor of her skin—no, not that prized Kashmiri, film star color, not that. Rather the muddiness of it, as if like a sadhu, she had smeared mud over her flesh.

"Should smear herself in garlic paste, that's what," Chinna muttered under her breath, as she caught me staring at the girl.

"So what's she doing there? Why not sell vegetables or go to school? Showing off, that's what. And she'll end up with more than coal dust on her face. See those stones?"

That's when I got closer, and got a good look. I squatted right in front of her and stared hard. No doubt about it. Her cheeks were filled with something. Not boiled sweets, for she didn't smell of that rancid taste, nor tamarind balls. She stared right back, and opened her mouth, and rolled one out. It was a pebble all right. I held it in my palm and gazed at it. It was beige but so clear you could see all the veins in it, blue and crimson, tumbling over yet never snarling up, stone skin licked clean with the saliva from the girl's mouth.

"Theru."

She wanted it back. That was the only word she ever spoke to me. I put it back in her hand. It looked a bit like mine, her hand. I wanted to look at her more closely, for it struck me that perhaps

I could smarten myself up, dress like her. Her sari looked finer than those Dacca cottons amma prized so. By its side, my frock, with the embroidery and special smocking on it, looked quite dull. I felt ashamed of the pink roses, tiny green leaves, knotty stalks, on the fine cotton, stitched in by the nuns in Tholaseri to raise funds for the new orphanage. Then it struck me I should try a few words, or even bolder put out a hand and touch the girl under the tree.

But Chinna yanked me away, raced me down the dirt road.

"Enough? Enough? Satisfied?" she seemed quite irate.

"What's her name then?"

"Name? Who can tell. She's a shameless thing."

"Shameless? Why?"

"Making an exhibition of herself like that. Mark me now. In a few hours that area around the tree will be filled with youths, drunkards, and not searching for garlic either."

I was dumbstruck, then recovered my wits.

"Your tooth hurts, is that it?"

Chinna nodded and popped a clove out onto her tongue to show me. She had been chewing it hard all the while. Then suddenly she tightened her grip on my elbow and yanked me back. It was just as well, for otherwise we might have been run over by a black Ambassador car.

Inside the black car sat a girl utterly erect. She wore a dark silk blouse and her hair was edged with two silver clips set with pearls in the pattern of jasmine flowers. I knew she had bought them in Kottayam. Now this was Vatsala, a distant cousin. Whenever she visited us, she wore pearls around her neck that clashed with the brocade borders to the elaborate pavade she preferred. Once she had held up the pearls and said in a high pitched voice: "They're from Tokyo you know."

I couldn't bear Vatsala. Her hair was always perfectly in place and the pearls that hung round her neck, brought all the way from Tokyo, had a pale pinkish gleam to them, like the inside of the love apple fruit. She wouldn't let me touch them, nor would she tell where she had bought her new chappals in rainbow colors that she flaunted so elegantly on her feet. I knew, though, that chappals like those wouldn't last long on my feet, what with all the outdoor running I did, but it did not prevent me from feeling a sharp pang of envy when I looked at her.

Now there was mud on my skirt and on Chinna's chatta from

that car wheel, and now the tiny malnourished children of the cobbler who lived by the train tracks were forced to crouch in the dirt to avoid the speeding vehicle. When the black car was well out of sight, and we had pulled ourselves forward and moved on to the garlic seller, Chinna, patting down her garments, expressed her approval of Vatsala's posture: "Such a good girl, now you should be like that, Mol," but having spoken out in this way, her own skepticism got the better of her thoughts, and she turned back to the stone-eating girl. "She'll never be a shameless thing like that one out there!" Chinna stabbed her thumb in the direction of the stone-eating girl.

The Malayalam word for *shameless* that Chinna used was the strong form of the word, the slang, the street use, *perachathe*, as in shameless-mad, as in mad dog, rabid, bitch, bitches being rabid, rabid dogs being known as bitches. I did not dispute her use, I just took it in. Amma had also used the word, not once, but twice, much to my shock. I wondered how she might have learnt such words from the Misses Nicholson's school to which she had been sent at an early age. Once amma had pointed at me when she said "shameless" in that way, but I was consoled since it was not quite what she had meant. In other words, it was not that I was shameless, but that, had I persisted in refusing to put oil in my hair and wear my skirts at a decent length so that they covered my kneecaps in the heat of Khartoum, I would become perachathe. It was a word that was to take on more and more importance in my life. At times it has seemed to me that the price for being perachathe—shameless—was to have one's mouth filled with stones and perhaps the reparation was to perform, in the theater of cruelty that is our lives, all our lives together, choosing stones, filling one's mouth with them, ejecting them through the miraculous gut we call the imagination.

Whenever I work at something hard, she comes to me, the stone-eating girl. It makes no difference whether it's a poem or rice and sambar, cucumber sandwiches, a torn hem, or a paper that must be graded. Or sometimes when I stand fumbling for keys for the double locks we use in Manhattan—though of course two locks will do nothing to prevent intrepid ones who might use a blow torch on the door and cut through the wood facades and the flimsy metal innards.

She comes through the doors, through the windows, through the walls of this apartment, sometimes keeping her body utterly still, sometimes gesticulating, mouth always filled with the small pebbles I first saw her roll around on her tongue over three decades ago in Tiruvella.

She comes to me in dark garments that seem to have been pieced together with bits from a Sudanese woman's tob, a Tiruvella woman's sari damp with monsoon rain, a Nottingham woman's schmatte—though of course she would not call it that as she hurries out of the local church in Beeston, into the pub—a New York City woman's scarf bought from the Korean vendor on the sidewalk, it jams in the metal subway doors and she tugs it out. It floats out, squeaking like oiled gold. And somewhere in that garment, I think, is a bit of silk from my grandmother Kunju's wedding sari, a frail pearly tissue, the most expensive silk you could buy in those days, amma said. But amma doesn't know the stone-eating girl, at least I think not, and the bit is so tiny that it is quite covered over by some rough stuff that hangs over her shoulder.

But when the stone-eating girl descends the steps to the subway—she frequents the Broadway local in Manhattan—that silk bit makes a manic flitter of light that catches the eye of the vendor of *Street News*, the mad saxophonist with antennae in his head, plastic, sprayed with glitter, bobbling. She hunches over in her garments of many colors, the stone-eating girl, eyeing it all.

Now all this is rather different, this bits-and-pieces covering, from the way she was dressed when I first saw her in Tiruvella, underneath a tree. She was dressed in a faded sari, washed so many times and bleached with sun, that the threads hung apart, letting her thin bones filter through. Surely the cloth had been of indifferent quality to start with, but with repeated washings with a few shavings of the cheapest soap, much water, much pounding on rock, the fabric became frail, the threads floated about her body, and were held in at the edges only by the stout handloomed borders.

At night, I lay under the cool white sheets in Tiruvella, staring through the barred window at the moonlight that flooded the bamboo grove, spilling over the speckled leaves of the gooseberry tree. The moonlight put me in mind of her frail sari. Asleep, I dreamt of the fine stuff, almost as fine as air spiked with moonlight, covering my own flesh, turning me into a magical thing. The next morning I sought out Chinna. She was sweeping out the ash in the ash room, shooing away the black hens with her big broom. I tugged hard at her hand so she was forced to stop:

"So?"

"Stop. Sit." I was choked up with the thought of asking her, even though I knew Chinna so well. She had come to work for us when I was born. At one stage she was my ayah. Now her only duty, as far as I was concerned, was to give me weekly oil baths and supervise my appearance. The rest of the time she hung around in the kitchen area, making sure the stoves were swept out so the ash didn't choke up the new flames, making sure the black hens that we bred in our compound in such profusion hadn't deposited another horde of eggs in the hole in the wall where the wood-burning fire for the outer bathroom was placed.

She was also in charge of making sure we had enough spices in the kitchen. The morning we sighted the stone-eating girl, Chinna had been in a tizzy. She had run around in little circles in the kitchen, scratching her head. Bhaskaran for some weeks now had been in a state of confusion. It was not entirely clear what ailed him. In any case, he had neglected to ask the boy who was bringing the vegetables home from the market to add an extra slew of garlic. Fish pickle was being prepared that morning for which the shiny cloves of garlic were always needed in great abundance. Chinna invited me to go shopping with her, so we set off down the road by the railway tracks towards the garlic seller's stall.

A sharp scent emanated from Chinna's mouth as she squatted by me. "Toothache?" I asked, just to calm me down.

She smiled back: "Garlic."

"What about her sari?"

"Whose, mol?"

"That girl's, the stone-eating girl's."

She laughed out loud, and as the black hens squawked about us, and in the middle distance Bhaskaran led out Susheela the cow to pasture, Chinna launched into her story. It came out in fits and starts, for she had to finish up work in the ash room, set the firewood in place, and then, purely as an act of kindness to help the cook, she started skinning some carrots—tiny finger-sized things, hardly larger than a big green chili. I held my nose as she worked on them, for I hated carrots, their color, their tepid flavor, even though Chinna insisted carrots would keep me from having brain fever. So as I sat at her feet, staring away into the tapioca leaves in the distance, Chinna told me the long, involuted tale of the stone-eating girl's sari.

The stone-eating girl's sari was woven by a woman in Pondicherry, long since dead of the exhaustion that can strike a poor middle-aged woman who has borne too many children, who is forced to fend daily for food. The weaver, whom Chinna called Ratna, was forced out of her work as a weaver by the new Hakoba Mills. Ratna had to make do as best she could, with a little housecleaning here, a little floor washing there, a few morsels handed out to her in charity, a few green mangoes a brother-in-law from the countryside passed onto her, which she was able to sell for a pittance in the marketplace and use for rice and a single vegetable, augmented with a few chilis for the evening meal. Her older children did what they could in terms of hiring themselves out for odd jobs, but the young ones simply waited for their mother, their dark eyes open.

One night as she watched the rice boil on the earthenware stove, the out-of-work weaver felt the skin on her palms, the fine colorless skin countless threads had run over, starting to vibrate, as if all the looms she had ever touched were whirring in her flesh. I huddled close to Chinna's ankles as her voice rose with the tale of poor Ratna of the vibrating palms. At night, the vibration grew unbearable and the fatigue rose within Ratna, a fever in all her limbs till she could scarcely breathe. By morning her mouth hung loose, then grew rigid, her eyes turned sightless, fixed into an eternity nothing in her could claim. At dawn, the youngest child rolled over on her mother, touched the cold flesh, and sat up in shock, hollering. Before they cremated her in the burning grounds reserved for those who are too poor to be sung over by priests or plenipotentiaries, they covered the weaver in a sari of the finest cotton they could find in her poor hut. The flames licked the cotton and burnt it into the same ash as wood and skin and bone.

The stone-eating girl never knew this Ratna who had once woven her sari. The sari that the stone-eating girl wore was given to her by Gomati, one of Chinna's associates. Gomati worked as a maid for a rich lady who lived over the hill, half a mile from the railway tracks in Tiruvella, and late one afternoon she had tossed the sari into Gomati's lap, tossed it just like that, without a single word uttered.

The rich lady collected handlooms and textiles, handicrafts and

icons of ancient wood—ebony and teak—that were carved into like-
nesses of the ferocious goddesses of death and sexual regeneration,
Kalimata with her string of human skulls, and Mariamma whose
spirit causes the smallpox to come and pit the soft cheeks of infants
with its dark stars. The rich lady had a husband who believed in
yearly pilgrimages to the Aurobindo ashram at Pondicherry to
cleanse the spirit. He was of the opinion that the spirit had to be
cleansed in much the same way as the body. He knew that yogis
swallowed yards of tape that they drew out of the mouth again, after it had entered the gut, so cleansing out the lower intestines. But
this upstanding businessman and estate owner, given to acidity in
his tummy, could never conceive of such rigors and decided instead
that a spiritual path, of periodic abnegation from things of the flesh,
worked much better for him, was more cost-effective in any case,
taking up only one week in the year. And the cool air from the Arabian Sea that blew him into the arms of a certain air hostess on the
Indian Airlines flight to and from Pondicherry, could more than
make up for the mortification of the flesh required in the ashram.

It was on one of these trips that he passed through the village
where Ratna the weaver lived, and came upon her selling a few saris
under the banyan tree. He jumped out of his taxi, pushed a few
rupees into her hand and made off with a striped handloomed piece.
On his return to Tiruvella, he draped it over his wife's plump shoulders, and loosening her hair in a fit of passion that took him by surprise, murmured, "Ah, Sariamma, Sariamol, Sarikochu, how
startling you are, my exotic coo-coo-coo. Wear this, wear this, little
moo-moo-moo." Whereupon she, not displeased, pushed his hands
away with as much gentleness as she could muster, wondering how
she could extricate herself in time for the ladies Sevikasamaj meeting that was to discuss the building of a clinic for the poor beggars
in the district. She undressed though and hurriedly put on the handloomed sari, sprayed some Chanel No. 5 over it—her brother-in-
law had brought it back from his latest trip to Geneva—and wad-
dled out to the car. All the way to the meeting she ran her hands
over the coarse cotton and despised herself for wearing the rough
crude thing. At the earliest opportunity she passed it on to Gomati,
the maid. Gomati, who was terrified that a curse might be attached
to the sari, handed it over to the stone-eating girl, who happened
to be passing by the gates of Satyam Vilas, the house where the
rich lady lived. The stone-eating girl, who made a living in those

days by selling okra and brinjal in the marketplace, was delighted to accept the sari. And by the time her obsession came upon her, that was the only sari she would wear.

When I saw her, sitting cross-legged in a pile of dirt by the railway tracks, wrapped in Ratna's woven sari, now frail and threadbare, she had given up her trade in vegetables and now concentrated on stones. Her skin, which had been the same color as mine, a darkish brown, had grown pale with dirt. Her lips had turned the same color as the earth in the dry season.

One of the tales I like best about the stone-eating girl came from a visiting social worker taking tea with Ilya and amma one afternoon. According to her, the government was at fault. In order to construct the new railway line, government officials had evicted the stone-eating girl from the hut where she lived. Hearing that, during the Nationalist movement to get rid of the British, satyagrahis protested by sitting in one place and refusing to eat, the girl took it upon herself to do likewise. It was then that in sheer hunger she started cramming mud in her mouth, then stones, and when the stones rolled round on her tongue, they satisfied some hunger she did not even know had possessed her.

Bit by bit, even in its satisfaction, the hunger grew, and the means to consume it turned into a stern discipline. Hearing this tale, my admiration blossomed. Once an ordinary girl-child like me, she had taught herself whatever skills she had, learnt to use them in her own way, and set herself up as her own authority so that in her unmitigated gluttony—strictly directed at small rocks and stones and soil—she became a female icon, creator of a stern discipline, perfector of an art.

It's much harder to eat stone than to eat fire. I've tried both after a fashion. Fire consumes substance and you have to be careful it doesn't burn up your tongue, but that's about it. Otherwise you can close your mouth over a small match flame without too much hardship. My cousin Koshy showed me how. It was the summer after I had met the stone-eating girl. He had bought two beedis off Thoma the woodcutter and sneaked them into the attic in the Kozencheri house. We lay curled up in a pile of cut rice that was drying out, husks and all, and he showed me how to eat fire. First light the beedi, and, when you stop coughing, pick up the burning match and pop it into your mouth. Poof, the fire goes out. "Fire-eating girl!" he sang out at me, the time I singed my tongue. And I was so pleased to hear him, I quickly hid the sharp pain in my mouth, or tried my best to.

Then I heard of the fire-eating girl who worked in the Gemini Circus in Cochin. She became my other heroine. When I returned to Tiruvella, for my Indian summers were divided between the Tiruvella house and the Kozencheri house, I asked Chinna for more information. She told me the fire-eating girl was once as fearful as anyone else and had kept water in her cheeks to wet down the flames she had to swallow. At first she emitted flames that were so weak she almost didn't make the grade as a circus fire-eater, though in due course she became world famous, best known in Dubai where a filmstrip with her act has been circulated.

Years later it was rumored that a group of our people, Malayalees in Oklahoma, had raised money to invite her to come and perform after their Pentecostal church service, as if the Holy Spirit they had learnt to revere in their stern churches in Kerala might, in spite of their years of comfortable North American life—backyards with barbecues, Barbie dolls with blonde hair, acrylic suits, pantyhose, refrigerators that popped out ice at the touch of a button, dollars made of gold that could be given away as part of a girl's dowry—be placated, eased into the body of a gaunt young woman dressed in ocher sari and gold slippers.

I still remember Chinna wiping her hands free of the ash she had swept up in the ash room where I often hid out, telling me that the fire-eating girl, the world renowned Kameshwari, had been invited to America. I'm sure she told me this to take my mind off the fact that Ilya was very ill and in great pain from his heart condition. Also Chinna was a little nervous that I admired the stone-eating girl far too much:

"The *Manorama* ran an ad saying so. 'World Renowned Fire-Eating Kameshwari Travels to America!' "

I listened to her, but said nothing. I hoped I didn't look as bored as I felt. I had already sorted all this out at least a year earlier. While it might be a good thing to start on the fire-eating path—a way to make people notice me, even make my strict Scottish schoolteacher in Unity High School, Khartoum, sit up and grip her skirts and those odd socks she wore in her heavy shoes, even clutch her beads in dismay—I found that in Tiruvella, which was the only place I could think of practicing my arts, I was unable to filch a single coal from the kitchen or from the pile where the cashews were roasted in the harvest season. For I was constantly circled by guardians: three ayahs, four maids, five cooks, a cowherd, a goatherd, a boy who ran errands, and amma in the middle distance sitting silently in a corner, taking tea with her one hundred and one cousins, who on the slightest hint of anything fiery approaching my mouth could be guaranteed to raise a hue and cry and come tearing down to the kitchen in her katau sari.

Even Ilya, whom I thought I could count on in a pinch—he was forever encouraging me to try all sorts of things—might draw the line when it came to fire-swallowing. Though once, right after my morning perusal of "Mandrake the Magician," the cartoon that ran on the back page of the newspaper, he had called me into his study where he was working on an essay about the social gospel. He gazed at me through his silver-rimmed glasses and when he saw me running my hands over the dark-colored wood of the shelf that held the books by the great bearded Russian Lev Tolstoy, friend of Rabindranath Tagore, inspirer of Gandhiji, he leant over and pulled out the book I had touched last. I saw a glorious woman in Russian clothing on the cover, her hair dark as coals, her eyes the color of burning fire. I touched her eyes with my thumbs, trying to touch the flame, trying to close those eyes.

"That's Anna," he said gently, and when he saw my bewilderment, for that was the name of my baby sister, he added "Karenina, Anna Karenina. She was married to a man called Karenin and they lived in Russia. A great, passionate woman. If you want to go away child, take it away, anywhere you want. Or sit here if you like, but read it, read Tolstoy's book."

I took it away and read it, cover to cover. I read it hidden high in the love apple tree. I was ten years old by then. I used to hide the book under my skirts as I raced past the well to the love apple tree, for I did not want Chinna or Marya or amma to see the coal-burning eyes of the Russian Anna. And the thoughts of passionate love driven to despair, of church bells and snow in Russia filled me. The night I finished the book and crept back to put it on Ilya's shelf, the sound of the train driving hard over the tracks from the Palghat Pass left me breathless, almost choking, for I saw in my dreams the eyes of the Russian Anna and her snowy neck flat over the rusty rails.

A high wind blew down from the Vindhya Mountains. I was

eleven by then. It blew all night as Ilya lay dying. The foxes flew out of their holes, crept into the kitchen, took fire in their tails and all that bushy fox hair burnt till the bodies were nuggets of solid flame and the foxes could not escape alive, not even by jumping into rivers or wells.

Lying on his deathbed, he asked me for water, ''Meena, Meenamol, theru, velam theru.'' I shut my eyes so tight. I turned away, choking. I could not bear his gaunt hand, his eye moistened with tears, the harshness that life made for him as he lay struggling to breathe. Night after night, he groaned, the iron tightness in his chest making the sound come out as if spikes from the lightening conductor on the prow of the Tiruvella house were poking out the eyes of the parrot fish Paulos the fisherman brought in, and the fish, still alive, squirmed in its basket as the unseen hand prodded in, with the metal thing, so tall and pointed and proud, that rode atop the house that Ilya built.

At eleven in the morning, I heard the death rattle in his throat. I hugged my ears with both my hands and bit my tongue so I should never speak again. I turned away, my heart a soiled stone. I wrap up that stone now, in paper, in sand. It shivers in my hand. I do not have the tongue to spell it out, or the gut to swallow it up.

I hurt amma too. She could not understand why I did not bring him water.''You used to do it Meena, so faithfully. You were such friends. Remember all the games you played with Ilya?'' Then she hung her head. But little Anna, my sister, came racing up, a glass in her hand, and passed the cool cup to Ilya as he struggled to sit up. It was Anna who helped amma put a spoon with a few drops of water into Ilya's mouth, while I stood staring, my back against the oxygen cylinder, that rusty red thing they had wheeled in to give him a little relief so he could breathe. There were the daily shots of morphine too, and long, interminable prayers to God the Father and the Son and Holy Ghost and no one knew that God had closed up his heaven and forced the fish to swarm out of the Pamba River and lie breathless against cold sand.

And in those days all that was in my eleven-year-old mind, and out of it, grew bleak and flat and dry like the white wall against his bed where Ilya's shadow lay, unmoving, as he suffered his last days into death. And it's all unmoving for me, that death, the funeral I refused to go to, locking myself in the bathroom and watching through the bars of the wooden window frame as they carried his coffin to the church.

I think it was in those days too, though perhaps the thought had arisen in me earlier, that I felt I must refuse life, become a stone, a hard unmoving thing, no motion in it, no force, neither hearing nor seeing. It seemed unbearable as the hot skies unfurled themselves, the morning after Ilya's death, that I should go on living, unbearable too, that we should all be creatures that are born into bodies and subject to death. It was a knowledge I could do nothing to alter. In dreams my whole body seemed to me, then, buried under a pile of rubble. And the powers of the stone-eating girl were very far from me.

7. Khartoum Journal

Khartoum, 1964. Blood seeping into water, a slow dark pool of it and overhead the sun turning the surface of the Nile into a sheet of burning metal. Then the blood vaporizes in water, vanishes into heat and I cannot tell what is water and what is the sun that burns up the sky anymore. This keeps recurring in dreams. Somewhere, at the banks of the river, they are fishing out a man's body, the head beaten to a pulp, the color of blood when it leaks into hot Nile water.

I hear her voice, calling, calling me, my friend, Sarra Annis. I'm sure it's she. "Meena, come quick, quickly." I hasten in the direction of the voice. I see a small crowd by an acacia tree at the water's brink, see Sarra there too and crouch with her by the edge of the Blue Nile where a corpse has been raised: a poor student from Wau, head mashed to a pulp, lifted out in the arms of three swimmers.

We whisper to each other: is this Lenny Deng's brother who, crossing into the Sudan, was held at the Chad border and tortured? Lenny had told the story at a students' meeting. There was a genocidal war being waged in the southern parts of the Sudan by the government forces in the north. Shatha, Sudanese red chilis, Lenny explained, were poured into all his brother's orfices. Then he was held in a room with a burning light and a slow trickle of water was trained onto his skull. After three weeks he was almost dead with the shock of the burning substance in his most tender parts, and the cold, relentless trickle of water. By the time he escaped— perhaps the guard's head was deliberately turned away—Lenny's brother Thomas was sick, vomiting, and half blind.

His nerve ends were shot and he trembled uncontrollably in the Catholic hospice in Khartoum that had taken him in. He had forgotten his mother tongue, Dinka. Or was it something more terrible than forgetfulness? What came out was a babble of tongues no one could decipher. Was this the same Thomas Deng being fished out of the Nile? I clutched Sarra's hand. Our friend Nurredin from the student newspaper was there with his old Kodak camera, snapping away, and then scribbling down notes. In the mounting crowd of students I saw a wisp of tissue-thin voile, and the garish red heels I had first seen in the dusty space by the Mahdi's tomb. I turned around, looked over Sarra's shoulder, but missed her, the mystery woman I thought of as my dark metamorphic angel in whose vacancy the imagination touches brutal north, smells death.

"Did you see her?" I asked Sarra as I held onto her elbows.

"Who?"

"The red-heeled woman."

I could not hear her reply, for the crowd was pushing back, away from the water and we were caught in the crush.

Sarra and I met in Unity High School in 1959 when we both entered the first form. I was eight, far younger than the usual age of students, which varied between eleven and twelve in first form. Sarra was five years older than I. Quite quickly, we became close friends. I was painfully shy in those days and used to rely on her boldness to get me through the day. If she was head of the rounders team, I counted on her to choose me. Once she didn't and I dissolved in tears, enormously betrayed, and wouldn't speak to her for days till she pressed some sim-sim sweets and a sachet of Gaon's perfume into my hands in the middle of our history class.

Our teacher was Sith Samia. So plump she could hardly rise to her feet, Sith Samia had a special blackboard brought in so she need not stand up. She sat there like a glistening white flower with a dark heart, face framed in her swiss voile tob, cheeks and forehead moist with sweat. Scents of rose attar mingled with Eau de Cologne 4711, a most unfortunate combination, emanated from her. Seated at our desks, lined up in neat rows, we shifted and giggled.

I tugged at my neighbor Elli's plait. Fatima passed out sweets from the Greek grocery store down the road. A striped toffee fell from her lips onto the desk, tumbled into the hole for the inkwell.

I hooted with laughter. Elli planted her foot on my toe. I shrieked. Sith Samia was oblivious to it all. The fragrant heat that came from her made a little halo. With an effort she lifted her right hand. The tob fell back revealing the green dress. Kobbles of flesh shook on her upper arm. Her elbow was so dimpled it was impossible to tell whether the bone had melted into the all-commodious flesh.

"Shu-shu-girls. Mathalb eh? Looki here. Suleiman. Suleiman the Magnificent. He came from here to here." The chalk squeaked on the blackboard. "All the way from Turkey."

Her fingers arced down, making a white line from the left side to the middle right. "All the way down. Girls. On his white horse. This is the conquest of Asia Minor." As I watched the chalk move, I made up an invisible white charger that bore the great Suleiman. He was dressed up like a Maharashtrian bridegroom with headdress and jeweled sword tucked into his sherwani. He could have been trotting down the main street in Pune where I had lived, Deccan Gymkhana, where the bridal parties came with their torches and drums and fanfare.

"All the way down, down, here. Looki."

As Sith Samia trembled into silence, my image of Suleiman the Magnficient, all his slaves behind him dragged in chains, his hands sparkling with bridal rosewater, vanished. There were voices in the street outside, in the harsh glare. Someone was shouting out, someone else was running away. The cries floated in with the scents of roasted peanuts a vendor was selling near the school wall. My gaze returned to the blackboard. I saw a white line traced from left to right, from top to bottom and that was what Suleiman was doing. A mere speck of dust crossing the board. Sith Samia shifted her bulk a little to the right. The fan had stopped working. Her brow was covered with sweat. It was clear she wanted to be rid of Suleiman and go home.

I could never figure out those scrawls on the blackboard, the names and dates I had to learn, all taken out of the old first-form textbooks. The books had faded, tobacco-colored covers. Imported from Britain, they were stored in the corner of the school library. I had nothing but mistrust for the facts and dates contained in those bound volumes—information about Bodicea, Julius Caesar, the history of the Britons and Celts, the Crusades, even Suleiman the Magnificent. It never struck me, how curious it was that in an independent Sudan, Sith Samia, fresh out of Teacher's Training College in Omdurman, would have to plod through these old British colonial textbooks. What I had as protection was a stubborn skepticism. At times it made for a barbarous ignorance.

Later I heard tales of how the British sent their men wandering through India, clad in pith helmets and ugly khaki shorts, knee socks folded down to reveal the knobby bone. They were measuring people's noses, the point, the bridge, the shape of the nostril, the width of the forehead, trying to make up facts about races. At the same time they were setting up measuring chains and triangles northward and southward, over the rich terrain of the subcontinent for their survey of India. What was surveyed could be known, controlled by sufficient use of force. Distances might be calculated for military purposes: how many troops to send, how large a quantity of supplies, how large a cavalry, to overcome intransigents like Tipu Sultan, whose tiger languishes in the Victoria and Albert Museum, useless, snapping its tongue.

I imagined meeting one of those surveyors. Walking towards him, I would turn quickly aside, hide behind a palm tree, only to stare better. After all, the Kannadical family name meant literally "glass stone," which could translate as "surveyor's stone"—*kannadi* in Malayalam being both glass and spectacles, the double sense of vision mediated ever present in my patronymic. "Probably one of your ancestors was a surveyor," veliappechan told me, as he lay on his bed with piles of prayer books all around him, blankets, bottles of strengthening potions from the Kottakal Ayurvedashala, the finest source of ayurvedic medicine in all of Kerala. "Yes, yes," he went on, "the family had a great deal of land in Raani, and it made sense to have it surveyed." I had listened silently, staring at his smooth old head.

And what of the head-measuring men? If I came across one of those trying to put a forehead into a bound book, I would rear to my full height, spit in his eyes, cobra-fashion, then drag him by the backs of those ridiculous socks with the stiff bits by the calves to keep them up, force him into the kitchen of the Kozencheri house. One glare from grandmother Mariamma and he would have blurted out, all red-faced and hot between the ears, incoherent words. "Sh-s-sh-s-sh-s-sh-s," he would stutter, the sounds that Kerala people think the English make.

*

In Khartoum we went to Sunt Forest for picnics. Seated at the edge of the blanket with its striped pattern and the hem of mango leaf design, I watched the shadowy line where the waters of the Blue and White Niles met. How restless it was with the dark silt under water, a muddy turbulence made visible when the Nile crocodiles shot out and started snapping at hot empty air. Ever since appa had stood me on a rock and pointed out the water line I could not forget it.

I knew that Allahabad, the site of my birth, was where two great rivers of India, the Ganga and the Jamuna meet: a sacred city, marking a sangam, a joining of waters. Now I was on another continent, in another city, hot, sun bleached, created by another sangam, the meeting of the ancient Nile rivers, the quick indigo waters of the Blue Nile mingling with the sluggish gray waters of the White.

Once when I sat in my dreamy way, a plate of idli and vegetable pulao on my lap, I saw the brightly painted prow of the Mahdi's ship cutting into the line. On board his hundred and one women, under the cover of their tobs, stood ululating. Surely the number one hundred and one is not right? Surely it comes from the number of petals the sacred lotus is said to have, the golden lotus one can see at the tops of temples throughout India, the mystic number that parts the veils of heaven, decipherable in the names that are given to the goddess Saraswati, she who is the purveyor of all wisdom.

Memory slips in me and I cannot recall the exact number of the Mahdi's harem any more, though I knew it once. Sarra told me, when I was eight and she was twelve going on thirteen and she lived on Kasr Avenue and I lived in Hai el Matar and we both studied at Unity High School in the first form. She whispered it into my ear in the terrible heat of mid morning. The temperature was at least 112 degrees and in our freshly laundered dresses, blue checks with white belt, white socks and shoes, armpits soaking with sweat that the best talcum powders south of Beirut could not prevent, we raced with what half-hearted energy we could muster onto the playing fields of Khartoum. At our side jogged the reedy Miss Bay, with a goiter in her neck, gym mistress of Australian origin. At our left, a whistle slung round her neck, decked out in shorts and tee shirt, hair all scraggly and gray, thigh muscles pumping like a cart horse's, sprinted Miss Reed our new headmistress, late of Cheltenham Ladies College, currently relocated to Unity High School, Khartoum: why no one could imagine except that having retired, she must have wished to extend her services beyond the tinkle of delicate porcelain and fine silver that the tea parties of Cheltenham afforded, turn her administrative skills to the great unwashed that we represented for her.

Indeed her best efforts were turned to teaching us not only "Onward Christian Soldiers," which she sang in a stout contralto and we mumbled under our breaths, but also to the arts of the playing fields, netball, rounders, and tennis. Twice I fainted on the netball field in the intense heat, and rounders, however slowly it was played, the girls traipsing around in the field, hitting the ball and running, became a form of masochism. When a slight wind blew over the wall and cooled our faces, the game almost stopped. But we had to wait till Miss Reed, secure under the cap she had purchased for herself in Paris en route to Khartoum, pulled out her whistle and blew: a loud piercing sound that startled the crows in the date palms and sounded far worse to our ears than the siren that sounded at midday in the factories north of the river. It was on such a morning, as I ambled by Sarra's side, in a pack of girls being chased out to play rounders by two aging ladies of the Empire, that my friend, no doubt to cheer me up, whispered:

"Listen, Meena, I have a cousin Samira who is related to Sadek. He says his great-uncle the Mahdi has...women in his harem. Suppose we were headed there instead of the rounders field. Just suppose." And she giggled in my ear. I could not bear the ticklish sound of her laughter and gripped her hand and laughed too, with sheer pleasure at entering the Mahdi's harem and seeing the ladies laid out on their rope cots with lion skins and velvet cloths, their breath laced with incense from the earthen censers between their toes, their tobs—the long sarilike swaths of cloth, nine yards though, instead of six, with which women covered themselves in public—hanging on hooks all ready to take out for their Nile voyage. When approaching land the Mahdi's women would stand in a ring and ululate for the old man, the hairy-chested white-haired old man.

So I held onto Sarra's hand and giggled with delight as we leapt over the channels for running water, proud that the present Mahdi's grandfather had defeated the British Gordon, though the thought of Gordon sitting alone in the midday heat under a thorn tree stopped me. Did he see his death approaching in the form of the Mahdi? Then a more troubling thought came up: what would our

Gandhi have said had he seen the fierce warrior, the Mahdi, sword raised in his right hand? Such thoughts rose in me as Sarra and I raced through the playing fields, hand in hand, then scraped past the tamarind hedge closer to the classroom. The number of wives the Mahdi had blurred in my head with the numbers Miss Reed was snapping out in her parched English voice, "Girls, Attennsshun, One-Two-Three-Three? Hear Me?" And Sarra and I, as if joined at the hip, snapped straight.

When I was just on the brink of turning eleven and had started to menstruate, it was Sarra who stuffed my mouth with sweets and congratulated me with wet kisses, and dragged me to meet all our friends. At the top of her voice, she proclaimed, "It's happened, it's happened," so that I felt proud as of a great accomplishment and forgot the discomfort of the thick pad between my legs amma had given me to wear; forgot too amma's hesitation, her soft words when she tried to explain why I was bleeding: "It's not uncommon," she had said, and I was left half-fearful that I might have contracted an unspeakable illness that made me bleed. But one of our teachers, an Englishwoman, on hearing of my predicament, had drawn me firmly into the wood-paneled library of Unity High School, sat me down next to the copy of Strindberg's *Road to Damascus,* a book that I kept peeking at, fascinated by the words inside. In her firm voice she explained how it happened to every single girl who was on the brink of becoming a woman, that it was part of the body's reproductive cycle. She pulled out an old book with pictures of ovaries and fallopian tubes and explained to me all about the egg and how it slipped down the bloody lining of the uterus if it was not fertilized. The pictures were in black ink, cool against the paper, and I was grateful to my teacher who explained that it happened to every single girl. So I did not need to feel odd, singled out by the blood that seeped from me. It was Sarra, though, who filled me with joy as she stuffed more sweets in my pocket. Soad tied a bright velvet bow in my hair, and, as she and Sarra, Fatima, Intissarat, Munira, and Antoinette and Nahid danced around me, I felt I had entered a bright circle of women.

Later that year, when Sarra and her sister Azza came along with us to see the sparkling lights and watch the fireworks display at the Moulid al Nabi festivities that were held in the wide open space in front of the first Mahdi's tomb, Sarra latched her sticky fingers in mine. We were both gobbling up the moulid sweets filled with sim-

sim and peanuts as fast as we could. She drew me into a dark place by a wall and whispered, "Look, Meena there she goes, Suraiya, she is part of his harem. Honest True Nancy Drew." And Sarra crossed herself.

I stared at the dark crack in the wall into which a beautiful woman with red high heels had passed, a fragrance as of rose attar wafting into the dusty air behind her. As the elusive woman vanished into the broken wall by the Mahdi's tomb I stared at my friend and felt a mounting excitement at the pleasures of life in red heels and Swiss voile tobs with tiny hearts stitched on in the latest imported mode. I had caught a flash of a dark face, high cheekbones, full lips, two dark scars on each cheek running vertically, dried wounds, fault lines in the flesh that enhanced her beauty.

Pondering the woman, I never asked myself why, if indeed she were part of the Mahdi's harem, she would be let to roam during a crowded festival of the prophet's birth. The festival was complete with a brass band dressed up in white and green, an oud player and a vocalist who had modeled himself almost to the point of parody on a popular Egyptian singer who had just died. The music rose in waves from the platform to the right, the singer's voice rose, orotund, the Arabic syllables lost in the curlicues of notes bent to an emotion that seemed to invade the skin, the hair, so that far from knowing what we felt, we were swept up in an oceanic thing, that left us speechless, senseless, intoxicated by a beautiful woman vanishing through a broken wall.

Straining to see the mystery woman, I entirely forgot my bewilderment at Sarra's addiction to what I put down as a North American custom, one that had stuck from her early years in a Washington, D.C. public school where her father, a kindly dental surgeon, had been posted as Sudan's first ambassador to the United States. His children had learnt to relish Superman comics, gooey bubble gum, and curious customs involving characters such as Ken, Barbie, and Nancy Drew, none of whom attracted me. But the mysterious Suraiya, if that indeed was her name, remained in my memory. Time and again she cropped up in my dreams, crossing the borders of the real.

A few weeks later I thought I caught sight of her again. This time across a broken alleyway where a red light hung, entering a mud door outside which hungry men hovered like flies. This was at the outskirts of Khartoum where appa used to drive to get us loaves of the long fresh-baked baguettes, that when broken and tossed into the open mouth, sizzled on the tongue. The bakery, run by Copts, was in a run-down neighborhood and from the parked car I watched the red lit door and the men in their long gelabiyas loitering in hot clusters. Was Suraiya there too? I never saw the mysterious woman's face, so how could I tell? But in those days, her figure became for me a quintessential thing, shining, female, metamorphic.

When I was in Unity High School, arithmetic with its rhythms of crude additions and subtractions and lumpish carryings over offended some internal logic in me. I could never manage it. Algebra with its finer music of compounds and metamorphic elements drew me, however, and once I was introduced to the figure x, I was fascinated by its possibilities. I would sit by the back wall of the Hai el Matar house, while amma or my sisters roamed around crying out for me to come and take tea and samosas, or come and get dressed for we were expected for dinner at the Kanagasundarams or Kannans or Gopalakrishnans and were already late. I sat in utter silence as they whirled about in the distance calling my name, secure in my hiding place by the white stucco wall, under the shade of a neem tree.

I fastened on the way the sunlight moved over the tips of the neem leaves, or the golden surface of the fruits; the way the pebbles were stacked near my bare feet, with streaks of cobalt under them scarcely visible as if a skin colored like my own, only a tinge lighter, had masked the essential properties stone held to itself. I bent over, laid my cheek against that warm surface, felt the sunlight ripple from tree leaf and bark over my body, or sitting straight felt the rough wall behind me. Each surface in turn echoed my own, made for a shining thing that rendered my own consciousness, held in a growing child's body, less arbitrary, less senseless.

Though I had not started writing poetry, it was in a mood akin to this that poetry began in me, words welling from a voice freed for an instant or two from the prison house of necessity—the calls to duty, the round of taking tea, sitting pretending to read a book at the edge of a circle of idle chatter about where the newest chiffons might be found, or how Mrs. So and So had received a pile of old kanjeevarams from her mother-in-law's tumbledown house in

Madras, or how Miss Such and Such was sneaking off to Geneva for a secret rendezvous—this in hushed tones—with a high-placed gentleman. Yet without those duties, those social rounds where I was held in a net of women's voices, what would have become of me? What if the x, the shining symbol I now gave to all that moved me—the gleaming intricate surfaces of the world, the feelings that welled up from too deep for words to reach—were to become all that I was, a spirit on the brink of dissolution, nothing, literally nothing. Such moods used to fling me into a wordless condition and amma would run out of the house worried at finding her eldest daughter crouched in utter silence at the side of the house, gazing at nothing in particular.

"What is this, child? Why do you behave as if the cares of the world were on your shoulders? What are you thinking of?"

There was little I could say in my defense for I had no language for what was passing through me. It might have pleased amma that the clear perception of beauty, in leaf and stone and sky, allowed me to join again with the gardens of my Tiruvella childhood. For by now Ilya was dead and amma was my thickest bond, the blood bond with that life. She turned to me not unkindly and said:

"Come put on that new striped dress, there'll be ice cream, I'm sure, at the party. The Vijaykrishnans have cousins who are coming from Canada to visit. They say there are huge forests in Canada and you can drive through and come to clearings with wooden benches and chairs and even metal grills where people can cook. Imagine that? What convenience. Could such a thing ever happen in our own countries? These Westerners have such conveniences!"

I stared at her, drawn back to the world of have and can, shall and shall not, the thought of metal grills, and charcoal in Ooty or Coonoor, Sabaloka or Wadi Sedna quite crazy to me. Who would put them there, who would use them? Amma, however, was charmed at the possibilities of such civilization, cars driven through forests without need of a driver like our ancient Rajan in Tiruvella, and magical cooking places. She knew she had hooked me back into her world, for she hurried on:

"Come, come. Manorama's brother, you know, is married to a Canadian, Chloe. This is her first visit abroad. She is said to be rather nervous. Perhaps you can speak to her."

At that dinner party there were tall lamps set out on the lawn at the edge of the house in Khartoum North, cries of mongoose and jackal from the area of darkness that surrounded the lamplight, and Chloe, beautiful, pallid in a low-cut printed dress, seated very still, her freckles and reddish hair in all that lamplight making her seem like a creature out of one of the books of poems I had found in the library. I was fascinated by her looks and wondered what it would be like to live in such a body and have a tall dark man like the Tamilian Tiru drawn to her. I do not think she opened her mouth except to him, and he hovered over her the whole time as chicken was borne out to the table in the garden, and golden brown puris and the chapatis, and dal and paneer saag, and as the expatriates from South India and Sri Lanka, Malayalees and Tamilians, hung together over glasses of whiskey and cold lemonade, laughing into the night. Over the hedges of acacia and tamarind, across the rough dirt road, wild creatures gathered: asses and hounds and jackals came in from the desert places, and scorpions summoned by the dim moonlight out of the cracks in the earth.

To my gaze Chloe was so pale, so exotic. I imagined all the men drawn to her, but foiled in the end by her childishness, her sheer need to be fed and sung to on a wooden bench at the edge of a Canadian forest, surrounded by metal implements with which the crudest of foods might be cooked. How did Tiru manage? They had been married just three months and he was immensely proud of her, bringing her first to the Sudan to visit his only sister, Manorama, whose husband was a veterinary surgeon at the university, then onto the family homes in Bangalore and Madras.

I heard later that Chloe was stunned by the chaotic moving surfaces of India. That she shut herself in a room in the Woodlands Hotel and refused to drink anything that hadn't been boiled three times and only ate food that resembled the mash that is fed to babies. Her poor mother-in-law finally took to making pots of kanji for her. Chloe languished on this fare. She was invaded by nightmares in which she saw a whole crowd of South Indians, their faces all scrubbed out, coming at her with cooking pots and ladles. And out of the cooking pots came dried turds, wet feces, excrement. They approached her, waiting to shove all this down her throat. She started to choke in her dreams and cried out that she could not breathe. Her condition grew worse. The learned Dr. Gunashekaran could not help her and Tiru was forced to flee with her on a night flight to Canada. Once she hit the cold air of Calgary and was restored to her newly furnished suburban split-level, Chloe seemed her old self again. Tiru, terribly nervous, resolved never to cross a border with her again, not even to visit Disneyland, the great dream of his life.

When I open the journals I kept as a teenager in Khartoum, the thin cardboard of the covers slips through my hands. I see lines of bold, upright script scrawled in between the pages of poetry and quotes from Marcel Proust, Albert Camus, Wallace Stevens. These lines tell of the misery I went through:

"If you want me to live as a woman, why educate me?"

"Why not kill me if you want to dictate my life?"

"God, why teach me to write?"

The invocation to God in the last was not to any idea of God, but rather a desperate cry aimed at my mother. The fault lay in the tension I felt between the claims of my intelligence—what my father had taught me to honor, what allowed me to live my life—and the requirements of a femininity my mother had been born and bred to.

Essential to the latter was an arranged marriage. It was the narrow gate through which all women had to enter, and entering it, or so I understood, they had to let fall all their accomplishments, other than those that suited a life of gentility: some cooking, a little musical training, a little embroidery, enough skills of computation to run a household. In essential details and with a few cultural variants, the list would not have differed from Rousseau's outline for Emile's intended, the young Sophie. Indeed, I was to be a Malayalee version of Sophie, or so it sometimes seemed to me. There was a snag though. Amma was living quite far from the decorum of her Syrian Christian peers, and the expatriate life of Khartoum set up singular difficulties in her path. How was she to cope with the parties to which I went in the company of Sarra or Samira, where I met boys, even danced with boys? And what of the University where she knew I read out poems I had written in secret, hiding out in the bathroom at home? What was I learning there? How would I live?

I poured my pain into my journals. I sensed that my sexual desires—which were budding at the time, though they had hardly been satisfied in the flesh—were essential to my poetry. But how did they fit within the rational powers that enabled me to think, pass exams, maintain some independence of thought? I had no answer here. I knew I could not live without passion; but passion burnt me up. That was the forked twig that held me. In dreams I was the snake struggling in that grip. The snake about to be beaten to death.

One night, filled with longing for a young man, a Gujarati whose parents lived in Omdurman, on the other side of the river, filled too with despair at the memory of a dead body, tortured, swollen, lifted out from the Nile River, I walked out into the garden at night. The brilliant desert stars came close, swooping down towards me. I lay down on the grass. I put my cheek to the ground, took the blades of grass into my mouth. I put out both my hands and ran them across the ground till I reached a slight crack in the soil. I was convinced by the evidence of my touch and of my beating heart, that there was a crack in the earth nothing could heal, a fault in the very nature of things, treachery in creation.

What I could not admit, as my parents wished me to, was that sexuality made for that fault, had caused the Fall of Man appa reverted to, time and again, in his discourses to me. Appa was pleased that I was being educated, that my rationality, as he liked to think of it, was developing, but he was clearly anxious about my desire to study philosophy, a discipline that he believed could only confound the religious sentiments he sought to inculcate in me.

"First acknowledge God," he said, "then all things, including human intelligence, can be perfected."

When I was fifteen, he insisted I go with him and amma to the sandstone cathedral the British had built in the center of Khartoum. Worn out with fighting, I went, but shut my heart and soul to the vicar of the Church of England who had confirmed me in the Christian faith, had checked my knowledge of its teachings over Sunday breakfasts of scrambled eggs and toast that I shared with him and his wife and their three boisterous children.

My struggles over received religion have caused me some anguish. Even now I am sometimes pierced with a longing to believe, but I know that were I to try to enter the steps of the American cathedral two blocks from where I now live, I would be swept out, as if by a hot dry wind, flung onto the stone steps, at the trembling feet of the man who has stumbled out of the methadone maintenance center. Sometimes I dream about trying to enter the cathedral and being flung out, onto the steps by a hot dry wind. In my dream the sandstone of the cathedral the British built in Khartoum turns into the rough gray blocks of Saint John the Divine.

I am out on the steps, clinging to the cold stone, cast out perpetually.

They sit around the long dining table that almost fills the room, appa and amma, side by side. Behind them, the long windows of the Khartoum house edged with white shutters. Through the windows the sky and the acacia hedge are visible. The sky is white hot. There they are, appa and amma, male and female, the beginning of me, discussing their daughters' clothing.

"They can't travel to Kozencheri like this."

Amma was worried. The lines on her forehead were just beginning to form. She was approaching forty. I sensed in her a heaviness of flesh, a settling in, a being there. A mother with freckles and small lines on the face, never picture perfect. So close at hand that she shut the light out. The fine bones in her face were growing coarser, as she put on a little weight, as mothering troubles rose up.

Appa sat there, arms crossed, looking grim.

"Of course they can't." The words seemed to be torn out of him.

"Why not?" I was being daring now, foolhardy even.

I leant across the polished tabletop. The sunlight from the window was in my eyes. I was squinting, trying hard to see. There didn't seem to be anything terribly wrong in what I was asking.

"Why on earth not?" I persisted, hearing my voice in my ears, as if it were going nowhere, as if it could not be heard.

He straightened up. He was an honest, decent man, but one who held in his passions with great effort.

"Know what they do with women? If you go sleeveless in the marketplace, they stone you."

Amma was appalled in spite of herself.

"Shh, Mol." She was trying to calm me down. "You're too headstrong. Just like Sosamma and see what shame she's brought the family. Of course you won't wear sleeveless blouses. You'll cover your arms up. You'll dress well."

The trouble was persistent, and it involved dressing well. It might have been simple if dressing well could work for all times and all places. But while one could dress without long sleeves in Tiruvella, in Kozencheri, twelve miles to the south, it was impossible.

How exaggerated it all grew in my fifteen-year-old mind, all hot and feverish and blurred. The thick-skinned grapefruit from the garden, the taut lemons, the slippery dates, shone with an internal heat. The blue painted ceramic bowl in which they sat grew heavy, bearing the naked fruit. I pulled myself round. "So what am I going to wear? Are you going to make a new set of clothes for us, all over again?" Amma nodded, mutely. I knew she was worried. Her mind was on Sosamma, a close relative who had contravened all the family dictates and married a Brahmin doctor. The man, however, was already married, and since he had a high government position, the double bond put him in trouble with the civil authorities. But they were wealthy, had a large house, several Alsatian dogs who were fed meat and raw eggs, more than the beggars got when they called at their gates. They had two lovely sons. Then the quarrels started. Sosamma left her husband to return to her father's protection. That was thirty years ago and it must have seemed to her like leaping from the frying pan into the fire. In order to live in the ancestral home, she had to be accepted back into the church; she had to sign an apology saying she had sinned. Her tall majestic back, her loud shouts of disdain, the bitter recriminations that passed between her and my veliappechan were vivid in my mind. Appa, too, was deeply involved. He was very close to Sosamma and even as he was dead set against her ways, he seemed to understand the will that drove her. But for amma, Sosamma with her proud self-determination, her car and driver that she commanded at will, was much too much. In secret, amma scolded me, crying out, behind locked doors, "You too will be perachathe like Sosamma, bringing shame on us. I can tell even now, how strong your will is."

That morning, at the dining table in Khartoum, I felt amma's nervousness and gave in. In my mind's eye I saw my arms, bare all the way from Khartoum to Tiruvella, covered up in cotton sleeves for Kozencheri consumption; my skirts suddenly two inches longer; the necks of the blouses cut so high I could hardly breathe.

It was only in Kozencheri, appa's ancestral place, that we had to be careful. Elsewhere women from the family dressed in diaphanous saris and revealed all the plumpness of their tender forearms. And who cared? Some even wore backless blouses at dinner parties on Pedder Road. But Malabar Hill in Bombay was one thing, the ancestral home in Kerala was another. I thought of my aunt Simi who wore sleeveless blouses and tissue thin saris and had her servants wear enormous turbans—a sign I always thought of desperate westernization. Her father, who was related to my grandmother Kunju, had a house not far from ours in Tiurvella. I remember being astounded at all the show to which his money had been put. The house was fitted out in the latest fashion: instead of the carved wooden shutters that we were all used to, the old man had installed glass windows. And not content with that, he had caused a long strip of glass to be installed above eye level in the veranda so that one could gaze into the house, consider the pirouettes of turbans as the servants passed with glasses on their trays.

Clearly, how one dressed was a problem. I was at Khartoum University at this time, and my girlfriends were caught up in the enormous excitement of shedding the tob. They were dressing in skirts and dresses and some of them, driving fast cars down the main street, behaved as if they were fit to turn into those women one had seen on international flights: at the drop of a seat belt they slipped out of their elaborate burkhas and, clad like liquid butterflies in fine Parisian costumes, sat downing drinks and sucking up cigarette smoke through ivory holders.

But Kozencheri and its demands could not be evaded. Watching a woman in a skimpy dress, her burkha shed to the side as she relaxed on a plane, was one thing; getting suitable clothing to gain permission to enter Kozencheri was another. Once puberty had set in, my returning home was fraught with anxiety. Ilya had been dead for four years and the Tiruvella house was locked up. Grandmother Mariamma was growing old and would soon herself die, quite peacefully in her sleep, dressed in her pure white garments. I wanted to lie with her in her great four-poster bed, learn the trick of silence, of female invisibility. How else could women protect themselves? Sometimes I felt it would be easiest for me, if I stood utterly still and disappeared.

In Kozencheri I had to learn all over again that girls could not walk outside the compound without appropriate escorts. It was hard to get the scary image of women being stoned out of my mind. Did appa get it from the Bible? From the Koran? Hunched over the dining table, staring at his stern, handsome face, I decided it probably came from his raw experience. Such things did indeed happen to women in the marketplaces of Kerala, in the inner courtyards of the ancestral houses. And sometimes women took it upon themselves to do away with their own shameful bodies: they jumped into wells. The image of women jumping into wells was constantly with me during my childhood.

*

A voice comes to me, out of mist and desert rain, out of well water and water in a blackened cooking pot where I looked in and saw my face: "You come from a long line of well-jumped women." Women come to me, countless women, some older, some younger: sixty-year-olds, hair bleached by time, stretched back tight over the skull, knotted at the nape; twenty-year-olds, their sweet hair hovering over the mouth, black hair blown back over the mouth in the monsoon winds; four-year-old children playing hopscotch, then swooped above ground on a wooden swing, hair brushing the branches of the love apple tree; babies too, plump, cheeks marked with beauty spots to keep away the evil eye, soft mouths dribbling milk.

And in the courtyard of a Kerala house I see worlds filled with women, women riding elephants, women like Princess Chitrangada with swords at their hips, bodies covered in rough jute—and who can see the softness of cotton underneath stained with menstrual blood? I see women in white starched saris, tucked in at the waist, hands sore with cooking rice and dal and fried fish, cleaning out the threshold stones that give entry to the courtyard, scrubbing out the cooking pots, popping riceballs into the mouths of young children. I see women, saris swept up shamelessly, high above the ankles, high above the knees, women well-jumping: jumping over wells.

I stare into well water. In that shining water no names anymore; the houses and places don't matter any more; no first there, nor second nor third; no foreground, background, left, right, or sideways; just the clarity of eyes shorn free of the bodies that held them in. Eyes bobbing in well water.

My amma's eyes, she who was born in Tiruvella out of whose womb I fell, blue, babbling. The eyes of both my grandmothers— appa's mother Mariamma born in the Kaitheyil house in Kottayam, amma's mother Kunju who died before my birth, she who was born in the Kurial house at the edge of Tiruvella. The eyes of my great-grandmothers, all four of them: how we grow in multiples of four, dunked into blackening water. Larger still, the eyes of my two sisters: I dwell in their sight, curious, fearful as I hang upside down from my tree.

Slipping, sloshing eyes of aunts, great-aunts, cousins, second cousins, third cousins and fourth, relatives by marriage from all the Suriani families to the east and west, north, and south. Eyes of other women, Marya and Chinna and Rameeza and Suraiya and Munira. Eyes of all the women they have ever seen. So many eyes crowded, jostling, bobbing, all female eyes. Why are they there? Why are there no male eyes? Why have these eyes popped free of their bodies? But how foolish to ask. These are eyes, not voices. I see them fluid, black, precisely as heavy as the water that bears them: the eyes of well-jumped women.

Born under the sign of Aquarius, I gravitate towards water: well water, pond, lagoon, river, sea. But the bond is uneasy. I am gripped by fear. I do not know what would become of me if I fell in. Perhaps I would dissolve, flesh devolving back into its own element, only my eyes remaining. Well water is most local, most domestic. Set at the threshold of the house, it calls all the girl-children to it. As a young child growing up in Tiruvella I heard countless stories of young women, beautiful as lotus blossoms in bud. At dawn they were discovered, black hair streaming, stretched fine as spider's filament over the well's mouth, bodies blanched and swollen.

Who discovered them? Why did they leap in? Eyes turned downwards, Marya would never tell. Nor would Chinna. Finally Bhaskaran blurted:

''The shame of it, Meenamol. The utter shame,'' and he gulped. He poked with a little stick at the ash that lay at his feet, at the shining fish scales Govindan the cook had lopped off the parrot fish we had for dinner two nights earlier.

''They were found with child,'' Chinna told me firmly, looking at me straight in the face. ''They could not carry the dishonor.''

We were standing beside the well as she spoke. Marya of the beautiful breasts had a bar of Sunlight soap in her hand. She was soaping up the clothes, before beating them on a rock set by the well. Bhaskaran stared at her uncontrollably as he gulped. He could not help himself.

''Kaveri, the blind girl who lived by the schoolhouse. They couldn't clean out the well after that! Who would drink from the water where his child had drowned? Some say the father pushed her to it.''

''Pushed?'' Chinna spoke up. ''Listen, I think it's time we checked the mangoes. Come with me.''

She pulled me away. As I walked with Chinna towards the tapioca patch I saw in a blur of light those great star-shaped leaves poised on the crimson stalks, high, higher than my face. But my pleasure was blotted out. Instead of feeling the stalks brush against my cheeks, I kept seeing the well. Over and over, like a mad flashback, I saw the well. First the wall, the brick painted over with gray mortar, streaked with moss, damp with monsoon rain, and then, as if the film had jerked, the inside.

Inside lay a woman. Once she must have been a girl-child like me. Now she was full grown, though she still had the slightly plump cheeks of a girl. I could see the tip of her nose, a fine pointed shape. Her oval face and floating hair framed by water were perfectly posed, like one of those calendar pictures sold in the marketplace. The water was a cloud on which she floated, hair splashing a little as the well frogs leapt. But this woman wasn't Paravati or Lakshmi. She didn't have four golden arms. Nor was she a film star like Nutan or Saira Banu, cheeks pink with paint. She was an ordinary Kerala woman, once girl-child, now full grown, skin wrinkled with water. Her eyes were wide open, staring shamelessly.

The almond shaped eyes were huge, black, lidless. Under the face, tangling the black hair, was the mound of a belly covered in floating cloth. Doubled up inside it like the baby dolphin I had seen in Trivandrum Zoo, was a creature, skinless, face blotched out. What manner of thing was it, forcing the poor woman to leap into water? Was her heart beating wildly as mine did now, this Kaveri or Mariamma, Meena or Munira? Had she locked her eyes so tight as she leapt over the hibiscus fence by the outhouse the servants used? Had she forced herself into the well, both hands clutching her nest of hair? Did she know that in well water her eyes would swing open wide, so shamelessly?

"Ah, the shame of it!" I glanced at Chinna. She was repeating herself, pointing to the golden coconuts on the miniature trees that grew by the hedge. The globes, heavy as a child's head, were tinged with green. They rolled in the sunlight. When I squinted my eyes they made glorious beads you could string together, clear, hard fruit, on a thread of sight. Gazing at the coconuts, I figured out how to freeze them in an instant of looking so the sun wouldn't blind me, so the poor pale thing in the well would flee from me.

Years later, when I read Wyatt's lines: "They flee from me that sometimes did me seek / With naked foot stalking in my chamber," I understood the poem immediately. The beloved, fleet of foot, was racing into water, and the lover was quite confused, bewildered by desire, but deciding not to do very much except stand where he was and make his poem. All dressed up in frills and furbelows and hose of apple green, the rage at the time, he stood his ground in his stately house, while she, poor thing, filled with shame, fled into the nearest tarn.

Sex and death were spliced and fitted into each other, quite precisely: like the milk-white flesh curved into the shell of the tender coconut as it hung on the tree; like the juicy flesh of the love apple rippling inside the purple husk that shone if you rubbed it against skirt or thigh. And shame lit the image. It was what women had to feel. Part of being, not doing. Part of one's very flesh.

Author's maternal great-grandparents with their children, circa 1910, Calicut. From left: (standing) Eapen, Sara, Elizabeth (author's grandmother); (seated) Anna (author's great-grandmother), Sosa, George Zachariah (author's great-grandfather); (seated on floor) George, Anna, Kuruvilla.

Author's maternal grandparents with their daughter, 1942, Kottayam. From left: Elizabeth, Mary (author's mother), Kuruchiethu Kuruvilla.

Author's paternal grandparents with their children, 1937, Kozencheri. From left: (standing) George (author's father), Sara; (seated) Annamma, Mariamma (author's grandmother), Kannadical Koruth Alexander (author's grandfather), Mary.

Author's parents, Mary and George Alexander, 1947, Madras.

Author as baby with parents, 1951, Allahabad.

Author with her maternal grand-father, Kuruchiethu Kuruvilla (Ilya), 1959, Tiruvella.

Author's family, 1965, Khartoum. From left: (standing) George; (seated) Meena, Elsa, Anna, Mary.

Author with her husband, David Lelyveld, son, Adam Kuruvilla Lelyveld, and daughter, Svati Mariam Lelyveld, 1986, New York City. Photo by Beryl Goldberg.

Svati and Adam, 1998, New York City.

Author, 1990, New York City. Photo by Colleen McKay.

8. Language and Shame

*I*t is summer in Manhattan and a hot wind blows. The wind blows in through the window. I feel it against my cheek almost as if I were in Khartoum or Tiruvella. I lay out my old journals on the white desk and gaze at them. Time contracts into the scrawl of my teenage years. The journals composed when I was a teenager in Khartoum contain within them a desperate awareness of my femaleness, a sense of shame, of power drawn back that in its very intensity was a threat to the order that governed my young life.

For not only did I bear the shame from the Kerala world within me, but I set by its side the burning horror of clitoridectomy that many of my friends had described. Some like Sarra had spoken proudly, of how, through the liberal education of their fathers, they had escaped it. Others had suffered its brutality and were silent. In my years growing up, from time to time I was filled with the image of what women might suffer— whether through mutilation or through shame—sufferings caused purely by being female. And I felt in a dim, unspoken way that there was a connection between how I came to language and what it meant to be cast out, unhoused.

As a small child in India, I had learnt to speak English along with Malayalam and Hindi. Syllables, phrases, sentences of English flowed along as part of the river of my experience. In Khartoum, however, as a young child of five, cut from the fluidities of my Indian world, I had to learn English all over again. Now it was not just one language spoken among many: it was the most important one and I was an outsider confronting it. No doubt my English tutor, Mrs. McDermott, had a lot to do with my feelings of utter ineptitude when faced with the complexities of her mother tongue. Over and over she made me repeat the words she felt I should learn till their sharpness overwhelmed me, made my mouth hurt. I see myself, a small child of six, sitting at a polished wooden table with a sheen so bright it reflected all that was cast onto it, an ivory vase with roses, a place mat, a knife, a fork pushed to the side, two faces, one small and dark, the other older and pale. The book I was trying to read was flush against the wood and so didn't make a double image: an old old book with pictures of Tom and Bess, little English children who wore knickerbockers and pinafores, carried caps in their hands and drank milk. They were forever loitering by ponds filled with ducks, racing down lanes towards windmills with red wooden slats. Mrs. McDermott leant forward. Over and over she made me say: "duck," "duck," "pluck," "pluck," "milk," "milk," "silk," "silk." It was hard for her. I pouted, I fidgeted under the table, knocking my knuckles against the wood, then tried over and over. It was a ruinous waste of time but she persisted. I was all wrong, I knew it. And I felt quite ashamed. The trouble was, I knew the words already but in a different way. And she tried her level best to polish out my Indian English and replace it with the right model. From her point of view she did a good job. Traces, perhaps even more than traces, of that speech linger on my tongue. How could she know that more than two decades later, that very diction would work against me, make me an oddity in the eyes of the white Midwestern feminist at a university in the colder reaches of this country who wanted nothing to do with me, who turned and said: "Of course they'll hire you. They'll trot you out because you speak such good English."

In Khartoum, after the year with the Scottish tutor, I enrolled in the Clergy House School, the first non-white child. At first they wouldn't let me into the school: it was officially known as the Diocesan School for British Children. But faced with the wrenching prospect of sending me away to Saint Joseph's in the hills of India, amma spoke to her uncle, C. P. Maathen, who had just come to the Sudan as the first ambassador from India. My great-uncle put in a word with the Anglican bishop and I was let in, by the side door as it were. For the first few months, when great-uncle and his daughter Sheila were living with us in Hai el Matar, while their large house by the Nile was being prepared for them, I rode into Clergy House School in the Indian ambassador's car, with the flag flying high. For great-uncle was there too, busily scanning his papers, running his elegant fingernails over the leather of his briefcase and his folders. When the driver opened the door for me, I hopped out, my lunch box in hand, my cotton frock come all the way from Tiruvella ironed straight, my two plaits neatly arranged on my shoulders. I was miserable in that school for the first two years. My blackness stuck out like a stiff halo all around me. I was imprisoned there, I could not move beyond it. I felt myself grow ugly under their gaze. The only friend I made was Christine from San Francisco. No one would play with her because she was fat, and so Christine and I had our lunch together under the outside staircase and we sat and watched the British and Australians and French and Germans toss their hair and ride on the roundabout in the Sudanese sun. Christine told me about Superman and Supergirl and the great golden bridge in San Francisco, and I remembered her, when years later, driven into Berkeley to give a poetry reading, I passed over that great metallic span and shut my eyes so the sun would not blind me and caught for an instant behind the sun's rays, the looming architecture of the prison of Alcatraz.

It should come as no surprise, then, that for almost a whole year in class I was dumb, I refused to open my mouth. It was my way of resisting. ''You were considered very slow, you wouldn't read in class when you were asked to,'' amma reminded me. ''I came to school,'' she explained, ''and told that English woman: 'My child is not slow, just shy.' She let you be. Then it got a little better.'' I remember amma walking me to the gate to wait for the school bus, helping me over and over with English words so I wouldn't be puzzled or get lost. But when I began to write poetry at ten and eleven, she grew anxious, perhaps justifiably so, about the disclosures that a writing life commits one to, quite contrary to the reticence that femininity requires.

As a child in Khartoum I used to hide out to write, either behind the house where there was a patch of bare wall and the shade of a neem tree, or better still, in the half-darkness of the toilet. I gradually found that the toilet was safer. There I could mind my own business and compose. I also learnt to write in snatches, a skill that has served me well. If someone knocked at the door, I stopped abruptly. I hid my papers under my skirts, tucked my pen into the elastic band of my knickers, and got up anxiously. Gradually, this enforced privacy—for I absorbed, perhaps even in part identified, with amma's disapproval of my poetic efforts—added an aura of something illicit, shameful, to my early sense of scribblings. School-work was seen in a totally different light. Essays, exercises, note-taking, reading and writing about the literary works on the school syllabus, were always encouraged. It was good to excel there, in-terpreting works that were part of a great literary past. The other writing, in one's own present, was to be tucked away, hidden. I had to be secretive about the writing that came out of my own body, but still a fierce pride clung to it.

Little did I know that years later the hot unease I had first felt as a small child learning to repeat English words, and trying to get them right, that dense tissue of feeling (unease, embarrassment, a fear of being exposed, a shame, finally, of being improper, not quite right, never quite right) would return sharply, enveloping me. Once again I felt that hot scent: forcing me back onto myself, onto a border existence. But this time it was my intellectual work that was called into question, not because of itself, but because of what my body made me: female, Indian, Other.

I was once called into the office of the chairman of my depart-ment at the Jesuit university where I worked. He leant forward in his black garb, stiff, quite clear about his own position. "It has been pointed out to me that you do not publish in the area in which you were hired, British Romanticism."

I perked up. "What about that?" I pointed to a book lying on his table. He picked it up, a little puzzled. "Look at the table of con-tents," I pointed at it with my finger. He glanced at me. I was sit-ting there, quite proper in my Kashmir silk sari, erect at the edge of the chair. His eyes shifted to the titles of chapters listed in the table of contents. There was a gap there, a split second. I shivered, not because I was cold—it was early fall and quite warm still—but because I suddenly saw something. There was no way the man who sat in front of me could put together my body with any sense of the life of the mind. I had fallen under the Cartesian blade. "Yes, yes," he muttered, looking at the chapters with names like Words-worth and Coleridge littering them. "Yes, yes."

I stood up. The trouble was what I was, quite literally: female, Indian. Not that I had not published in my designated area, but that I had also published outside that docket. A paper on Jayanta Ma-hapatra had just come out in London. Some senior colleagues had seen it. Was this stuff really literature? Also, I was active in the read-ing series, Art Against Apartheid, and my poems were coming out in journals. It was all quite improper. Later, when I was denied tenure in the spring of 1986, when my body was swelling with a second child, going into work I sometimes smelled that old shame. The sharpness of the recollection excited me, but by then I was too tired to sort it out. I left it hanging there in memory.

When I was a child, barbed wire ran across the back of the Tiruvella compound where the cashew nut trees grew, where the mango trees arced their boughs of speckled fruit. In July the cashews started to ripen. First there were streaks of yellow in the soft fruit out of which the nut descended, then as the season gathered force, green turned ocher or red with the sweetness of the cashew sap. This was the signal for the young boys who lived in the railway huts to turn up in little clusters, armed with stones. If I stood quite still in the back bedroom where my grandmother's mirror stood in its rosewood frame, I could hear the sharp sting of stones against the cashew trees. If Bhaskaran or Kittan were not there, I would have to run out and start shouting at the boys, ''Stop that, you, how dare you, scoot, scoot,'' and other such strings of words that rushed out of my mouth.

Once, I grabbed a young urchin by the foot as he tried to slither out from under the barbed wire, a horde of juicy cashew fruits under his armpit. I felt the air from his ankle lashing at my hand. But as his foot slipped out under the barbed wire, I felt another ''I'' slipping out with the dusty child. After all, why shouldn't he have a few of the fruits? What did he have to eat at night? A mess of gruel and a few chilis with these fruits as supplement, and once a week, if he were lucky, a small slice of fish. Isn't that why his ribs stuck up in hunger? Wasn't that what Ilya and all his friends were talking about when they had those meetings on ''The Needs of Our Children''? I was torn in that way by my own behavior. I was a divided child and felt my own precariousness: born to privilege, I clearly had only one foot in my grandfather's garden. I had returned home for the holidays from Khartoum, and what I saw, however intense my vision, was colored by another life.

Quite soon after, my own divided stance was brought home to me. It was the same summer. The children next door were having a birthday party. Their father had returned after several years in the United States, and had invited a colleague, another mathematician, to visit India. The professor had duly arrived with his red-headed wife and freckled, carrot-haired children in tow. It was a miracle. People came from miles around to see them. "How could anyone be that color," people whispered. "An unknown jinni? Too much henna applied raw—what then of the spotty skin?" Some even wondered if it was an advanced European form of leprosy that invaded the bodies of these visitors, but they seemed perfectly healthy and no one lacked body parts. No toes dropping off, nothing like that. At the birthday party, the little American children, three of them, stood in a lonely group by the marigold patch. My friends pushed me forward.

"You go ahead, Meena."

I dug in my toes, quite firmly.

"Why me?" and even as I knew the answer that would come, "No, no," I muttered. "Not me, not me."

"You must." They pushed me on. "You've talked to people like that in Africa."

"Well..."

"No, don't be worried, really," the oldest, Reeni, took me by the hand, almost leading me there. She wanted the birthday party to be a success. The visitors should at least try to play a little, loosen up, share in the sweet papaya that was being brought around. Still I shrank back, not wanting to be picked out, the childhood desire for conformity turned into a prickly fear, for the little boy Bubu was hissing in my ear:

"You speak like that too, *sssss*," he made the sounds with a sharp tongue, "*sssss*, the Madama language." I stood, smiling hesitantly at those children, and even put out my hand, but I resolutely refused to open my mouth.

I knew what I was: a child from Tiruvella. That is what my flesh made of me and I saw no reason to let my mouth betray me. I was well aware, though, that at other times, in other places, I had to rely wholly on the language I had learnt with such pain, to carry me through the invisible barbed wire of a burden I had not chosen. Later, as I became a teenager, I realized the forked power in the tongue I had acquired: English alienated me from what I was born to; it was also the language of intimacy and bore the charged power of writing. Through it, I dared to hope, I might some day unlock the feelings that welled up within me.

*

I was just thirteen when I entered Khartoum University. My father had to get special permission from the University Senate, so that I could enter. I had graduated first in my class from Unity High School and there was nowhere else I could go. In the mid-sixties, politically and pedagogically, Khartoum University was an exciting place to study. Reading groups recited Arabic poetry; drama groups put on everything from Wole Soyinka's *Dance of the Forests*—I remember the great thrill of helping construct the papier-mâché masks for the production—to *Caligula*. There was the energy of trying to figure out Sudan's place in the outburst of power flooding the Arab world. Nasser was at the helm of Egypt and there was a strong sense that the world was changing. At the same time, the issue of an African identity was not lost in the debates the students engaged in. A civil war was smoldering in the south of the Sudan, and southern Sudanese were being tortured and killed by the northern troops. Although General Abboud's so-called ''benevolent dictatorship'' had prohibited all discussion of the ''southern question,'' the students' union decided to go ahead with its debate on the issue and, when refused permission, hundreds of students took to the streets. The townspeople joined them. Then the tanks started rolling.

I had gone to the street demonstration with my friends, Sarra and Azza Anis. It was my first public march and indeed my introduction to the larger, more vital life of the university. There was tear gas in the air; two students ahead of us, Babiker and Bedri, were shot to death. More and more tanks rolled out of the army barracks and the stench of the tear gas became unbearable. But in the face of overwhelming support for change the army backed down. A bloodless coup, everyone said, when democracy was restored for a few short years.

Raised by Ilya on the stories of civil disobedience that had finally forced the British to leave India, I was prepared in my own way for the oppositional struggle my friends were embarked on in the Sudan. It seemed to me then, nearly fourteen, that the whole of the known world must be participating in these struggles. My sense of poetry, even in its uttermost privacy, drew strength from struggle, from tumult. I felt that it must be possible for all human beings to struggle towards equality and social justice, to live in a world without unnecessary suffering.

The language I used, English, was part of my reaching out for this new world. It was braided in for me with the Arabic that was all around me, the language that my first poems were translated into, the language in which I first heard words of love and anger. English was woven too with the French I had learnt in school and chattered with my friends, the language of Verlaine and Mallarmé, of the most exquisite lyricism imaginable, of tears, of storms of tears, of betrayal.

> Le ciel est, pardessus le toit
> Si bleu, si calme!
> Un arbre pardessus le toit
> Berce sa palme.

I loved those lines, for quite early I understood the necessity of beauty, of an atmosphere of silence, of a void even in which the imagination might blossom. And without the space made for beauty, of what use was the political struggle? The heart would grow hard, numb, turn into a desert stone.

I existed then, in my unfolding sense of what it might mean to speak and write, in the tension between my multiple worlds. In my teenage studies I was deeply attracted to the poetry and prose of the English Romantics, whose intense, even tormented probings into the nature of image and language were underwritten by the call for a revolutionary knowledge. I will never forget the first time I read Coleridge. It was in Khartoum, and I carried with me the magical thought of what he, borrowing from Schlegel, developed as the notion of organic form, the idea that any living existence, a cloud, a plant, a poem, a person, might have its own unique inner teleology, apparent only in the flowering of the fullest form, a logic, a *svadharma*, that could not be questioned. Given this, no one could say: you're all wrong, you don't do things right, you don't get the final syllable in the stanza right. The inner form had a logic so powerful it was best spoken of in the language reserved for passion and it tore through the mesh of decorum, of the principled order the disparate social worlds had established.

Yet even as these liberating thoughts came to me in English, I was well aware that the language itself had to be pierced and punctured lest the thickness of the white skin cover over my atmosphere, my very self. The language I used had to be supple enough to reveal the intricate mesh of otherness in which I lived and moved. My very first poems were composed in French when I was twelve and thirteen: I felt this was the way to attain the heights of lyricism Verlaine had opened up. Slowly I revised my thoughts and turned to English.

In the late sixties, I was part of a small group of poets at Khartoum University. My friends all wrote in Arabic and were strong supporters of the use of contemporary language. They felt that the decorum of the classical meters could only violate the quick of the spoken form, the pressing needs of the poet. These friends easily translated my poems into Arabic. My first publications were these poems printed in the Arabic newspapers in Khartoum. While this gave me a great deal of pleasure, I was also surprisingly compliant about accepting my illiteracy in Arabic. During childhood, I lived in Hai el Matar near the poet and scholar Abdullah Tayib, who had encouraged me to study the great classical poetry in Arabic. Somehow, I was hesitant to learn the script. I wanted only to listen, to let the spoken language wash over me. Dylan Thomas's lines concerning ''the force that through the green fuse drives the flower'' made utter sense and I held fast to the same impulses that had allowed me to escape my grandmother Mariamma's elaborate mesh of proprieties, and to escape also the study of the Malayalam script.

It seemed to me, then, that one script was enough, the one that I had been forced to learn. And I truly believed that I could translate myself in and out of it, together with all the languages that welled up inside me. Perhaps there was also something else at stake, a greater fragility than I could acknowledge, a need to protect the quick of the self.

Through an inability to read and write the script in Arabic, and even in Malayalam my mother tongue, I maintained an immediacy of sound and sense in those two great languages of my childhood years that enabled me to dissolve and dissipate, if only in a partial, paradoxical fashion, the canonical burden of British English. And so a curious species of linguistic decolonization took place for me, in which my own, often unspoken sense of femaleness played a great part. I set the hierarchies, the scripts aside, and let the treasured orality flow over me. After all, that was how Malayalam had first come to me: in chants, in spoken voices that held a community together. Perhaps deep within me was a fear that learning the script would force me to face up to the hierarchies of a traditional society, the exclusionary nature of its canonical language. Wouldn't that script imprison me? How then would I ever be restored to simplicity, freed of the burdens of counter-memory?

I did not know any women who were writers, at least not firsthand, though indeed, I was aware that such beings existed in the libraries of the world. And it was only dimly, if at all, that I was aware that the illiteracies I clung to helped me steer clear of the elaborate hierarchical machine that set women apart, lower, different from men. In those days, my friends in Khartoum were slipping out of their tobs, or refusing ever to put them on, and struggling against the old strictures that ordained clitoridectomies for women, that barbarous mutilation my two closest girlfriends had escaped. Women were refusing to carry a bride price; almost in jest, they were renting the elaborate gold jewelry needed for weddings, the cost of which would have burdened the family with debt.

They were seeking out the rights of women. I recall a student union election at Khartoum University when, without the slightest hint of irony, an ardent Communist argued that women have souls. The Communists were campaigning for women's equality and won overwhelmingly that year against the Muslim Brothers, their chief opponents. The struggle to modernize was everywhere, and I entered into the exhilaration of it.

I was fascinated by the corrosive magic of the first person singular: its exuberant flights, its sheer falls into despair. Still there was always a desire to tell the stories of my life, to write of Ilya's garden. My experiences as a young child, as a guardian of the cashew nut grove, were sufficiently troublesome to lead me to want to set down those feelings in words. I needed a fictional form that would allow me more than the intensities of the lyric voice: I needed others, many voices, a plot however simple, a form from which history could not be torn out any more than a heart could be torn from a living animal. At thirteen I thought I would write a short story. But in my first attempts the supple skin of language turned into a barbed wire that trapped me.

I was sitting in the stacks at the bottom of Khartoum University Library. The library was made of sandstone. Large columns held it up and made for a delicious coolness in the basement where the stacks were. I could run my palms over the bricks and feel the pleasure of release from the intense heat outside. I had a favorite spot, right by the poems of Sylvia Plath. To my right was the shelf of contemporary poetry in English translation, and my favorites: Yevgeny

Yevtushenko, Hans Magnus Enzensberger, Paul Celan. My own scribblings in poetry seemed quite trite, so I turned to my other life, tried to put down the words of the child I was in Tiruvella, years ago and the thoughts of the child he was, whose name I never knew as I gripped his ankle under the barbed wire.

Something tore inside me. No, I wouldn't. I couldn't do it. I could not turn the Malayalam utterances into English. Why would I even want to do it—turn those words of the language where I lived and moved in my inmost being into an English that could never carry that emotion, that would only distort it? But there was more too. How could I translate the words, the feelings of my mother tongue, the only one I had, into the discrepant script of English? English was so powerful, even Celan and Yevtushenko were translated into it. That is how I read them, knew of them. But I could not bear to set myself into that trench, tear myself limb from limb.

And at least two things became clear: one was that I could never write fiction, for that would mean translating the words of the people I knew best, the life and the practices I was closest to; and the other was a sudden bitter realization of the sheer force of English and how I had been made to learn it. I had had no choice in the matter. It was presented to me quite literally as the only way to go. Living in Khartoum as an expatriate Indian child, I had to learn English. How could I possibly have received an Arabic education? What would that have equipped me for? And in any case the Sanskrit and Malayalam tutors were far away, across the burning waters I had traveled with amma.

Bit by bit I realized that the form of the poem offered something I needed, a translation out of the boundaries of the actual, a dance of words that might free me from my own body. And I took to reading poems day and night so that history might not consume me, render me dumb. But that realization came slowly when, years later in North America, I had to strip my partial knowledge away so that I could learn to write the truth of the body, pitted, flawed, unfinished.

I called up a friend. He has a poem about a bear, hunting it, tearing up the skin, eating its blood and turds, then going into its skin, becoming that bear, the stickiness of its blood: poetry. His poems had opened up America for me when I first came here. I had read "The Avenue Bearing the Initial of Christ into the New World" and *The Book of Nightmares* many times. And in the year after I arrived in New York, sitting and drinking coffee with Galway Kinnell, off and on of a morning, speaking of many things, including poetry, I had glimpsed a little of what survival might mean here, what blossoming might come of a writing life.

We spoke on the phone. I had not been able to sleep for two nights. I had felt the back of my head was being blown off, a nameless violence creeping in I could not understand. But his voice settled me. Something of tenderness at the life all around flowed back.

I sat at the window in the living room, looking out onto the windows and roofs of 113th Street. I saw a pigeon open its wings, as if those wings were spilt petals. The ligaments of the bird did not spill apart. The creature let its body-weight down on a fretted stone ledge across from my window. The sun glanced off the chimneys of Broadway making a purple sheen on the pigeon's claws.

I went into the next room that serves as a study to get pen and paper, to make a poem of the bird, but what came instead was a piece that ended up with the title "No Man's Land," about the aftermath of war, women washing their thighs in bloodied river water. This is how the poem I was working on runs in the final draft I completed several days later:

> The dogs are amazing
> sweaty with light
> they race past the dung heaps
>
> Infants crawl
> sucking dirt from sticks
> whose blunt ends
> smack of elder flesh
> and ceaseless bloodiness
>
> The soldiers though
> are finally resting
> by the river
> berets over their noses.
>
> Barges from the north
> steam past nettles,
> cut stalks of blackthorn

and elder, olive trees
axed into bits

Women wash their thighs
in bloodied river water
over and over
they wipe their flesh

In stunned
immaculate gestures,
figures massed with light.

They do not hear
the men
or dogs or children.

But it did not rest, the spirit that rode me. Out of that compulsion a music came and I could get a little of it, a tiny fraction, with my words. Writing as best I could on scraps of paper I had tucked into my coat pocket, I busied myself, getting ready for a day's teaching.

I dropped little Svati off at the Family Annex across the road and crossed Broadway and got onto the No. 4 bus. As we passed Central Park on 110th Street, I saw the dry rough earth where Harlem Meer was drained out. The leaves, such as they were, survived in coils of brown, littering the bare ground. There was a concrete ledge that ran all the way around the drained lake. I was surprised at its shallowness. Once boats had sailed there. It was a city lake, a man-made device to please the eye and ear, cool the senses. Now it was emptied out. The ground where water had been was sprinkled with leaves, pocked with odd-shaped gashes in the ground. There were bits of metal and plastic and newspapers blown in from the barrio and upper Fifth Avenue and God knows where else.

News of the world in a dried-up lake.

I could make out a child's tricycle with bizarre handlebars, half-bent, that someone had pitched in. I balanced the poem in my lap as the bus turned the corner onto Fifth Avenue. The title, "No Man's Land," that I had given the poem, troubled me. In the long, difficult conclusion of "Night-Scene," which I just completed, I had used the same phrase. And somehow passing Harlem Meer all dried out, the phrase returned, worrying me. Is that all I had, is that all I was, this torn territory? I was carrying the long poem with me, as a kind of talisman, a protection for the mind, and now I opened up the pages as the bus turned the corner onto Fifth Avenue. My eyes fell on the image of barbed wire.

After Ilya's death, the Tiruvella house had been empty for many years. Wild grasses took root everywhere, and delicate orchids my grandmother had planted around the guava trees lost their hold in the laterite soil. Brambles choked up the rose beds and the sweet-scented laburnam that fenced in the five acres of compound on the north side started to rot, eaten up by large black ants. The house was empty all those years when appa and amma were in Khartoum, and then, when they returned to India in 1969, amma rented out the house, first to a doctor and his wife, and then to a priest with many children. The priest cut down the fragrant woods in the side garden for firewood and planted tapioca all over the flower beds. Years later, in 1983, when my parents were living in a small rented apartment in Trivandrum so that they could be near my sister Anna who was teaching there, a great misfortune occurred.

A broker, to whom amma had entrusted the sale of some plots of land at the side of the house closest to the road, had suddenly turned up at the Trivandrum apartment and threatened appa with death if he did not give him control of the Tiruvella property. This man had a gang of armed men in his pay. He also had funds with which to bribe the first set of lawyers my parents hired. It took three years of hard struggle for my parents to get the house restored in my mother's name. Desperately ill as he was with polycythemia, the rare blood disease he had contracted, and with the asthma that came over him in the dry season, appa traveled again and again to the state supreme courts and to the High Court in Delhi. There were times when I was scared that the strain of it would be too much for him to bear, and the great house seemed just a millstone around our necks. Lying awake at night in New York, I wondered if it wasn't a penance we had to pay.

When finally the house was restored by the courts, it had been half-destroyed. The crooked broker had installed a drunkard and his family there, as well as a few of his armed men. All the wiring had been ripped out of the walls, the portraits and porcelain had been smashed, and my parents and those who came to their assistance had to remove yards and yards of barbed wire from the finely carved windows of my grandfather's house. The barbed wire had been hammered in to turn the house into a fortification should the police try to storm it. It seemed to me almost a miracle, the care and patience that my parents and Anna and Elsa put into cleaning the house and restoring it to some measure of grace. But the marks remain.

I thought of the barbed wire inside the Tiruvella house as the bus jolted on Fifth Avenue, then in front of the Museum of the City of New York. I looked out at the museum where a banner hung and realized that, for me, poems made real places. They had to. My life was so torn up into bits and pieces of the actual that I depended on the poems, irruptions of the imaginary to make an internal history for me. I focused in on the silk banner outside the museum entrance. It had a sign advertising "The Golem in Jewish Art." The mud monster. Wasn't that what the golem was? Mary Shelley's monster came to mind, the creature made with bits and pieces of flesh and stapled together with Frankenstein's miserable magic. I shut my eyes to cut out the ugliness of it, the grotesque joints, the stitches that showed, the split seams.

When I was little, amma had tried again and again to show me how to stitch properly. How to fold the hem under and curve it over the stretched index finger, fix it tightly in place with the thumb and then make the stitches all as evenly as possible, tight and hard so that the silk could blend into the fabric and the frayed bit turn invisible in the well-groomed sheen of the skirt or blouse. But I was much older now, and I felt I was living in a world where amma's kind of stitching did not make sense.

I had no house here with pantry and parlor and silver neatly wiped and polished in rows. My kitchen was a spill of bread and peanut butter and onions and garlic barely in place on the racks. Herbs I had dried freely dropped their leaves onto the linoleum floor. I needed my stitching like my writing to show its seams, its baste lines, its labor.

I opened my eyes and Harlem Meer shorn of its water was behind us. There were poky trees, fragile with winter. A torn kite stuck its shiny stuff in a branch and dribbled its string down, ounces of it, falling to the cold ground. As the bus passed Harlem Meer an image came to me: and with it, as with all images now, in the dislocated life, landscapes superimposed each on the other, a veritable palimpsest, time's turmoil.

I saw barbed wire just before combat, a pale flag falling. It was 1967, I was sixteen. Ilya had been dead five years and the Tiruvella house was still locked up. Grandmother Mariamma too had died and only veliappechan survived of that older generation. In the summers, instead of returning to Kerala, the family had taken to traveling westward. That summer the five of us, two parents and three children, were all together in a black car, with a driver, traveling from Jerusalem to Bethlehem.

Suddenly on the right came a line of barbed wire. There was no warning before it. It went on and on. The thin trees rose behind. I saw a man in combat uniform. I forget the color of his uniform. A UN solider, appa said. We stared out of the car windows. The driver, sensing our interest, slowed slightly and the car started coughing. Slowly, methodically, the soldier dragged at a coil of rope, pulling the flag down. The thin blue and white rectangle, as delicate as the mist around it, fluttered and fell. The rope pinned it in place. A few weeks later the war burst out. There was news of grenades and firebombs and artillery so old that it backfired onto the Egyptian soldiers. By this time we were safely at home and in Khartoum the excitement came, a mirror dashing itself sideways into our lives. The sharp bits glistened and fell and I could not put them back together again.

Was English in India a no man's land? No woman's either? I could not be sure in those tumultuous years of the early seventies when I lived and worked there. At the Central Institute of English in Hyderabad where I started work in 1975, there was much discussion of precise speech, correct pronunciation, appropriate usage, the status of English in India, the function of the language, how knowledge imparted in English, including technical knowledge that had to do with modernizing the country, must surely have a trickle-down effect as it was called, from the elite—who unabashedly saw themselves as such—to the rest of country. English then had this superior status in the eyes of some who taught there, superior that is to any Indian language. But there were others who realized that the future of English in India lay in its ability to blend itself with the life all around, the world of the streets, of the marketplaces.

Often I would spend long evenings with my dear friend Susie Tharu, thinking through what it meant to write in India, what sort of art could come out of the streets, the marketplaces. In her company, I learnt to think afresh of aesthetic forms and consider how they are bounded by the public spaces of our lives. Susie too had spent her childhood in Africa—in Uganda, rather than the Sudan—and then, after her studies in Britain, had returned to India. In those days I learnt from her about femaleness, about resistance, and the possibility of political action. In 1979, just before I left Hyderabad, she took me to the first meetings of the women's group, Shree Shakti Sanghatana. Even after I left Hyderabad for New York our friendship, stretched taut by absence, survived, deepened.

In India, my quest to make sense of poetry written in English—what role would it have in terms of Indian literature, who would read it?—took me to Cuttack, to meet the poet Jayanta Mahapatra. First, I wrote to Jayanta, whose work I admired, and asked if I might call on him. It was 1976: I was twenty-five years old. I took the train to Cuttack and then set out in one of those high-backed rickshaws in search of Tinkonia Bagicha. The rickshaw driver took me to the gate. I peered in through the bamboo that grew by the house and saw a bay window filled with books and then Jayanta's slight figure dashing out, calling me. I spent several days there, immersed in the life of poetry, feeling the soil under my feet. Jayanta and his wife Runu grew to be dear friends. Through Jayanta, who had lived his whole life in Cuttack, I learnt to understand the poet's bond with place; learnt to understand how the elegaic voice could gather sustenance from the landscape around; learnt, too, how to accept the ravages of time.

The years when I taught at the Central Institute in Hyderabad, 1975 to 1977, were the years of the Emergency in India, when Prime Minister Indira Gandhi withdrew civil liberties and people could be jailed on mere suspicion of an oppositional stance. Behind my office window was a police station and sometimes I could hear the cries and the hoarse whispers of those who were taken there. I wrote a poem about a police station called "Within the Walls," which appeared in the *Democratic World* in Delhi, but the next poem I sent in and they accepted, "Prison Bars," about prisoners being beaten, was never published. Instead, in the spot where it should have been, the magazine maintained a blank white space, the exact size of the poem, a signal of censorship.

In 1977 I moved a few miles away to Hyderabad University, a very new institution, and there, in an atmosphere of academic excitement, I debated the question of poetry all over again, particularly poetry written in English. My special friend there was the poet Arvind Krishna Mehrotra, who was reading *After Babel* in those days and thinking hard about multilingualism and the composition of poetry in English. For my part I could not forget my Khartoum experiences and how English, the language in which I made poems, had come to me.

Colonialism seemed intrinsic to the burden of English in India, and I felt robbed of literacy in my own mother tongue. The English department of Hyderabad University was housed in "The Golden Threshold," home of the poet Sarojini Naidu. Reading Naidu's poetry and her political speeches—she used English for both purposes—I noted how the discourse of her poetry stood at odds with the powerful language of her speeches. The former was pained, contrived, modeled on the poetry of the English Decadents, filled with images of the female body wasting away. Her speeches, in contrast, were impassioned, concerned with the British abuse of power, with the possibility of a new Indian beginning: they were forcefully directed to her audience, a people struggling for national independence.

I was fascinated by how English worked for her, and how in her political speeches the language could be turned to the purposes of decolonization. What would it be like if Naidu as a poet had been able to break free of the restrictive ideology that bound her in? What would she have needed in order to make poems of resistance, poems that voiced the body?

The questions have not left me. They reverberate in my head. Sometimes a voice rises in my dreams, as floodwaters rise, subsiding suddenly. And the parched landscape of Hyderabad, in the season before the rains fall, starts to crackle with flames and the flames become the blue gas flames in the stove in my New York City kitchen and in my dream I have to hold myself back with both hands, tie the end of my sari to the refrigerator handle to prevent me from tumbling over the slopes into the fault lines that split my imagined earth.

"We must imagine the earth again. Poetry must be like bread," Faiz Ahmed Faiz once said to me. I can still see his face, his eyes, that grand old man of letters, eyes green-blue, the color of the sky after rainfall. It was 1977 or perhaps early '78 in Hyderabad. He was in the large, ornate drawing room, in the home of Indira Devi Dharajgir. It was an intimate gathering, and I had been invited to meet Faiz, asked to bring some poems along to recite to him. A musician was there, with a sitar, a tanpura player, to perform some of Faiz's ghazals. Faiz patted the place next to him on the sofa, so that I could sit down. He spoke of the poems he had composed during the Bangladesh War, he spoke of Beirut, then suddenly laughing at some comment about translation and the Third World, said, "English, of course, is the language of love!" We were charmed, feeling that at least some times he must speak to his English wife in that tongue and she, of course, living in Lahore, was surrounded by Urdu. Now, years after his death, I want to turn to him and say, Faiz, how can poetry be like bread? How?

Shelter, unhousedness, the multiple speeches that surround us, broken walls, prison cells. The thoughts turn jagged in me. Everything is overcrowded. Everything is emptied out. I dream of barbed wire.

There are images of barbed wire in the long poem "Night-Scene, the Garden." I started work on the poem in the months after Svati Mariam was born when the experience of childbirth was still with me. In that poem I am haunted by "ferocious alphabets of flesh." They have to do with the female body, but also the limbo the violence of combat breeds: the blasted terrain of the West Bank, houses blown up, olive trees uprooted; the bombed-out streets of Aden I saw as a child; the ravaged hillsides of Sri Lanka; the fields of the Punjab where massacres bloom as millet and wheat once did. These spaces of radical dislocation are bounded by barbed wire. In the poem, though, the barbed wire is at the edge of the Tiruvella garden, quite close to the heart:

> My back against barbed wire
> snagged and coiled to belly height
> on granite posts
> glittering to the moon
>
> No man's land
> no woman's either

I stand in the middle
of my life...

Out of earth's soft
and turbulent core
a drum sounds
summoning ancestors

They rise
through puffs of grayish dirt
scabbed skins slit
and drop from them

They dance
atop the broken spurts
of stone

They scuff
the drum skins
with their flighty heels.

Men dressed
in immaculate white
bearing spears, and reams
of peeling leaf

Minute inscriptions
of our blood and race

Stumbling behind
in feverish coils
I watch the women come,
eyes averted from the threads
of smoke that spiral
from my face.

Some prise
their stiffening knuckles
from the iron grip
of pots and pans
and kitchen knives

Bolts of unbleached
cloth, embroidery needles,
glitter and crash in heaps.

***

Slow accoutrements of habit
and of speech,
the lust of grief
the savagery of waste
flicker and burn
along the hedgerows
by the vine.

The lost child
lifts her eyes
to mine.

***

Come, ferocious alphabets of flesh
Splinter and raze my page

That out of the dumb
and bleeding part of me

I may claim
my heritage.

The green tree
battened on despair
cast free

The green roots kindled
to cacophony.

9. Long Fall

As if seeds were blown out of a
dried poppy pod and shook roughly, dispersed, flying; or as if the
insides of a silk cotton pod had broken and the tiny dark life within
had blown out, removed itself, and fallen a great distance from the
upswept branches of the tree. Trembling in the long fall the delicate hairs around the seed, embedded then for a while in moist particles of soil. Life like that, driven by anxiety, excitement, the
structures of the world out there into which one falls.

In 1969, when appa and amma left Khartoum to return to India,
to Pune from where they had left in 1956 for the Sudan, I knew I
was ready to leave too. I was exhilarated at the thought of what
might come, but also felt I had no option but to move on. I did not
see how I could continue to live in the Sudan where I had grown
up, come to consciousness, where my dearest friends lived. Many
were fleeing already from the increasingly repressive regime of the
new government.

Sarra left for Edinburgh University where she was to study for
an M.A. and from there she traveled with her husband to Kuwait
to find work. My friend Isabelle Raoul, who was a Sephardic Jew
and had never had a real Sudanese passport, only traveling papers,
fled in the middle of the night, just the month before I left. She fled
with all her family to Geneva, then on to Brighton. When I visited
her a few years later, she was living with Bertrand—her parents had
arranged a marriage for her—in a luxurious penthouse, with gold
wallpaper, and an entire library filled with fake books. Bertrand insisted she stay home, as befit the wife of the proprietor of numer-

133

ous garages that catered to Jaguars and Bentleys. He would not permit her go to the university to complete her studies. Isabelle sat upright in a leather armchair. She had grown lighter in color, put on weight. She had a large number of photographs from Khartoum carefully pasted into her albums. Look, she pointed. There was one of her pale, and me dark, arms entwined, dancing our version of the sixties twist. "Remember 'Twist and Shout'?" she whispered. "How we used to dance those late summer nights in Khartoum."

Our friend Ernest Solomon left from Birmingham, where he had gone to study, to work in Israel. He used to write me long letters, imploring me not to tell our other close friends where he was. "How unhappy I am," he wrote, "they treat us dark-skinned Jews so badly. But what life was there in Khartoum for us?" His mother escaped from the Sudan and joined him. Then he married Riva, a young woman in the Israeli army and he sent me a proud picture, of him in his checked shirt and Riva with a rifle by her side, her army beret cocked on her head. I never heard from Ernest after that. George Constantinides went off to Cyprus to work in a hotel, as a manager. He had to do a stint for a while in the Cypriote army. Samir, whom his cousins had wanted me to marry, joined the Egyptian air force. How tall and straight he was, his face taut with the pleasure of his new job. He used to take me out for ice creams and sit there quite silent, looking into my eyes, smiling at my odd words. He was quite content to let me talk, and I took a great pleasure in his trust. When his cousins Madiha and Samira, both tennis players—Madiha had even reached Junior Wimbledon—wanted me to marry him—"That way you'll stay in Khartoum forever"—I was touched to the core and even considered the possibility seriously for a day or two. Perhaps married to Samir, and there were a number of Indian women married to Sudanese, I could give up the burden of what I was, be driven around in a car, live in the large house in Khartoum North where his family, Turkish relatives included, all gathered. I could indulge with them in shopping trips to Alexandria and Beirut for slippers and cosmetics, even Rome or Paris every now and then; I could have the sweet-scented halava run over my legs and arms ripping off the small hairs, so my skin felt as smooth as a newborn baby; I could place cotton balls with rose attar or Chanel No. 5 on my skin. But what would become of me, my mind, myself?

And always the longing to return to India haunted me. In the end, in one of those choices that help define the shape, the texture of a life, I took the long route back. At the age of eighteen, I went to England, to Nottingham University to study for my Ph.D. Initially, amma had had other thoughts in mind. She was keen that I join Madras University where she had studied and where grandmother Kunju had studied and taught. Her fond hope was that I could be drawn back into the web of traditional life as if the fabric which had been stretched, even battered, by our life abroad, might be woven afresh and I wrapped up in it again, a fresh generation entering adulthood. An M.A. from Madras University was not wholly inappropriate for an intelligent young woman. It should certainly be possible to find a good husband after that. And then would follow a life in a comfortable home, with servants and children, somewhere in India. But to amma's shock, for she had started all the investigations herself, through her many cousins who lived in or near Tambaram and Chinglepet, Madras University refused to accept a degree from Khartoum University, which must have seemed in its eyes a poor, postcolonial cousin. London University would accept the Khartoum degree, but not Madras. So I was left with the old colonial route seemingly the one credible possibility: go to England, young woman, they all said. Then you can return to India.

The external examiner at Khartoum University had come from Nottingham University. Jim Boulton, a handsome man, shortish with a shock of white hair and piercing blue eyes. He had been a fighter pilot during World War II and, landing his plane in Madras, had been billeted in Pune. He met us at the cathedral where appa and amma in a renewed spirit of Anglicanism took us each Sunday. "I will meet you after the service and then come home for dinner," he said. After dinner, sitting on the lawn, under the desert stars, he spoke to appa privately. "You have a very talented daughter. I have just marked her papers, and she would have got a first anywhere. I would like her to study further, to do her Ph.D. in England. She can certainly come to Nottingham, but perhaps she would like to try for Cambridge, where I am sure she would get in." This is the conversation that appa, in fullsome manner, relayed to me a few days later.

I did not go to Cambridge. When one of my professors who had studied there wrote to Girton College, Miss Bradbrook, on learning that I was just eighteen, wanted me to fulfill the second half of the Tripos exam. I was dead set against it. The thought of ever doing exams again filled me with irritation: I did not see how reading a set text had any connection with the learning requisite to the composition of poetry, which was what my heart was set on.

My poetry professor, Alasdair Macrae, also counseled against it. "Don't go there, Meena. People who go to Oxford or Cambridge always think of themselves as superior, as set apart for the rest of their lives." Alasdair, who had read us the words of Hugh MacDiarmid and sung ballads in Gaelic to illustrate the music of poetry, had grown up as a proud Scotsman and had studied at Edinburgh. He was a great influence on me. I took his words very seriously, for, apart from my poet friends at Khartoum University, it was he who first nurtured in me the specific music of poetry, and taught me to value the condition akin to a waking dream in which the rhythms of a poem first enter the conscious mind.

At night I used to lie awake and wonder what the high tower of Trent Building was like—I had seen a photo in the brochure that the university sent me. I used to wonder if the whole city was filled with Raleigh factories and what was left of Lawrence's coal mining town, and the poverty he had written of in *Sons and Lovers*, a book that had moved me greatly.

Khartoum airport, August 1969: the travelers waited by the concrete wall with their relatives, just by the runway. Amma was fighting back tears, then let them spill. She turned her face all puffy with weeping. Anna and Elsa stood arms linked, a little to her side. Appa, stepping forward to hug me, seemed tired, his eyes slightly red with the glare off the metal airplanes lined up on the concrete. My suitcase, the blue one with the expanding frame that we had taken on all our trips to India, had gone already into the metal hold of the plane. I think I was calm, ready to move on. I had already cut my bonds, I would fly loose.

"Meena, don't forget our people, go to church too," amma had begged me. Now her arms were wide open and empty as I stepped away.

I will never forget that plane ride: the temperature dropping precipitously at each stop—Khartoum, 110; Cairo, 90; Rome, 70; London, 60 with frozen fog—so that in the little semidetached outside Heathrow the body trembled in its thin covers, then trembled all through the next day, entering another life.

At Heathrow, Prashant and his sister Mamta met me. I had only seen him once before in Khartoum. There he stood in his cheap shirt, the lower button loose over his potbelly, his head balding prematurely. He waved at me forlornly and I walked as quickly as I could towards him, my bulging suitcase in hand. He was one of the Indians tossed out of Kenya by Idi Amin's edicts. He had fled with his British passport to London. Now relocated in a newly purchased semidetached not far from the airport, he was trying to get his laundry cum grocery store off to a good start.

His eldest sister Rani was one of amma's friends in Khartoum. Rani was married to Prakash Mehta, a South African of Indian origin who taught in the zoology department at the University. They lived a two-minute walk away from us in Hai el Matar. With Prashant so close to Heathrow, Rani thought he would be the perfect person to meet me.

That night I sat in the bare kitchen with the yellow linoleum floor, the single metal sink, and stared out through the window frame at a yellowing peach tree. Its leaves were minimal, three or four at the most, and the ones that hung there were a dull ocher color, twisting sullenly in the slight autumn breeze. I could not reconcile that tree to anything but the shivering that took hold of my body. Mamta was solicitous, running forward with her bright green cardigan, insisting I lie down. All that night on the small metal bed in the bare room, in the bare house that told so clearly the tale of dislocation, a calendar, a telephone, a television, suitcases open on the floor, a few oddments in the cupboard, none of the detailed densities, circlings of dust and books and fallen flower petals that tell of a house lived in, I struggled to figure out where I was and what I was doing.

Nothing made sense. All that night, as if bitten by a low fever, I shivered in my skin. I hugged my arms around me as if that might afford a minimal protection. The thin blanket Mamta brought in did very little.

I do not recall how I passed the next day in Prashant's house. Everything blurred in the peculiar English weather I was to learn so well in the years that followed, the threat of rain, but the heavens never opening, the ground and air sucked into the innards of an immense wet cheek, light filtered through a porous grayness.

After the dazzling heat of Khartoum, the roads, the edges of the desert lit by the white light that distills all objects into their edges, date palms, cars, stones, passing feet, camel hooves, the partial darkness that frequently washes over an English afternoon was hard to take. I kept gazing out of the window at the peach tree, hearing Prashant behind me. He had drawn up a metal chair in the kitchen and was going over the details of some business transaction on the phone.

As a student in Nottingham, I had a room in an old house, national trust property, so no one could tear it down though the wood was falling apart in the basement with the pressure of water that seeped in from underground. On the ground floor lived an old lady, delicately featured, partial to long lace gowns. She had gone to kindergarten with Bertie Lawrence and was filled with wonder at the goodness of his heart, his brilliant blue eyes, and the machinations of the German she-devil who had robbed him of grace. Below her lived old man Carver who stored his beer bottles in the mess of black water that coursed through the cellar. Once, hearing the cry of birds from the cellar, I ventured down and stepping over the bottles found a whole nest of swallows that had made their way down through a broken window and taken shelter in darkness.

At Nottingham, Jim and Margaret Boulton took the place of a second set of parents, and I grew to depend on them greatly. I appreciated their rose garden and the delicate herbs Margaret placed on her roast beef, the Yorkshire pudding they cooked up. Jim gardened for hours and often, spending Sunday at their house in Beeston, I would talk to him of the difficulties I was facing. For instance, trying to make sense of the fitful audience in the old marketplace, as a small group of artists and writers whom I had joined worked on a performance piece complete with animal blood and the head of a dead pig—all to smash the notion of aesthetic space and awaken the populace. Or in a somewhat different vein, my difficulties in figuring out the symbolic structures of poems like "The Red Wheelbarrow" or "Anecdote of the Jar" (I was fascinated with how minimal a text could get). I also shared with him troubles caused by various young men who kept asking me out, one even going so far as to say he would kill himself if I did not marry him. I felt quite helpless in the matter. I did not know what to do. Shovel in hand, or trimming a rosebush, Jim would listen patiently, and his acute intelligence when he responded always clarified my confusions.

In all these narratives, without consciously intending to do so I kept my sexuality carefully out of the picture. I painted myself as the passive recipient of male desire. I was not touched deep inside; they wanted me, I told myself, and told others: such percipience seemed the feminine part. It was with a shock, a year later, still in England, when I realized that the world I had so carefully constructed, of intensive study, of a few late night parties that I attended more out of a sense of duty than anything else, beers, cigarettes, heady intellectual talk of the sixties, all the accoutrements of a young student's life, could all blow apart. I wanted a man, and I had not wanted anyone so much since the friend I had met in Khartoum when I was seventeen. The intensity of sexual passion forced me back into my bodily self, made me turn against the "reason" of the world. Though all the Romantic texts I was studying seemed to work against the sorts of Cartesianism that split mind from body, I could not move from those intense visualizations of personal space into my own ravaged history.

I felt I had nothing to hold onto and was falling and falling through empty air. I felt I had transgressed in some unspeakable way and the arms of the father could not hold me. That is how I couched it in my journals: "father" or alternately "Father," as if I had fallen through the arms of God or as if my own father, in lifting me high in the glittering air as I ran off the ship at Port Sudan, had suddenly vanished and I had dropped through hot air. I struggled for familiar sensory attachments that might hold me, but there was little my eye or ear could attach to, little to revive a web of memory that might connect me to my past. The whole world had caved into the apocalypse of the mind.

Even when I could not read, I held tight to my well-thumbed copy of *Fear and Trembling*, often tucking it in under the bedcovers, where it would get lost in the pale pink blankets the University Health Centre favored. For that was where I found myself, heavily sedated, so I would sleep. Indeed I was grateful for sleep when it came and willing to give up my nervous pain for the pacification the sleeping tablets provided. Awake, I was acutely conscious, my mind trembling with knowledge it could not piece together. My research into the structures of Romantic self-consciousness, into the refined articulations of internal time-consciousness, had led me here. I did not know who I was. I felt as if I were paying with my life.

Tormented by a sense of having transgressed a boundary, a

code, an edict—something in the law as it stood—I was aware at the same time that what had befallen me had nothing to do with my own actions, and everything to do with my being, what I was in and of myself. I felt the force of passion buffeting me and wondered if the heights I was falling from were not precisely measurable in terms of the physical distance from the hands, the lips, of the beloved. I think there was a truth in that intense, even numbing sensation, thought turned wholly to bodily knowledge, that it has taken me till now to spell out.

Walter Benjamin writes of how raising up the truth of the past means seizing a memory as it flashes up at a moment of danger. I believe this to be true. Perhaps the long fall that has haunted me is a symptom of crisis, of a time of convulsion, where everything still is to be worked out, elaborated, survived. My migration to Britain, and with it the sense that the future was not really comprehensible, had fused with my well-concealed fear of God the Father; the theology of my Christian upbringing forcing a terrible fragility into the self, rendering it groundless.

I cannot forget here the great guilt that has remained with me: when Ilya was dying I could not bear to see his terrible pain—heart pain—and called upon what God there was to make him die. In his last days when Ilya, laid flat against his pillows, hardly able to raise his head, asked me to give him some water to drink, I turned away, hardening every inch of me, filled with fury that he should suffer so. It was my little sister Anna, just four, who in her innocence ran forward with a glass of water. I did not weep at Ilya's death; I went forward in the throng of other mourners at home and laid a single red rose on his chest and I looked at the face I had loved so, the chin wiped clean with the mortician's blade of all its white stubble, the proud, regal forehead, the long nostrils stuffed with cotton wool, and I lost all remaining faith in God—in that deity whom I had called upon to put an end to Ilya's suffering. Sometimes, at night, I feel I can hear him cry out in pain, as the bands tighten around his chest, and he gasps for breath. I toss and turn on this old futon in Manhattan and put out my hands, and reach into the night air as if by reaching out, I might touch his hands again, for the last time.

Somehow, in my mind's eye, the crossing of borders is bound up with the loss of substances, with the distinct pain of substantial loss: with the body that is bound over into death, with the body that splits open to give birth.

In my Nottingham journal I had jotted down *"Si le grain ne meurt..."* over and over again, though I did not know when that falling to the ground, of the small dark seed, might come. The entry into the future seemed irrefutable but, at the very same time, shorn of all possible images. My terror was that I felt I had no history. It was precisely to discover, to make up my history, that I had to return to India. But this was not something I was aware of when I was going through my spiritual difficulties, my "nervous breakdown." Indeed, much was unraveled from me in those years in Britain, and what coiled up again threatened to destroy the quick of my feeling self. I could not accept my own body and my desires and what those desires might lead me to. The world was already too fractured, and when I went to England as an eighteen-year-old, I clung to the clarities of a realm marked out by male poets, even though in abstract terms I was thinking about the body and how it permitted a place through which internal time could sway.

There was nothing in the refined notions I set about to elaborate (drawing on Husserl and Merleau-Ponty, the notions of intentionality and *corps vecu)* that might be inclusive of what I was—no color there, no female flesh, no postcolonial burden. In those days in England, in ways I would not even acknowledge to myself, I longed to cut free of what I actually was, a female creature from the Third World with no discernible history.

Sexual passion then became an extreme danger, for it threatened to let loose all the emotions I was struggling so hard to cut away from my person. The summer I turned nineteen I had what was termed "a nervous breakdown." I could not read. I could see in a hazy sort of way, but near books my sight twisted, firing the alphabets of English till they became utterly Other. Some letters even took on the swirling syllabic forms of the Malayalam I had left so far behind. I could not sleep. I was afflicted by nervous headaches. Perhaps I was working too hard, trying to finish my thesis. But it wasn't just that. I had formed a passionate relationship with a man and it tormented me. I had no idea, or so it seemed to me at the time, how obsessive passion could be. I could not give myself, as I phrased it then, to him, nor could I turn away. I felt as if my body were taking vengeance on me. All my thoughts of "the intentional inexistence of the object"—a good Husserlian phrase—were swept away in unfulfilled desire. There was also the brute fact of the academic discourse I had chosen: no way could be found within it to acknowledge anything of what I was. My study of Romantic identity was predicated on the erasure of my own. It was many years later that I wrote a book on women in Romanticism, choosing as my beginning Mary Wollstonecraft's radical questioning of woman's place: "We fearfully ask," she wrote in her novel *Maria or the Wrongs of Woman*, "on what ground we ourselves stand." Marginalized, considered mad by the illogic of the world, her protagonist struggles on, mind intact, fighting fiercely. A banned creature, she questions the laws of the world that render her such.

Returning to India after my studies in Britain, as a grown adult in 1973, I had to unlearn my tortuous academic knowledge, remake myself, learn how to read and write again as if for the first time. Thinking this out, I take courage from Rassundara Devi, who in 1876 published the first autobiography in Bengali, *Amar Jiban* (My Life). As a married woman, held within the confines of domesticity, she taught herself to read and write in secret, hiding a page from the *Chaitanya Bhagavatha* in the kitchen and scratching out the letters on the sooty wall. It took me many years to get where she got, many years to find my own sooty wall on which to scratch these alphabets.

To help me recover my strength I went away from Nottingham for three months, into the countryside outside Basingstoke, to Pamber to live with an old bricklayer and his wife. I had never seen such poverty, such plainness of living close at hand: a small cottage, no books, just the beds and chairs and table and a small pile of vegetables, a few cheap cuts of meat. Old Mr. Long still slept with newspapers tucked into his bed to keep him warm, a habit he had picked up in wartime, his wife told me.

I took *The Prelude* with me. "When I am able to read I want to read this first," I told my friend Robert, whose sister-in-law's parents had so kindly taken me in. One afternoon, as I lay on my back at the edge of the delicate woods of oak and birch that rose by the Longs' house, I opened a page of *The Prelude*—this was after two months of being unable to read—and miraculously found my eyesight clarified, sharpened to the syllables of the poem. Somewhere towards the end of Book One of the 1805 text is where my gaze fell, but quickly, with shaking fingers I turned to the eleventh book, lines I had long loved, and I repeated them over to myself: "So feeling comes in aid / Of feeling, and diversity of strength / Attends us,

if but once we have been strong.'' I wondered at the sudden in-
fusion of vigor I felt, and a trembling pleasure, as if it were my own
past that was on the brink of being restored. Slowly, but certainly,
my eyes gained strength. For another couple of weeks I continued
to work in the Longs' garden, picked plums, took walks in the
woods, painted, wrote long letters to the Boultons, who all the while
had treated me with great kindness. ''You needed a change, that's
all,'' Margaret comforted me. ''Very soon you'll come back to your
studies.'' I did return. I did finish my thesis on Romanticism and
the structures of self-identity, pondering how memory was opened
up by the complications of lived space, how the ''now'' of recollection permitted internal time to unfold, a moment, constantly shifting, constantly returned to, much as the opening note of a piece
of music is held always at the brink of consciousness, guaranteed
by the fragile, living body.

That last year in Nottingham I grew close to a poet from Amsterdam, a scholar of Gaelic who was doing his research on translation theory. Maxim and I traveled through Ireland, living in Galway
where his mother was. We spent several months in Amsterdam
where I poured myself into the art galleries, studying the Dutch
masters and the fierce works of Van Gogh that I had learnt to love.
Time and again I would return to a series of early paintings done
around the time when Van Gogh had very little money, the al-
lowance from Theo only trickling in, the paints spread out so thin
the canvas almost poked through. The paintings I particularly loved
had to do with a garden with forking paths. The back of a figure
was visible, but ahead, the road split into two and one of the paths
would have to be picked out, traveled. The brooding grays and
greens of those early paintings remained with me, and looking out
into Wollaton Park, or in the Arboretum, when Maxim and I
returned to Britain, I seemed to see them replicated. Then, though
I was happy with him in so many ways, I left Maxim to return to
India. The thought of living as the wife of a man in Brussels or Lux-
embourg, bringing up young children, cooking Dutch soup even
as I struggled to write poetry, sat hard with me. If I had stayed with
Maxim, I felt I would have lost India. The grief at parting tore me
apart, but I knew I had to go.

In 1973 I returned to Pune where appa and amma were living.
The city was recovering from a bad flood that, coming after a season of drought, had devastated life. I saw women picking up shards

of glass, bits of broken bottle, wire, paper, anything but stones, to recycle them for a few paise, and this with the right hand while the left scrounged around for scraps of food that might have been thrown out of the houses nearby: rice, dal, chapatis, half-cooked vegetables. Seeing all this, I could not eat and grew very thin.

I needed a job, so I could live my own life, but it was several months before I finally found one, in Miranda House in Delhi, in 1974. I had just turned twenty-three. Delhi made me. I cannot conceive of myself without those years, 1974 and 1975, when I threw myself into the life of the city. I was young enough to be taken for a student and enjoyed the life of the hostel and cafes. I used to attend the meetings of the Philosophy Society at Saint Stephen's College, at the home of Dr. and Mrs. Gupta. Old Bose Saab, the elegant philosopher, used to attend regularly and we would sit in silence and hear him speak of Spinoza and the intellectual love of God, this very old man whose bones seemed to be shining through his frail skin.

It was at these gatherings in 1974 that I met Ramu Gandhi. It is hard for me to conceive of what I would have been in my thinking, feeling, being, had we never met. Through him I learnt to see India for myself, started to glimpse the deep troubling truths about the land of my origins. Through our conversations, I sensed afresh something of the pain and pity of what it meant to feel one's self spiritually cast out. He taught philosophy in those days in Delhi University and we would sit and talk under the trees in the campus gardens or in the coffeehouse. He came from a distinguished family, his father's father was Gandhiji, his mother's father was Rajagopalachari and he might have considered himself part of the most privileged in a new India. But Ramu, with his intensity of soul, had a true empathy in those days for those who were truly cast out, considered polluted. And knowing how new I was in Delhi, indeed in India, at least where adult life was concerned, he pointed out all sorts of people to me: the poor children picking rags by the truck stops, the beggar squatting by the pile of garbage outside Saint Stephen's College, the mother with three naked infants clinging to her back. His brilliance broke loose from the language of the Oxford philosophers—he had studied with Strawson—and turned to the concrete, vivid landscape around him.

It was in Delhi that I met my dear friend Svati Joshi. We first greeted each other in the English department at Miranda House where I had my first job. The English department in those days was filled with talk of kanjeevram saris and chiffon saris; where to get the best quality rasmallai; how to arrange a sumptuous tea party after the fifth viewing of *Gone with the Wind*, a movie that had reduced many of the English teachers to tears. Those who were not involved in this sort of chitchat sat on the edges, in some visible discomfort. While indeed there were serious, gifted people teaching in the college in those days, in the English department the noise of socializing dominated. I was the proud possessor of two cotton saris, which I wore on alternate days; two pairs of jeans and three tee shirts. Having come out of the late sixties in Britain, to possess little seemed to me the mark of a fine mind: clearly I was set on a collision course with the givers of tea parties. But there were fine compassionate women there too, political women who were involved with the teachers' union and the strike plans. I joined them in Boat Club Road, in a protest march against Mrs. Gandhi's government, my first experience of courting arrest.

Svati and I became fast friends. I remember when I caught sight of her first, her fine brown hair flying into her face, her string of amber beads glistening on her neck. She had recently returned from Harvard and initially it was the love of poetry that bound us together. When I lost my job at Miranda House—it was a leave vacancy and the woman who had gone away had returned, her husband's dairy farm having failed in some fashion I could not quite grasp, something to do with the cows, their feed and the rising cost of both—Svati and I took to the streets to see if I could find another job: as a journalist, working for a magazine, an art gallery, anything that seemed suitable. The world was wide open in those days and we were filled with excitement at the protests against the repressive measures of the government. I had to move out of the Miranda House flat and for some time I stayed with Svati, in her flat in VP House: we would sit in the cool room and listen to Joan Baez or read Neruda, and then walk the streets, drinking in the sights and sounds of Delhi, attending poetry readings, theater festivals, showings of recent Indian movies.

I met her father, the poet Uma Shankar Joshi, whom I too called Bapuji. And I met her sister, the Harvard-trained economist Nandini, who was filled with thoughts on how an economy appropriate to India might develop, how the spinning of khadi might help alleviate the terrible poverty in the villages. From Uma Shankar I learnt of the fine pleasures of poetry, of a life bound to the creation of literature. As he cut vegetables to make kichdi or stirred the rice and dal, we spoke of poems and the political world. A follower of Gandhi even as a young man, he had lived and worked in the Sabermati ashram, I sensed that Bapuji belonged to the same world as Ilya had, filled with a shining belief in how India could be made anew. It was a world I appeciated deeply, though I did not see how I could be a part of it. There was an amazing quality of light about Uma Shankar, a true refinement of soul that touched all those around. It was clear that poetry for him was part of the illumination that came from the shared world. It was inconceivable that it should be something cut apart.

With Svati I went on the great march that J. P. Narayan led in 1974, in Delhi, and we watched in wonder as very old ladies clad in khadi came out of their seclusion and climbed onto jeeps that moved them in slow motion, through the hot air, towards India Gate. When my little daughter was born in the summer of 1986, Svati and Bapuji were visiting the United States and they came and stayed with us and Svati held out her lovely arms and picked up her little namesake and sang songs to her, and walked with me, the week after the baby was born, in the summer heat of Broadway.

Why did I leave India? Why did I feel as if there still were a part of my story that had to be forged through departure? I am tormented by the question. All I knew was that something had broken loose from inside me, was all molten. And what was molten and broken loose had to do with India as I saw the land, and to write I had to flee into a colder climate. Else I would burn up and all my words with me.

"I am falling," I said to David when we first met. "I keep dreaming I am falling." It was a long time ago, 1979. We were sitting at Manju's, the new bar on Abid Road in Hyderabad. It had a dull orange light and excitable men who had left their wives behind to come and drink. It had a bar lady with a cleavage and fish that swam sullenly in a neon-lit aquarium with water two feet deep and enough artificial pearls to smother even a fictive Nizam of Hyderabad.

"I am falling. I keep seeing that, falling off the edge of a cliff. I am holding on with two fingers, wrapped around a bit of rough grass." He was very tender. "I'll hold you," he said. "I'll be a safety net for you.'' And he told me about the extreme cold of Minneapolis where he worked, where breath froze, and the car froze, where just for the heck of it bearded men went out on the ice when the temperature was minus forty, punched holes in the ice with metal picks, and sat and fished for pike, all red with cold, never trembling, never falling.

I was fascinated by those tales and by his own gift of narrative. David loved telling stories, and wrapped me in his voice and held me there. We had met at the home of a mutual friend in Hyderabad and very quickly, in three weeks, had fallen in love and decided to marry. We used to meet in his high room with a balcony in the Taj Mahal Hotel. He was retracing all the steps that he had traveled ten years earlier and had gone from Athens to Jerusalem and now was in India. On his old Hermes typewriter he set up pages of the Jerusalem journal he was writing. I was fascinated by the sense that through narrative he was making up his life, his autobiography.

There was a neem tree outside his balcony and the quiet shadows of a garden of marigolds and roses. I felt a peace, a great pleasure in that room with him and knew I could be there forever. But when we reached Minneapolis a year later, where he had his teaching job at the university, I felt chilled by this strange new world: baby food in jars and shopping malls and at home books stacked high in piles with no time to read them. When my cigarette dropped into a wastebasket in the attic room of the house David shared with a colleague in the history department, and the basket started smoldering, the thought sprang to mind: I am this basket, this burning thing, how shall I bear my life here? And I tossed the basket out of the high window to put out the flames and to cool off, pushed my little Adam—who was born in New York just two months earlier—around and around the sidewalks of the neat suburban area and watched other wives lay out the washing and roll out their carpets and thought, I am a wife like that, I am, I am. And I saw the mailman come with the mail, and lay it down in a neat pile under the laurel tree and heard my son cry out with delight. But in my mind's eye I kept seeing that basket burning, filled with waste paper from writings that never had time or space to come to anything, torn pages of a Sears catalog, fourth-rate junk mail, bits of soiled tissue paper. Where was the life I had led? Who was I?

Later that summer, Trish Hampl spoke to me of a place where she used to go to write, a little cabin by the North Shore. ''Why don't I find you a cabin there?'' she suggested. So I found my way to the small cabin by the quiet waters, ringed with massive green of fir trees, rocks, solitude. I had tea with Trish and she spoke to me of her life, her writing. I can see her large eyes, her face, as we sat hearing the waters move against the rocks and I understood how haunted she was by the sense of beauty. But when I returned to my own cabin, what came out onto paper was all the confusion of my crossing, and before David and little Adam came up to meet me, for I missed them so, I sat in the little cabin on the North Shore of Minnesota and started making notes on the rocks of Banjara in Hyderabad, the dried-out river bed where I was attacked, the police station where Rameeza Be was raped, where in rage the people had risen up and set the place on fire, so that it stood in the midday heat, the white-washed station the British had built, all its rafters burning.

''I feel as if my soul had collapsed, as if there were no distance there.''

I was speaking on the phone to Erica. We had first met ten years earlier when I was newly arrived in America and she lived in Westbeth and ran the Woman's Salon. When I first visited Erica I told her my adventures: crossing the streets of Manhattan, finding the right subway stop. We sat over coffee and shared our thoughts on writing as the sun set over the Hudson River, over the old rotting piers where Melville had strolled years ago and where still the gulls wheeled.

''I cannot bear to write this part, let alone breathe, think about appa's illness. Why?''

''Because you cannot let it go—the pain, but also it's yours, nothing can touch it. Let it out into words and then you have lost it in a sense, and you must grow through it, beyond it.''

As she spoke I thought of a snakeskin, sloughed off so the new skin could emerge. Her words cut in, ''Its a liminal stage, a flux in creation, when you look at the pain.''

''And if you don't, it destroys you?''

''Exactly...'' and she spoke on in her moving way of what it meant to draw something out of the psyche and look at it, and set it to words, and how what was not set into words would remain literally unspeakable. Listening to her speak, I drew courage to go on.

*

The phone call came in the middle of the night. I tremble thinking about it. I try to make it all blur and vanish. Thinking of it, I feel as if I were falling, falling through empty air. "Your father's in the hospital. He had a heart attack killing a snake. It was threatening your mother and sisters. There was no one else around. He picked up the big bamboo stick that lies behind the almirah and hit it. Once, twice and then fell down as the snake writhed and died. Your father collapsed. He could not breathe and cried out in pain; stumbled to the dining room and fell unconscious. He had to be carried out to the car, taken to Pushpagiri Hospital. A few minutes later and he would have been dead. He's there now, in a critical condition."

"He's still in intensive care."

"Yes, he was killing a snake that was threatening your mother. He had to kill it. There was no other man there."

I pieced the story together, through the nightly phone calls, my chest hurting, for I felt as if iron bands were ringing it around, tightening as the phone rang so I could not really breathe as I picked up the receiver and heard the phone line swaying as I imagined it, across several oceans. Other times I felt as if my body were a piece of transparent fabric and I could hear within it my father, thousands of miles away, crying out in pain, struggling for breath. And sometimes, in those weeks, when he was very sick and my small child cried out in her bed, in the room next to where I slept, I felt as if the two cries, at opposite corners of the transparency that my soul had turned into, were all that was, that there was nothing else left.

Appa was very ill that summer, but he did not die. When I got there two months later with both children, he was well enough to sit up for a while at the edge of the bed or lie against the pillows and talk to me. He spoke to me about his life, about history, about the battle of Tessenei.

"Did you know about that battle?" he asked me. "Ten thousand Indian soldiers laid down their lives. They fought Mussolini and his soldiers. Else the Fascists would have advanced. I went near that place."

"Went there, you traveled there to see the monument?"

"Flew over it on the way to Asmara."

He was half sitting up now, propped against the pillows, his lean face haggard with exhaustion. He put an Isordil tablet in his mouth. Then he relaxed and I saw the wonderful bones in his face, resting quietly in the light that shone in from the window and I thought, this is my father, he is speaking to me, giving me his life in words, letting me into history.

He sat up and the oxygen cylinder strapped to his bed shook a little.

"It was an old connection between Sudan and India. Mussolini had taken Ethiopia and wanted to march into the Sudan, so the British army went in; and the Indian army came too. It was a pitched battle. Ten thousand Indian soldiers were killed. In recognition of that fact, after India became independent, the British gave ten thousand pounds to build the main administrative block in the National Defence Academy in Khadakvasla. It's called Sudan Block, or Sudan House, I think."

"I think I've seen it," I said softly, my mind casting back to our visits to the NDA after I had returned from England, the large gray stones of the military training quarters, cold, crepuscular as the night winds rose. "I'd forgotten though that it was Sudan Block."

His energy rose a little in him, an old impatience, though the lack of oxygen in his body that the polycythemia caused made it hard for him to go on.

"Sudanese officers used to be sent there for training. I met President Abboud on the plane when he was returning from India and Europe. I even considered going to him for help when they wouldn't let you into the university because you were too young. But you had done excellently in the exams."

"To Abboud?"

"Yes, indeed. He always used to ask our ambassador about us."

"Appa, you know he was thrown out."

"Of course. In any case there was no need for me to call on him. You got in without too much difficulty."

I sat up, embarrassed, confused. This was something I had known nothing about. At the same time I was deeply touched by how seriously appa had taken my studies. He had understood that my mind needed to grow, sharpen itself. In the early days, when I was twelve and thirteen and used to write my poems in the toilet, it was always appa who encouraged me to send them out, get them published, allow my work to find a place in the world. And he had encouraged me to go to England to study. Returning to India, I had shared with him all my difficulties in landing a job.

His voice was coming more softly now, a little blurred with the difficulties of breathing. "It was because of the Bandung Conference that we went to the Sudan. Azhari and Nehru met there, and became friends and India sent technical assistance to the newly independent Sudan. Even our Election Commissioner, Mr. Sen, went out to help with the first Sudanese elections."

He was tired and lay back against the pillows and I sat watching him, his body so thinned by the ravages it had survived. Ten years earlier, when appa was working for the United Nations in Somalia, he had suddenly collapsed. Elsa, my little sister, only nineteen at the time, was visiting him there. They scooped him up, put him in a little plane, and flew him to Nairobi Hospital. Elsa was all alone in the city, stranded, till Fauzi's sister Rehana took her in. It was a miracle appa survived, with acute hepatitis, kidney trouble, and the polycythemia that had already taken hold of him. And now another brush with death.

I seemed to hear his voice as I watched him lie there, his eyes closed. His voice came to me from almost thirty years earlier:

"He makes us put our foot on the head of the adder; He will not let us fall." We were sitting on wicker chairs, in the lawn in Khartoum and appa with great gusto, a glass of beer in his hand, was telling the story of how, in the Pink Palace, where he stayed when he first arrived in Khartoum—it was Emperor Haile Selassie's old quarters—he had walked out to the bathroom, felt something squirming underfoot, and realized that the heel of his sandal had struck the head of a poisonous desert snake.

"If it had been anywhere but the head, we would have been bitten. And there was no cure for that poison." I had laughed in relief, the story of my father's strength filling me with new life. And I had clutched my friend Mala's hand, for she too was listening to the tale enthralled.

Now in Tiruvella, he was lying breathing gently, arms by his sides, almost dead after beating a poisonous snake to death. He had killed it so it should not bite my mother, and had almost paid with his life. Lifting up his stick to strike the snake a second time, as it rose in the pile of coconut husks that were stored at the side of the veranda, appa, almost sixty-eight now, did not know if it was the snake he was seeing again, that brown thing thrashing, or his eyes were doubling, shimmering in the blood clot that rose.

As I watched him rest against the pillows, I straightened myself in the chair, shut my eyes only to feel the tears hot against my eyelids. I opened my eyes and let the tears fall. Above appa's head, to the right of the desk, to the right of the window that gave onto the incense tree in the garden, was a portrait of grandmother Kunju. I had grown up with that portrait: her large dark eyes, the clear cheekbones, the perfectly formed chin, the pearls in her ears casting a slight shadow, it seemed, onto the image, all gathered into the composure that marked the whole, as a slight uptilt of her lips, a half-smile drew the viewer's gaze in.

A week earlier, entering the room, exhausted after the long journey from New York, little Svati in my arms, I had embraced my parents and then sat in silence against the far wall. Amma was reading Psalm Twenty-three for the night's prayer, and appa, tired like this, had sat up in bed. I felt I could not bear it any longer, this near death, this slow wasting away of appa's body. My eyes moved to that portrait. I felt a radiance come down to me, something from her dark eyes, captured on thin, perishable paper, falling on me like grace. I sat there, worn out, unable to move. "Put yourself in the way of radiance." I heard those words as if a voice had spoken them. Past and present vanished for me and I felt the release, the absolution of having fallen a great way.

In New York, in the weeks before I was able to leave with the children, in weeks when appa hung between life and death, I had tried to go on with my life. Rashida invited me to lunch one afternoon, a week before I left for India. She called me up quite early in the morning.

"Come to Zula Restaurant, Chinua will be there and Nurredin. You know Nurredin lived in India in his student days." So we walked down to the Ethiopian restaurant on 123rd Street and greeted Chinua Achebe, who was teaching at City College, Chinwezu, who was visiting, and Rashida's friend, Nurredin Farrah.

I sat next to Nurredin who kept heaping food on my plate. "Eat, eat. We both come from countries that we don't know when we'll next see, my friend." The talk turned to snakes. I spoke of how appa had had a heart attack killing the snake. "Was it a relative?" Nurredin asked. "No, I hope not," I replied. Chinua was listening intently, large, dignified, one could almost hear his mind working in that silence. The talk of snakes seemed to please him. Rashida entered into a tale of how growing up in Dahomey she had crossed the path to get the sweetest mangoes and come upon a snake. Chinwezu nodded. Over Mexican beer and Ethiopian flat bread the talk was of snakes that wove into our memories, live snakes that might help or hurt, and then the conversation turned to dictators, students gunned down in Africa during demonstrations, repression in India, poverty in New York City, our speech crisscrossing continents.

"Appa." I turned to my father.

He was sitting up in bed. Outside some visitors had arrived. We could hear them climb up the stone steps, greeting amma. "It's all part of colonialism, isn't it? Its aftermath, I mean. Your going to Sudan. Otherwise it seems so arbitrary."

He nodded, understanding perfectly what I meant. After all, he had spent thirteen years of his adult life working in North Africa.

"But don't forget there was trade between India and the Arab world for hundreds of years. And the British took Indians with them, wherever they went, as clerks, as railway workers. We of course went to the Sudan after independence. Do you know that the neem and the mango went to Sudan from India?" I nodded.

"And your mother's family. There was Syrian blood, wasn't there?"

"Even quite recently. My grandfather Wilson Master, veliammechi's father.'

"Yes?"

"His brother Kurien had a Syrian wife."

"Why?' I gulped out.

"He married her and brought her back. Just like Sudanese men going to Egypt to get a fair wife. We have that too." He smiled. "Of course she learnt Malayalam."

"And your cousins?"

But the visitors burst into the room in a flurry of good wishes, and hot tea borne in by the young Regina. Appa tried to rise, but quickly, almost without thinking, I pushed him back against the white pillows, the wooden bed, and felt my elbow knock against the oxygen cylinder, cold metal painted maroon, perhaps the very one they had wheeled in for Ilya so many years ago.

After tea and sweetmeats, after leave taking, the house was quiet. I was all alone for a little while and pondered the curious ways of history: my grandfather Kuruvilla who saw an Englishman whip an Indian in Bangalore, in 1917 or 1918, and knew so clearly his work was cut out for him. The problem of evil tormented him. He used to visit prisoners, in particular a murderer in prison in Kerala. Why does evil exist? What is it? Why does God exist, he had once asked me as a child, and broken into telling me how he and grandmother Kunju used to invite the beggars into the Tiruvella house, to sit around the dining table, once a week, to break bread with them. The plasticity of their lives in the early decades of the century, the sense that the future could be remade in the image of justice, fascinated me.

Appa, chosen as a husband for Ilya's only daughter, decided that, after the political activities of 1937, his intermediate year in Alwaye College, protest marches, meetings, demonstrations against the British presence, he needed to study hard, do well in college. My father's fascination with the British, with their sense of order, but also his distance from it, his awareness of the sense of racial superiority that underlay their claims to Indian territory, came back to me. He was describing his passage to Britain as a student, just after independence, on the passenger liner, *The Empress of Scotland.* "It was difficult for us Indian students. We ate with the British officers, but of course they never mixed with us, never." And then laughingly he spoke of how as a gazetted officer in the civil service in Madras, working during World War II, he had walked in the heat of midsummer to the office, dressed in full suit and tie including a solar topi, the uniform the British required of all Indian officers. The thought of walking dressed in that fashion in the Madras heat amused me and I laughed. I spoke out loud of how fanciful it would be to dress like that in Manhattan, or Brooklyn, and go into work.

"Those were the days when the war-time operations were being conducted in the Bay of Bengal and the German U-Boats were active there. Know something?" he mused. "Professor Boulton must have passed through Madras at the time. He did in fact land there, didn't he? I remember how Mountbatten used to fly in, he had two whole planes for his use," and my father's voice rose a little in memory of the grandeur of that whole affair, and he described the medals Mountbatten had pinned to his military garments. Then, tired out, he lay back against the pillows to rest.

I walked out through the drawing room onto the veranda that skirted the back courtyard. I felt my father's words falling, ever so gently dissolving in the great imaginary silence that constitutes all that we know of the soul. I looked up and saw the brown arms of the silk cotton tree, rising beyond the red tiled roof of the house, sixty feet tall, and from the topmost branches, the thick pods had broken open and delicate silk parachutes that encircled dark seeds were dropping, down towards the ground.

10. *Seasons of Birth*

*I*n September 1979, ten years after I left Khartoum never to return again, I made another continental crossing: from Hyderabad to New York. By this time I was twenty-eight years old and I was not alone. David Lelyveld and I were married. I remember the evening we first met. It was February 21, dark, clear, so that the rounded moon and stars were visible. A cool breeze was blowing as I entered Syed's house. David was sitting on a mura, talking to Syed. I recall something being said about the fake books in a Nawab's library, walls filled with them, concealing liquor cabinets; the old stables in Rampur converted to a garage for antique cars.

David is a historian of India and he had come to Hyderabad to work on his ideas of nationalism and the formation of Urdu as a public language. In the daytime he would wander about the marketplace, talking to people, scholars, ancient graybeards who gave orations. He was also deep into the Hyderabad archives. After that first meeting, our friendship picked up quickly. We were lonely, each of us, deep inside and our meeting made for a sheltering space. There was a great innocence to our falling in love, a sheer sense of possibility. We felt we had each lived our separate lives and now could come together. I had just turned twenty-eight; David was ten years older. Within three weeks we decided to get married. We traveled north to spend a long summer in Chail at the foothills of the Himalayas. Already in Chail, I was filled with excitement at the thought of coming to America, a country I had read about, but never seen.

Our first stop on the route west was Paris, where we thought we could combine a holiday, part of an extended honeymoon, with some work at the Sorbonne. But after a few weeks in Paris, under the green leaves of the plane trees in late summer, I grew so dizzy I could hardly stand and was forced into the University Hospital on Boulevard Jourdain. I did not get to do any of the work on Walt Whitman that I had wanted to do. "I am fascinated by his notion of the body," I had told Professor Roger Asselineau, "surely it is relevant even now. All that space stuck out flat, the bits and pieces added onto the body, the corpses carried out of the old house. But how?" He had listened carefully over coffee. But my own body, heated by the malarial virus that had developed during the long trip through India, overtook me, stopped my intellectual questioning. The nausea of early pregnancy coupled with the headaches and chills of acute malaria made Paris in the summer a fearful thing.

I lay in bed in the hospital, next to a young woman of eighteen, the veins in her arms swollen a jagged indigo with all the heroin she'd shot up. She was unbearably thin and her blonde hair stuck up straight in the air making her a spiky white doll. Each morning Laure painted her thin lips a brilliant shade of red. When I leant over I could catch myself in her little plastic framed mirror: a woman with one eye, face split by the glass, dazed but still curious. We chattered away in French. I was calmed a little by the quinine that was pumped into me in large doses and could refuse with seeming equanimity when Laure counseled me to take as much of the wine as possible. She was a great believer in anodynes of any kind. The spirit needed to be replenished and her poor veins were all smashed. She did not know how long she would last. Wine was offered by the nurses in delicate plastic cups. I was nauseated and refused. The bell tower I could see out of the window, the gray-blue swallows clustering there, with darker birds mixed in, tilted in the air. The two arms on the clock face were fierce, cleft apart. Something was out of joint. I looked at Laure for reassurance as she sat up in bed, hooking the intravenous tube over her scarred wrist.

She cajoled me: "*Je veux y aller. New York, Los Angeles. C'est magnifique ça. On mange le biftek là bas, non?*" Twisting her thin body to face me, she smiled in angelic sweetness. I was nervous about those unreal cities she mentioned. Inverness in Scotland was as far west as I had been. I would almost have traded places with her, if it weren't for the purple scars scrawled over her arms.

The nurse from Surinam who came in was very gentle. She would find the sachemere, she assured me. They could check if the baby was all right. So, as David held my hand, they put the monitor to my belly. Under my pounding heart was another, clearer, swifter. As we listened to the tiny chop-chop-chop of the little heart under my own, I felt I might bear it all, the sickness, the anxiety of passage, even the tilting clock face outside, if the child were all right. I was doubled now, a cover, a stretched skin, an envelope of life, all buzzing inside. I was also still very sick.

Five weeks later I stood in the Boston airport behind the line of large Portuguese women dressed in black. I longed to fade into them, my difference absorbed into their warmth, their sheer substance. I recall having to step aside for the photograph for my green card. "Congratulations, welcome to America," the man said as he took my hand. The image sticks in my mind, darkened, floating free of the plastic frame. My face with the hair tied back, tired out with the malarial attack, just about visible above the numbers printed onto the card. Then we were outside, in the sharp air of Boston.

I recall bright lights in the streets, signs in violent neon, the quivering jumble of colors cut as if from a movie I might have seen in Khartoum or Hyderabad, huge Texan hats in lights outside a taco shop, Colonel Sanders painted in black and brown and white, apple pie and see-through lingerie shining in sequins on billboards in the honky-tonk part of Boston, as Michael, my new brother-in-law, drove us through at top speed. "Your first sights of America," he reassured me, as the car jolted and almost crashed against the fenders of another on our way to Lexington.

Then it was New York. Safe in David's mother's quiet apartment high on the sixth floor, I gazed out at Riverside Drive through the blur of dilated retinas. The drugs for malaria had almost driven me blind, and the autumn leaves, the tall trees by the river, blurred into each other, massed and bled into an inchoate scenery, a backdrop that trembled precariously. I watched my mother-in-law's hands lay out the glassware for our meal and I sat and watched, hardly trusting my legs. I was trembling with the exhaustion of travel and could hardly believe I was in America or start to ponder what that might mean.

When I arrived in America I was carrying a mass of papers with me, the first draft of a novel I thought of calling "Nampally Road." I had composed it in Chail, at the foot of the Himalayas, in a room filled with mountain light, sharp glints of ice from the rocks in the middle distance, the guttural cry of hawks. In my life that work

marks a crossing, a border. Sometimes the border has barbed wire
strung over it. I made a wager that almost destroyed me: the book
will be done before my child happens, before he is thrust out, mouth
open, gulping the air of Manhattan. I laid out sheet after sheet of
paper on the floor, all my scribblings unpacked from the suitcase.
I made more signs on paper to add to those and made a little moat
around my growing belly with paper. Once when David's older
brother Joe and his wife Carolyn visited—their visits always pleased
me, I had a sense of a larger family with them, a continuity of which
David was a part, into which this new child might enter—I pointed,
crying, "Look!" at all the messy paper, the unkempt pages laid out,
"Look, it's my novel." And there was an edge to my voice as if
having all that paper visible might justify me, a woman without history in this new world, a bride made pregnant, an almost mother.

But I lost my way in that morass of paper. At night I would lie
by David's side and look out the window, out across the terrace on
the twenty-third floor of the Master's Institute, at the dark sky. Racing across the black waters of the Hudson, across the jeweled lights
of the George Washington Bridge, I saw the tinier, harder lights of
the cars. I watched, transfixed by the minute motions of those cars
with human beings in them crossing into New Jersey, metal bodies
crawling between two borders, across a bridge that seemed to have
no ending.

Those were the days of Chinese takeout and Häagen Dazs, Yonah
Schimmel's knishes, long walks in Central Park, several viewings
of Woody Allen's *Annie Hall*, which was David's way of teaching
me about Manhattan life. I remember watching the movie at the old
Thalia on West 96th Street with creaking fans and popcorn machines
that spluttered and fumed. I was sitting in a red seat that tilted back
at an odd angle, my feet propped as high as I could muster, for my
body was swelling and my circulation slow. I'll never forget the thrill
I felt when I saw the scrawny hero stand in front of the very theater
we sat in, trying to scrounge his way into Diane Keaton's skirts.
I knew I was in a great city, in one of the greatest cities of the world,
and I wondered what it might mean to make an art, kinky, screwy,
edgy, co-equal to the city. At the same time I felt myself a looker-
on, a watcher. Neither Jew nor WASP, I had no way into the story
that Woody Allen and Diane Keaton were playing out.

I tried, hard, though to understand a filmmaker obsessed by
rabbis who stuffed pork in their mouths, a fantasy we'd seen on

the screen in Paris a few weeks earlier, another Woody Allen flick—and wasn't there something in it about a wife with a wig and black lace undies whipping the poor old white-haired man? David had buckled over with laughter, peal after peal of helpless laughter in an entirely silent theater. I could hardly see the humor in the whole affair, a poor shaved woman holding a whip in her hand, or was it a plateful of pork?

Those were the days when I kept adding to the first draft of my story, scrawling page after page of a section in Kerala, page after page about a movie in the making, a crazy theological shot in Hyderabad. And all the while I felt more and more distanced from my own life, swollen out of recognition, my body grotesque in the new world. I noticed homeless people curled up in the subway stop, bottles flung out of the high windows on 103rd Street, the young mother with two infants begging in the street by the Good Luck Deli.

David gave me Tillie Olsen's *Silences* and I could not open it without feeling the tears sting my eyes. I felt my whole life was blanked out by this newness I had been thrown into, I felt I would never get to write the real stuff of my life. I knew I was one of those women, mouths taped over, choking on her own flesh. When many years later in the company of Florence Howe I met Tillie, I was struck by her small erect figure, the clear beauty of her eyes. I did not say to her, it took me so many years to read your book, your book of fragments. My own life made a mess of me when I tried. Eight years later, in the summer of '88, two babies and two books later, I completed the novel I had begun in Chail. The pages I had added in my early days in Manhattan, my moat of paper, my counter-world, was cut so the text could lie taut, the sentences stacked against each other.

How very far it seemed from our summer honeymoon in Chail. Then, an imaginary land had enticed me as David sang me songs from Danny Kaye and Fred Astaire, told me tales of the Bronx High School of Science and summer camps in Maine. In Khartoum my childhood friend Sarra, who had returned from her stay in Washington with a cache of Superman comics, Barbie dolls, and American clothing, all frills and spots and checks, had presented me with a hardbound copy of the adventures of the Hardy Boys. That was in the back of my mind somewhere and I was curious as to how boys in America lived. I had read of bunk beds and fishing and swimming and what it was like to race around half-naked in the heat.

David told me how his hair, when he was a small child, was bleached almost white and it fascinated me, as did his discomfort at being so blonde a Jew. "I have always imagined myself as dark," he explained to me in Chail as we wandered through the elaborate gardens the old maharajah had carved out for himself, roses and tulips and the dripping laburnum all woven through with twisting paths of crazy paving and clumps of pine trees. Surely it was such an advantage to be blonde, I thought, though of course in the Indian scheme of things a level of pallor that verged on the pink didn't really count.

"The Jews are the chosen ones of God," appa had told me quite clearly. Those were conversations we had during the Six-Day War, when we had returned to Khartoum from our visit to the Holy Land. "You know that surely, Meena." Amma had pitched in, "It says so in the Bible." And I, filled with the problems of the Palestinians, the diversion of water from the River Jordan, the Israeli propaganda that was beamed over Radio Omdurman, all of which we had discussed in heated fashion over the student union tables at Khartoum University, struggled to discuss history with him. My father always rose to the defense of Israel, but before appa got started on that, or the behavior of the Indian army in the last Indo-Chinese war, amma chipped in: "Think of all those geniuses that come from the Jewish people. There's Einstein. There's Yehudi Menuhin. And so many others. Count the Nobel Prize winners. We Syrian Christians don't have that brilliance, now do we?"

Now quite apart from the fact that there was no Syrian Christian Einstein, had there been such a creature he would surely have been called GeeVarghese and inducted early into the priesthood, I felt she might have a point. The exile and the genius of the Jews, those twinned fates, troubled me. The Jews had been cast out from country and territory. They had suffered centuries of persecution and, in our own century, mass killings at the hands of the Nazis. The genius seemed a kind of compensation, at least as amma explained it to me: "There are no other peoples as gifted as the Jews," she insisted. "They are God's chosen. The Bible says so."

Years later, when amma came to America to help me after Adam was born, when I had a job in New York, and David was commuting from Minneapolis, I grew somewhat anxious. What would happen when Toby and she got together? What could they possibly speak of? And Toby so elegant and well arranged. David reassured me that amma had just the style of his grandma B, Toby's mother, but without all that iron will, and that they would manage fine together. And so they did. With the plump little Adam to share, Toby fixed apple pie and took my mother to *West Side Story*, and to Bloomingdale's and Saks Fifth Avenue.

I thought of all this, yet felt the bitterness rise in my throat as, after an evening out with Toby, amma returned to the small apartment in Van Cortlandt Park and stood staring out at the snow that was falling, stood there clenching and unclenching her small hands. And I could not bear it, for I felt she was thinking of her own mother's death, and her dislocation, and now alone in New York with her eldest daughter and the newborn child, what did she have, what home for herself? My father was in Somalia in those days, working for the United Nations, and amma, instead of being with him, was taking care of Kozencheri veliappechan, who in his large house on the hill was taking an awfully long time to die. Only an anxious letter to my father, for I had a new job in New York and did not know how to manage with the baby too, had released my mother for me. He cabled her to leave and come for a few months to America, to help me out. His Madras sister would take over the filial duties. So amma came and stayed with me in New York.

But what right did she have to bring her anxieties to me? I felt I could not bear the bond of blood. There was nothing stronger than it, but I was left no breathing space. I stood behind her at the window and heard the elevated subway clatter in the distance. We saw the lights turned on in the housing projects on the other side of Van Cortlandt Park. My marriage and movement here, to a small apartment in a lower-middle-class neighborhood in the Bronx, what did it all amount to? Was this what a woman's life had to be? I watched my mother watch the snow fall in the delicacy of the first flurries then mass over treetop and roadside. And as she stood there utterly still, watching all that sweet frozen water, saying nothing, nothing at all, I felt all torn up inside and had little sense of what either of us might turn our lives to. The fact that I had married a man of my choice, come with him to another country, given birth, and found myself a university job, all in short order, none of that counted. What I felt was the burden of her on my soul, a gravitational pull, a mother-weight. What she felt inside her gave me no room, and I did not have the suppleness of spirit to speak to her, to comfort her.

Those days were difficult. My job helped a little and so did writing. In the bus on the way to and from Fordham University where I taught, I immersed myself in the madness of Edgar Poe. Somehow he touched me to the quick. Moving to the Bronx where the air was clearer; his child-wife Virginia dying of tuberculosis; his exotic belief in electricity. So when I met my friend Joel in Cambridge a year and a half later and sat with him in the half-darkness of the Harvard Club, I listened attentively as he explained the crack that ran through the house the Ushers lived in, that half-crazed brother and sister, and I listened to him explain their entombment to me. I identified with that burial, I felt my Syrian Christian past was like that. I wanted to breathe the clear air of America. But where would I find it?

Where indeed, I asked Joel. He and I had first met in Hyderabad in 1977. He had quoted lines of Emerson to me, and told me of how he loved living in Cambridge, strolling through Harvard Yard. Now I asked him where his parents lived. For I knew he had studied first at City College and had been born to a Brooklyn Jewish family. "They kept moving," he replied, in answer to my second question. "It was cheaper to move than to have the house painted. I was born during the Depression and that was the way my parents managed." I could not forget that story of his parents moving so often. After all, David and I had done almost that. In the first two years of our marriage we moved eleven times and after those two years I was burnt-out.

I did not understand what it meant to keep house in this inconstant fashion, to hold on, to keep going. Often I did not recognize myself. I felt I had lost my soul: that it was sucked into the vortex of an Otherness I had no words for; that all I was had contracted into being a wife, being a woman who had crossed a border to give birth in another country. Seasons of birth have stripped me, formed me afresh.

March 1980. Near midnight, Roosevelt Hospital on 59th and 10th. A slab of a building made of red brick and stone. It has swing doors that you have to push hard, especially if you have a large belly that trembles with the pressure inside it, or if you are worn to the point of blankness, a new baby in your arms.

We had just given birth, she and I. She woke me from my stupor screaming, "Why? Why?" But I could be mistaken. Who could tell what her words were, what languages she spoke? I could not shut her cries from my ears. Her child had been born with a malformed head. It would not survive two weeks. She wept and wept. The white corridors of the hospital stank with her sweat.

In my head I hear her still, green gown flapping, the white strands that should tie it in front streaming at her sides, bare breasts heavy with milk, fit to burst with all the nourishment the poor child would never suck. There had been a snowstorm two nights before, just as I had gone into labor. Waking up, looking out through a window onto the high roofs of Manhattan, in sudden sunlight I saw the fine slate-colored tiles, the precise tinge of the underside of a Sudanese dove, top feathers hot with the sand from the desert, underside gleaming with cool air currents from the Nile valley. I saw that delicate blue-green shot with gray in the irregular surface of the tiles shimmering through a dirty trickle of snow.

They must have stuck a needle in her, for when I turned from the window they had already brought her back, her face ashen but without the substance of ash, like that water trickle really, a see-through thing, her two hands limp. They pulled the covers over her, set the screen over against her bed and it was as if nothing had happened. Nothing.

That night a child was brought in to me. The nurse from Jamaica held up a screaming thing. Its hair stood on end. Black hair turned into electric needles, shock straight, each blade gleaming, face contorted purple, mouth an angry welt, each eye screwed tight, heavenwards slanted as if gashed with a blade. Out of the lips of this thing held bolt upright in its swaddling, came sore stings of breath. Then the air sucked in let the body shudder and swing as the nurse held it so that the screams, low and guttural, came out again and again, not from the mouth that seemed snapped shut, but from the whole surface of that swaddled body. I sat up in bed and stared in horror.

Nothing came out of my mouth. No words. Finally I heard a voice murmuring:

"Take it away."

Puzzled but polite she stands there waiting.

"That's not my child. It must be a mistake."

I cannot take my eyes off the little mummy, only its head brutally alive. She is gentle now. Waits for me.

"It's a mistake, a mistake." I feel the hot tears prickle my eyes but I keep on. ''You know that's not my child. It's someone else's.''

Worn out with the day and a half of labor, the three hours of hot pain at the end, the small bullheaded thing butting through, the iron jab in my back, the ball of lead in the brain, I clutch the side of the bed and bite my tongue. No words come. The cut still marks my tongue.

''Look, let me show you.''

Without the slightest fear she stands and with her small brown hands, starts unpacking the bundle. The motion must reassure it, for the shuddering breaths stop. As the bands ripple off in her hands, and the little palms are set free of their cotton covers, the creature sucks in its breath.

''Look!'' She points to the plastic band on the plump little wrist with the letters sealed in: ''Boy Lelyveld,'' it says in clear black script. ''Boy Lelyveld,'' she mouths for me in a delicate singsong way. As I stare at her, she sets the baby in my hands.

The pillow is behind my back. I sit up, the hair over my mouth scooped away.

In that strangeness of flesh that assaults us, making us all touch, making the very quick of our selves adhere to the surfaces of life—a metal railing, the knobby trunk of a guava tree, the lover's wrist, his upper arm where the coarse hair curls, his thigh—in a knowledge that sweeps over the particles of sense, a grace not voiced as such, a light that does not declare itself, a true sense without cipher or prefiguration being as it is wholly of the body, I lean forward, I set my right palm to the heft of his neck, as she offers him to me.

My left hand and upper arm cradle his weight, almost nine pounds of solid muscle and bone and circling blood, twenty-three inches long and the shoulder blades so huge the mid-wife summoned in the doctor to check they were not broken in the bruising he received as he butted his way out, out of my womb and vagina, the midnight of the birth passage torn and bloodied, the skin at the vulva's end slit clean so it would not tear, slit with metal instruments I saw, for I wanted to watch her slight hands, Nancy Cuddihy, the mid-wife who worked on me.

Out out, the blue cord wrapped tight around his neck so the veins bulged in his struggle to breathe and she leant forward, concentrating hard, the small Irish woman murmuring, ''I'm going to cut the cord while he's in you, its wrapped around his neck, we don't want to lose him,'' and I struggle half up and feel the loose bands around my feet as they are held in the stirrups. And still it's another twenty minutes of breathing and toiling before he's pushed out clean, intact, dark blue, Lord Krishna's color, my son, life of my life, and they rush him to the oxygen machine and he breathes and stirs and whimpers and roars and then is handed, still naked, to me. I set him to my right breast, the one with the small mole on the left, set his mouth there and feel the lips quaver for an instant then work for the first time in air. His strong pink mouth is so tight, the lips, the infant gums, so hard, I start to hum and hurt and stir sideways, uncontrollably so David wants to hold me, hold my shoulders, for my groins too are shaking as the afterbirth is pulled out, an iron-colored thing I scarcely see.

But now Nancy has started stitching and on and on she stitches into that numbness of my secret flesh as the sweetness fills and starts to flow out of my nipples, pale yellow colostrum the color of the first petals of the narcissius in springtime, the color of tender winter jasmine flowing into his small mouth and she stitches and stitches brown head bent into the time that needs to heal, the eruption that I am sutured, closed back by a woman's strong hands wielding needle and thread. Shall I learn to be his mother? I cannot tell. All I feel are his lips set there and my breast beneath, and we make a being so pure.

That memory is nowhere in me as I take the child the nurse hands me. I set him to my breast. His mouth is even stronger now and sucks and sucks so hard I hurt but let it hurt as the milk slips into him and I feel his body shudder. On and on he sucks and the nurse leaning against the chair watching so carefully till then, whispers, "He was so hungry!" and walks out.

When that breast is drained I set him to the left side and when he is satiated and falls into a deep sleep, I sit up very straight and in my trembling hands take the edge of his swaddling clothes and gingerly roll off the bandages that hold him in. I stare at the soft flesh, the curve of shoulder, the belly with the angry bruise of flesh, an inch of cut cord held down with a plastic clip, the remnants of the life that fed him while he was in me, not dried yet into a pruny thing, but raw still. Further down I look at the delicate penis with the brown whorls that flesh makes as it curls and under it, upholding its slight tapering form, the great orbs of his balls that hold in the sperm sacs, his thigh, the curve of his hip, his ankle curved too, the great toe and the little ones all in their intricate order, and up on his head with the bumpy thing on his skull not quite subsided from the pressure of his birth I see the black hairs, gleaming, a gentle cap of hair now, pacific on his head.

He trembles in his sleep as I hold him to the space between my two breasts and his toes reach to my navel where I was joined to amma. But the slack worn belly after childbirth trembles with all those rushing hormones and I start to shake and shake as if a fever were in me. So after holding him there on my skin I pick up all his clothes and wrap him up again and then exhausted drop back. We are wrapped in a soft sleep all that morning and into the late afternoon.

When David comes to visit he sees us there, all worn and shiny with sleep. "He was so hungry, that is all," I whisper in my happiness. "Look at him now!" Arms marked with all the pinpricks from the blood lettings and takings, snarled in old lace amma bought me a lifetime ago, I hold out our son.

When David leaves, when the nurse returns and takes the baby back to the nursery, I fall into a heavy sleep. I dream of the clouds, light, flaky as dried milk over the clock tower, the fragrant gray-green of the tiles, my mother's hands so close suddenly, the heavy wedding ring visible on the worn finger. She holds out her hands to me, she comes forward.

She holds out her hands in the blue air to me.

Behind her face is a window. Is it a window? A porthole surely? A mirror? I cannot tell. The wooden frame shifts as if my eyes were a dark, unstable water that held it. Behind her face is darkness, a mirror of ink. She is going now. No, no, she is returning. She is coming and going, in and out of my eyes and I cannot bear it.

Each summer after Adam was born, we would travel to Minneapolis where David taught, to spend the warm season there. I had taken the job in New York so that I could breathe and live a little. But I had a six-month-old baby, I was relatively new in the country, and bearing the strains of a commuting marriage. Still, I was clear I did not want to be a faculty wife in Minneapolis, I did not want to be swallowed up in the cold. In the midst of that welter of Scandinavians where David with his blonde beard was often called "Sven" in bars, I stuck out like a sore black thumb, a grotesque thing.

I remember walking along a street in Minneapolis when Adam was not yet two. We were just strolling, he and I, on a lovely summer's day, with clear blue skies that stretched for miles all around and in the flatness the scent of cut grass, the growing stalks of wheat, the buzz of summer flies. We were quite close to the university campus. There was a motorbike leaning against a tree, so we walked a little to the side to avoid it. I do not know where he stepped from, the white man in the black leather jacket and the slicked back hair. But the hate in his voice stunned me. "You black bitch!" he yelled at me, apropos of nothing except that I had almost brushed his motorcycle and he had seen it from a shop window. I held onto the little boy. Where did that man's fury come from? I was shaken to the core.

I could not tell David. It would have hurt him far too much and there was no way he could become me, enter my skin. I did not want him to know about it at all. But when our friend Prakash from Bangalore came to visit, the words tumbled out. Prakash heard me out in silence, but somehow the fact that he listened was enough. Later that year, his Ph.D. completed, he moved to New Jersey to teach in a college there.

Did he understand that white man's rage as he listened to me? Or figure it out better, speaking to the Indians who have lived through racist stonings and murder in Jersey City, who live in fear of the Dot-Buster skinheads. What would they tell me, I wonder, the Indian women who are forced to give up their saris and wear western clothes lest they lose their jobs, or the Asian children in the city schools, or the black youths who strayed into Bensonhurst, or the brown youths, or the Asian youths who pack our city streets? What does it mean to be Unwhite in America? Can I make lines supple enough to figure out violence, vent it, and pass beyond?

We went to Puerto Rico the spring Adam turned two. We lay on the delicate white sands on Loquillo Beach to sun ourselves. I carried Conrad's *Heart of Darkness* with me to read. At night after David and I made love, I dreamt I was carrying the pages of the novel I had laid out two years before on the floor, all around my pregnant belly. In my dream I was carrying the parts all tenderly wrapped up in the Pashmina shawl Toby had presented me with when I first arrived in America.

I treasured the shawl woven in the mountains of Kashmir, with its fine embroidery of bird's beak, mango leaf, and vine, and saved it to wear on special occasions. In the dream, which consumed me as I lay on the flat bed in the Parador Martorell with the hibiscus blossoming outside and the cry of birds crossing the shore at dawn, a landscape so much like the west coast of Kerala, I stooped, I picked up the shawl. Quite tenderly I used it to wrap the pound load of paper I had written. My feet were possessed with a life of their own and carried me out of the orange painted door of the Bronx apartment, down the narrow corridor to the small metal hatch set into the wall. Pull the hatch down and shove it in, my own voice said. As I shoved the shawl down the incinerator the scent of burning tissue filled my nostrils. Back in New York City, it was many weeks before I could pass by the corridor without a burning scent rushing up my nostrils.

Svati Mariam was born in New York City, late at night, on May 12, 1986, almost born in the taxi cab. I will never forget the full moon behind the Guggenheim, a pale lemony color as the cab raced down Fifth Avenue. David didn't know I was fully dilated, nor the cab driver, whistling through his teeth. I bit into my lips to stop the pain. One red light, I thought, and that will be that and the child will be born here, now. But we got into the emergency room and I was on the stretcher, and in another half minute she shot out all blue and gray and mottled, my little one, and I trembled and laughed, all at the same time, an experienced mother now. "What is her name, her name," Dr. Wolf asked, when he got there. "Here she is, she must have a name." I took the strength of speech into my own lips and said, "Svati, Svati Mariam is her name."

She was all mottled and discolored then.

"That was before you became a beauty," I tell her, when she asks me what color she was when she was born. "I am varnish now," she replies or sometimes she fixes herself a color change: "peach." And then continues: "You are brown mama, papa is blond papa, Adam is brown Adam, and I am peach Svati."

What shall I be for her, my little one? I push her each day towards Broadway. The days pass. She is still so young, packing in her years, one, two, three, four. Sometimes I worry for her, a little Indian-American girl-child. Whenever I can I hold onto the reality of mechi and mechan, her grandmother and grandfather in Kerala, her aunts, her cousins. Another soil, another earth. But what might she wish to be, that other soil cast into invisibility years down the road, when her small breasts flower and boys line up for her? What will she make of me, her South Indian mother? Will she recall I loved her, loved her brother too, throwing my arms around them, trembling at the sound of trucks roaring past, ambulances that halt to the stench of burning rubber at Saint Luke's emergency room?

In a dream Adam comes to me, as he did when he was a little child. "Mama, I am losting," he cries out, making me blindfold him and then twirl him around. His little arms stick out, he wanders around the room, relying on me to steer him away from tables and chairs and books lying in heaps, all the while singing out in his deep little voice, "Losting, Mama, losting," and when he signals, flapping his arms up and down like a pigeon might, I know he's had enough and I hug him to me, shower kisses on his cheeks. With my free hand I tug off the blindfold and watch him, pleased and anxious all the same time, rubbing his eyes, staring at me, once again, as if we had just met, he and I, for the very first time. He used to play that game all the time when he was three, even four. Was it to repair a memory he could not bear?

I cannot forget Adam just before he turned three. He lay on the airport floor at Trivandrum. Words tumbled out of his mouth, mixed in with the tears. He beat at the cold floor. "No. No. Don't take me away, no, no." He was a well-built child with rosy cheeks. His tears made a mess on the floor. He could not bear to leave Kerala and his grandmother and grandfather and the rough and tumble of all that love, scents of cows and chickens and goats, the safety of so many arms to hold him.

I bent to pick him up, preparing for the passage through the metal detectors and body searches, then over the tarmac into the plane, all ready for the first step, in long return to New York. But as I stooped I felt myself dissolving, a sheer bodily memory I have no words for. I was all tears. I cupped his struggling little form to my breasts and looked at my mother's face. Through her tears, she looked back at me quite steadily.

A few days after Adam returned to New York, he lay on the floor in his American grandmother's house and drew a little picture: his map of the world. On the brown paper there were squiggles running up and down and a square shape somewhat at an angle to the up and down lines.

"Kozencheri, Delhi," he explained, reading his map to us, "India, sixth floor."

"What's the sixth floor?" We peered over his shoulder.

"Grandma's house, right here."

He beamed in delight at his own creation, the hereness, the honey of life included in it. Looking at him, I learnt to forget the little clenched form on the airport floor, the pain, the refusal. How close to danger we so often are, I think to myself, how little the present reveals the complicated amassing discord out of which alone our words can rise to music. In the little kitchen behind us, Toby was warming up a zucchini preparation she had cooked for our homecoming. That tangy, alien fragrance, and the sweetness of bread pudding steaming on the stove top distanced me from those thoughts and I shifted my weight in the new shoes I had bought for our return to this island city by the Hudson.

A little over a year later, when Adam was four, the doorman at Toby's building on Riverside Drive leant over and engaged him in conversation.

"What are you?" asked the lean black man from the South, bending towards my child. A few days earlier Frank had complained bitterly to me about white people and how all they thought was that blacks chewed watermelon. He had grimaced, elegantly spat out the bit of tobacco he had chewed into a bit of silver foil, and folded the whole caboodle up into a triangle, tossing it into the bin at the foot of the marble fireplace in the foyer.

"So what you, child?"

Adam, shy as ever, had just looked at him.

"You American, child?"

"No," said my son very boldly.

"Indian then. You Indian, child?"

Adam shifted his weight "No." He stuck his fist into his little mouth as he sometimes did. I was growing tense. What did my first-born wish for himself? Some nothingness, some transitory zone where dreams roamed, a border country without passport or language?

"What you, then?" Frank insisted, his old man's voice growing tetchy as he waited.

Raising himself to his full height Adam replied, "Jedi, I'm a Jedi knight!" His head filled with Luke Skywalker and Darth Vader and the citadel of Death Stars, planets of lost origins, Adam knew exactly what he was talking about. Perhaps Frank knew what the child was saying, perhaps he didn't. But his face creased in smiles and he pressed a silver nickel into Adam's grubby little hand. The next time I saw Frank was several months later. He had moved to another apartment building. He was limping now and visibly aged. His cough was worse too. "How's the Jedi knight?" he asked me in a hoarse whisper. "How's the little knight?" "He's fine," I replied, "growing taller by the minute."

Svati too is growing taller. Born six years after her brother, she is now the age he was when he thought of himself as a Jedi knight. Just the other day she came home from preschool with a picture she had made of her Indian grandparents: mechi, mechan and her aunts Anna and Elsa and the dog and cat, all in the Tiruvella house. Her grandparents had round bodies and round eyes. Her grandfather and her two aunts had short crisp hair colored in with crayon strokes, all dark. Mechi had a sari, her hair drawn back in a bun. But through her bun, poised on top of her round head, ran a stick. At least that's what I took it to be.

"Svati, what's that?" I pointed.

"Bone."

"Bone?"

"She's my bone-and-arrow mechi, you know that. Bone-and-arrow Indians, mama."

Her voice rose in the utter certainty that sometimes grips her. I bent down and picked her up

"Darling, mechi and I and you are a different sort of Indian. She doesn't have a bow and arrow running through her hair like that. Who told you?"

I carried my child into the living room and turned my palm as I often do, into a map of India.

"Look, Svati, India is here—America there." I pointed a little to the right of my palm, somewhere near my ribs. "And Native Americans live all over this country. They were here first."

"And mechi?"

"Mechi lives in India. You know where she lives in Tiruvella."

"And Mechan?"

"Yes, he too."

"And the well?"

"Yes, the well and the guava trees and your aunts. And know something else? Native Americans don't wear their hair like that."

The next day I went into school and spoke to the teacher, an attractive young woman, filled with good projects for the children. Had she really thought I was Indian from the plains somewhere west of Manhattan? "I am Indian," I said, "from Asia. Heard of Columbus?" "Sure." I spoke about Columbus and his obsession with finding India. How he thought when he landed in America that he had struck the Indian coast. And then I mentioned Vasco da Gama, searching out the spice trade in the ancient kingdoms on the west coast of India. A child like Svati I added, was caught in the crossfire of the white man's naming patterns. All of this took about a minute as children entered the classroom.

"Come and tell a story to the children, will you?" she invited. I promised I would. A week later I went back to tell the children a tale of India. I opened up my palm once again and drew invisible pictures on it. Two weeks after that the teacher invited a Native American from the Community House, and he came with a peace pipe and pictures of herbs and headdresses and ancient rites and talked to the children of his people who had once inhabited Turtle Island. That sacred geography all built over, bits and pieces of it burning, I thought to myself as Svati told me of the visitor to her school.

Who are we? What selves can we construct to live by? How shall we mark out space? How shall we cross the street? How shall we live yet another day?

A vivid scent almost as of paper burning, a bitter, meaty smell, fills my nostrils. In the kitchen something left over is actually burning. I pick it out of the oven. I pick up a knife to cut up scallions for a salad. I am alone at home now but we have to eat tonight, all four of us together, and I may as well make the salad a few hours early. I am going to do tomatoes and lettuce next. The radio is on loud, louder with the whine and roar of winds in telegraph poles, winds tearing off rooftops, smashing up walls, destroying kitchens, bedchambers, writing machines, small salad bowls. Hurricane Hugo hits Puerto Rico, causing enormous damage to life and property. No deaths are mentioned as yet. The excited voice on the radio describes a fifteen-foot wall of water smashing into fences, walls, school buses, trees, the lot. Charleston, South Carolina could be next, the voice predicts.

Listening to the male voice describe the hurricane, something thrashes in my head. I feel I cannot bear to slice tomatoes for the salad, tear up the lettuce with my fingers after draining out all that cool tap water. At the pit of my stomach something crashes, as if water were churning into milky chaos. I pick up the phone to call a friend I have not seen for many months. Perhaps he will understand what I am going through.

"Sometimes I cannot even cross the street," I said to him many months ago when we met last. "I look at the trees on the far side of the hill past Saint Luke's Hospital and I can't put one foot in front of the other to cross the road, get to the other side." He seemed to understand. We were speaking about being Indian and living in the United States. Just now I needed that sense of something shared, a special displacement, an exile.

My fingers were all wet with tomato juice when I picked up the phone. From the courtyard below a child was crying, over and over, "My ball, my, my ball." The super's grandchild. He'd come from Miami to visit his grandparents in Manhattan.

I got the connection I was searching for. "Yes, yes," the voice listening on the phone replied, "But why assume living and writing will be easier in India? Might it not be harder even, with kerosene and gas out of stock, with lines for sugar?" "But I could just stay home and write, someone else would do that for me," I replied quite crassly. "Yes but you'd have to supervise the someone else!" I laughed, in enormous relief, at the sheer fantasy of return to a life I had never led. "I live here because I can work here, Meena. But you writers are different. I think you're pushed from inside. Something tugs, pushes you hard."

That night several New York City writers who had published poems or prose pieces with Red Dust were to read. Joanna Gunderson had arranged the reading. She had invited Robert Pinget to read and he was there too, just arrived from Paris. Pinget with his leather tie and balding head was spry, dour even in his humor as he read out the paragraphs of *M. Songe*. Going ahead of him, reading her bit first, was his English translator, Barbara Wright. Her pleasure at his lines couched in her English was infectious. As she threw back her head of bobbed black hair, and raised her voice, we were captivated by the lightness of her mood. I was freed of myself, and the intensity of having read lines from "The Storm" about warfare. Reading the elegy of names—"Khartoum and Cairo, Columbo and New Delhi, Jaffna, Ahmedabad and Meerut"—had hurt my throat, made me catch my breath. Now in the delicate refinement, the plainness even of Pinget's nouveau roman style, I found a solace, an exit from the self. I loved the savor of the French language I had not used for so long. It was some time after ten-thirty at night, after the words, after the peanuts and wine, the banter of a literary evening, that I walked briskly, the wind in my leather coat, down Broadway, towards 113th Street.

On the traffic island right in the center of the street, I confronted a friend. She rose out of the darkness with her long dark hair, her dark scarf, her books clutched to her. There were bushes behind her, magnolia and the newly planted holly. So at first I could not tell her from that blur. But soon we recognized each other. There was an empty bench prepared for us and we sat there in the darkness on a traffic island on Broadway, two displaced creatures greeting each other. She spoke of her loneliness on returning from Madras, on the harshness of the city. And I replied, "Sometimes, Gauri, I cannot cross the street, for I look down and see the trees, way over there, beyond Saint Luke's Hospital and I wonder to myself, Where am I? When am I? And there is no point in crossing the street. None at all." I went on to explain how one morning I had gone out to get some bagels for breakfast from Mama Joy's. But I could not bring myself to cross the street, to return home. I will remain stuck here, I thought, fighting back tears, staring at the trees all the way beyond Saint Luke's Hospital, stuck here at the edge of 113th Street for the rest of my life.

People were passing us on the traffic island and giving us little stares. But I felt it was all right to be there, a New York City housewife on a bench after dark, chatting to her friend. But I needed to explain something to Gauri. "You know, I don't think I could survive if I didn't write. Just now reading the poem set in the Tiruvella of my childhood, and in Kozencheri too, standing in a small bookshop on the Upper West Side, I felt I was breathing again. But it stings me to write all this. In India, I rest, I just am, like a stone, a bone, a child born again." Then I added hastily, "If my husband saw us he'd think us bag ladies."

"That's all right, Meena." She was very gentle with me. "We have the right to change our identities." I think we were happy in that moment, Gauri and I, on a city bench in Manhattan, the great island city where the poor cry out of tunnels, and the rich frolic in their limos and luxury penthouses, where just as in my birthplace children hunt for scraps of food in waste heaps.

11. Transit Lounge

In Manhattan it is hard to make the bits and pieces hold together. Things are constantly falling apart. The city is dispersing itself, jolting, juggling its parts. There is no ideal of poise in its construction, just the basting together of bits. Sometimes bits burst open, split apart, and one does not quite know how to go on. How to construct a provisional self to live by. How to make up memory.

"Return to Khartoum," Talal Asad counseled me.

"What do you mean?"

"No, really."

He made it sound so simple. I had gone to him wanting to know more about Khartoum, the city in which I lived off and on for more than thirteen years of my life. Talal is an anthropologist with a special interest in colonialism. He lived in Khartoum in the sixties and taught at the university in the years when I was a student there. He even had a house across the road from us in Hai el Matar, and though I do not think we were ever formally introduced, we had surely passed each other by, heard of each other. Talal was in New York City. I called him up and spoke to him. He said he would help me remember what I could of those lost years of my life.

"You should get a travel grant or something and return and it would demystify something for you."

"Demystify? What does that mean?"

We were sitting side by side in small metal chairs in an art gallery in lower Manhattan, Art in General, that was showing an exhibit of box works by women of color. All around us were boxes of intricate artwork in glass, glue, paper, metal, stone, bone, eggshell, filaments drawn from a spider's web.

177

"Demystify? Look here, in a dream I had I kept returning to Lahore but suddenly, realizing that my mother and father were no longer there, that I was no longer a boy, filled with emotion, I wept. I went back thirty years later and it was a dusty town with little streets and so much smaller than I remembered. I was utterly unmoved by it."

He continued and listening to him it was as if his voice were a voice from within, breaking my own heart:

"It's the imagination, really, isn't it, working within us? Surely all exiles are like that? Surely you have those dreams too?"

There was something urgent in his voice. I stopped utterly still to listen. At the celebration for the exhibit Gale Jackson, Maritza Arrestia, and I had each read our poems on the theme of Ancestors Known and Unknown. The reading was over. It was time to leave and I was standing next to a pedestal. On it was Tomie Arai's work of crushed glass and metal, *In Memory of Hiroshima*. A mushroom cloud on glass and, in front, a woman cut into metal, her hands folded, weeping. I stopped. I looked at Talal.

"Yes, of course," I nodded quickly. For I didn't know how to say I don't think I dream of that at all; or if I do I don't recall those dreams. I only have the voice that comes out in poems or in bits of prose, cries of the occasion, the voice singing against itself, against time.

Memories nearer at hand flood back. I was standing in the transit lounge at Bombay airport on the way to Trivandrum when I saw a group of men dressed in the rough brownish fabric that is sometimes used to make the garments of the very poor, baggy shirts and loose-cut trousers. They squatted in a heap in the dark alcove of the transit lounge of Bombay International Airport. The floor of the immensely long room is covered in ridged plastic, with little suction cups built in to prevent soles from slipping and they squatted right on it, at least thirty persons, their faces in shadows, propped against each other, seemingly sleeping. When one of them rose, the others stirred.

I saw a man, his face gray with exhaustion, getting up, stretching a little. From his neck hung a name written out in Hindi, in neat Devanagari script. When a few minutes later the men pushed themselves up, little knots, welts of human beings all dressed in identical clothing, I saw that each man had his name written on his chest. Some had cords around the neck to which the name tags were tied, crude postcards with lettering on them. Others had their names and destinations—Kuwait City, Dhahran, Abu Dhabi—attached onto their shirts with safety pins. Some of the pins stuck out at angles from the pockets to which they were attached.

These illiterate men from a Bihar village, like so many others before them, had sold their services to a middle man on the promise of several years of paid labor on construction sites in the region of the Persian Gulf. So there they were, resting after the long, hot ride in a lorry, after finding their way in through the overpainted lounges of the newly refurbished airport, hands sore with clutching the parcels wives and mothers and sisters had tied up with old cord. Now, in the early hours of the morning some stood rubbing their eyes, others shuffled as if an immense tiredness were welling out of them. A man in a gray safari suit, obviously the middleman's agent, bustled about not far away.

I raced forward and pulled Svati away. How little she was then, not yet three. In order to approach the group of men in the half darkness of the lounge, she had evolved a whole system of movement. First she tossed her plastic dolly with the blonde hair and blue eyes forward, and then crawled after it, as fast as she could manage on her plump knees. When she reached the toy, she laughed with delight, only to scoop it up again and fling it away. It was by following her into the half darkness of the alcove that I came upon the bonded laborers. So I stood there, in the shadows, clutching my child's hand, not moving. Then swiftly I pulled her away.

When next I saw the men, roughly two hours later, they were walking onto an airplane with black and green paint on its nose, bound for the Gulf. A slightly manic man I had noticed, with black glittering eyes, hand fretting nervously all over the hem of his roughly stitched shirt, walked ahead. He held his head erect as he walked. The name tag, slightly torn with all the fingering, was still fluttering on his chest. By the time they left, it was ten or eleven hours since I had first entered the transit lounge. My first feel of Indian soil, as it were, was the ridged plastic of the transit lounge in Bombay airport where I waited with Adam and Svati. The flight from New York had taken twenty-one hours and now we were all set for three more hours of flying time, south into Trivandrum, which was seventy miles south of Tiruvella. There was a go-slow strike.

Plane after plane was canceled. Following the messages on the loud intercom system and the confused words of the airline people sitting by the gate, the line stirred wearily from one departure gate to another. Men and women and children thrust themselves forward as best they could from one queue into the other. Old women squatted on the ground, the younger folks leant against each other, children started to stretch out on the black plastic floor. It must have been almost five in the morning when the pale rose of the morning sun, rising over the Arabian Sea, flooded the unwashed glass windows of the transit lounge. We were still waiting for the plane that would take us to Kerala.

Exhausted by the long wait, near the front of a new queue that had formed by Gate 14, I stood as firmly as I could, holding tight to the handles of the McLaren stroller into which I had buckled Svati. She seemed content for the moment. Adam was a little to my right, watching a group of Indian children play frisbee. I could read the longing in his eyes. Once when the frisbee came near him he leapt up and caught it and held onto it for a brief instant before sending it skimming off. The frisbee-playing children were chattering away in German. Their parents, obviously Malayalees, perhaps even from the neighborhood of Tiruvella, were standing ahead of me in the queue. How oddly the German sounded on those children's lips. But why was that any odder than English in my son's mouth, the pristine North American sort, of the Manhattan species? He was a New York child, conceived in India, born in the city, and now I was taking him back to his grandparents, back to my ancestral soil, an old house, a large garden, a well with clear water in it. Perhaps he would learn to speak Malayalam again, I thought fondly. As a small child of three and four he had babbled phrases, after six months in India. But now all that was forgotten. Where did a language go once it was forgotten, I wondered. I often forgot Malayalam, at least little bits of it, but on my childhood returns to Kerala from Khartoum, it always revived, the deep buried roots stirring again. Why shouldn't that happen for Adam? But I was forgetting that he never was bathed in that language as I had been. After all, as a child it was my first spoken tongue. And during the years in the Sudan my parents returned home to India for three months or sometimes my mother returned for six months and immersed her daughters in the life of buttermilk and chilied fish and more garrulous cousins than could fill two alcoves in a transit lounge.

Where were they, all my cousins now? One of them was a cardiologist, I knew. He was working in Kuwait, earning masses of money by all accounts. By now the sun's rays were brighter, glinting on the plate glass as I stood clutching the handles of Svati's stroller. My thoughts turned to the laborers bound for the Gulf. They could not read or write. They did not know how to speak Arabic or English, the two languages that surrounded me when I had moved as a child to North Africa. There were whole families, waiting in India, dependent on the money these men would send home. Their plane must have risen over the waters by now, over Bombay harbor, cutting its way north and west. Perhaps the men were less weary now, exhilarated even, seeing the morning sun for the first time, over the shoreline of the Arabian Sea. But what would they find on the other side?

And writing this today, sitting in a room in New York City, I wonder how many of those men are still there, stuck after the Iraqi invasion of Kuwait, herded into the refugee camps set up outside Amman. Was it yesterday, or the day before, that the young man with the glittering eyes ran as hard as he could towards a water truck long run dry? What will he do when he is airlifted out of the deserts in a wide-bellied Indian air force plane and flung back into Bihar or Haryana? What can he and others like him, men and women too, do with lives burnt up by the hopes of a new world? Where will they live? Who will tell their names?

Somehow all this is in my mind as I try to stitch together the life I have lived, to recall Khartoum where I spent my childhood years, a city of sandstone, brick and mud, in the heat of a North African desert I have forgotten and remember. What can I see? A white painted house with a terrace on top and lawn in front, with the prickly acacia hedge at the back. Haadia who lived next door to me racing about in her blue cotton dress. She was about a year and a half older than I, with her hair parted in the tiny braids that women wear now in America. We were about the same color and shape, except that she was somewhat heavier set and my knees stuck out more. We romped and played and raided the fridges in each of our homes for Coca-Colas and sweetmeats and hid out under the neem trees, as Abdullah Tayib, Haadia's uncle, the Sudanese poet, called out to me from across the yard.

He knew I had newly arrived in the Sudan from India, that I was five and a half, the right age to learn a classical script:

"Come here, come here you young thing and learn the syllables of Arabic. How can you live unless you learn the syllables of Arabic?" Those were the days before Abdullah Tayib became vice-chancellor of Khartoum University and it was rumored he used to go into senate meetings in his absent-minded poet's way, one shoe off and one shoe on.

"What should poets do? Let them stick to poems," someone high up in the civil service laughed out over drinks as he told that story. How cruel I thought that man's comments, and how untrue. And how I treasured the memory of Abdullah, as he sat in his chair reciting poetry to me. His old man's voice, as he stood tall and erect on the other side of the yard, still sounds in my ears. And the voices of many old men crying out to me from many yards, on many continents, echoes in my ears:

Come, child, come and learn the great languages of the earth. Unless you learn, who will speak your name? How will you know yourself? How will you keep your face from being burnt by the sun? From bursting into filaments of pearl when the moon comes too close on full moon nights? How will you write, child, how will you read? Who will know your name, girl-child, who will know your name?

I think it is the pain of no one knowing my name that drives me to write. That, and the sense that I am living in a place where I have no history. Where all I am is surface and what is not reducible to a crude postcard dangled round the neck, a torn card with name and address pinned to the blouse, cannot exist, has no place.

In Manhattan, I am a fissured thing, a body crossed by fault lines. Where is my past? What is my past to me, here, now at the edge of Broadway? Is America a place without memory?

I observe the teenage girl in the Burger King at the corner of 110th and Broadway. She smiles at me through terribly white teeth, a sweetness visible, and hands back jangling change. She forgets what I ordered for the third time round. I think of asking her name, then forget myself. An old man, the one from the makeshift shack at the corner by the subway stop, comes in. He has a stench about him, he is crusted with dirt. Where on these sidewalks of Broadway will he find water to sweeten himself? He stretches out his hand.

We are on the upper reaches of Broadway, in Morningside Heights, just six blocks from the wrought-iron gates of Columbia University with its polished white statue of a woman with naked breasts. A few years ago they did a survey at the university and decided that Morningside Heights did not have enough gourmet restaurants to attract high-flying faculty, the kind that wear leather jackets, deconstruct with a vengeance, and eat fine foods. However, we have Dynasty.

Dynasty is Chinese fast food at the corner of Broadway and 110th, flanked by the bagel store and running slantwise, all plate glass and spindly hanging plants, down the avenue with stone houses, half a block to Burger King. The floor is done up in ridged plastic stuff, a bit like the transit lounge I have left behind, somewhere in my head. Holding my head with both my hands, I hopscotch to Dynasty where the diners sit with their bowls of swift fried food, behind unwashed glass. You can see most everything about them from the sidewalk, right down to who's butting whom with knees or gleaming toes.

Dynasty has problems. The food isn't so hot. It's hard to keep up appearances at 110th and Broadway. Perhaps further downtown, in the fashionable reaches of Columbus or Amsterdam in the seventies, an enterprising restaurateur might try. But here the homeless and the doped out ones are with us, with nowhere else to go, and it's hard to keep up appearances through glass.

Inside the Burger King where I have gone in search of a quick meal for the children, an old man approaches stretching out his hand. I stop short, quite close to him now. I have my two specials in my hand, gummy with ketchup and the sour pickles they wrap up. I decide to move away. I have what I need. The children are waiting. I last saw the old man ten minutes ago near the entrance of Dynasty, the Chinese restaurant at the mouth of the subway stop that keeps appearing in my dreams. The subway stop, I mean. Sometimes I people that underground passage with cousins I have not seen for decades, ancient aunts from Kerala, bonded workers on their way to the Persian Gulf, all of us migrants and even those settled in ancestral lands, jolted by time.

The old man doesn't halt. He approaches, shuffling his feet. They are tied with bits of newsprint and cloth. The makeshift cord he has used looks as if it were ripped from inside a rubber tire. His clothes have been tied together with thread, a tweedy thing patched up, a yard of torn plastic, a bit of cardboard expertly bent, doubling as a crude scarf and a protective piece, a ridged carapace.

We are our outsides, I think, that's all, skin and clothing and bits of hair poking out from under headgear. He spent the night under cardboard cover, by a bit of wall by Dynasty. Perhaps he crawled out of the subway and set up this impromptu shelter, a contraption of his own making with just enough of a breathing space, a habitat of cardboard, torn up and fitted together to make a place for a crouching man.

Walking by earlier I had noticed that the whole caboodle was shored against a bent shopping cart. It gave him some protection, broke the wind as it blew the two straight blocks from Riverside Drive where the bare trees and stout stone wall did little to curb its ferocity. I dropped a quarter in the old man's tin. A coffee can with a man, a mule, a black poncho over the man's hat. The can was carefully set to the right so that the Dynasty folk wouldn't trip on it. I hurried on.

Now, I see myself, see myself seeing as the old man inches closer. I hear the orange-capped girl crying out, "Carlos, Carlos," summoning the manager-in-training, a young lad in his twenties who hurries down, frowning. The girl behind the counter is oblivious to me now. As I move past the old man I glimpse the young lad with his manager-in-training badge. He draws himself erect. Not far from the counter, the old man looks up. His mouth is open as if he were having difficulty breathing. I open the metal door handle, step back out into the cold.

By the black wall between Dynasty and the bagel shop I avoid the cardboard shack, broken down now without a crouching man's warmth inside. Fingering the white paper bag with the children's dinner in it, I speed past Love Pharmacy. For an instant I stare at the neon-lit window and catch myself—a scurrying thing packed in coat and leather hat, a Gujarati shawl, white with black tie-dye dots, covering her upper body for extra warmth, face plump in a flat white light, cheeks a soft brown, hair parted and messy. The feet are covered in soft leather boots the same color as her skin, a ripe brown.

I look what I am, hastily put together, hurrying in the cold, a Broadway thing.

I live here now at the edge of Broadway. My familiars in the street, like the old pavement dweller, the girl in the Burger King, the newspaper vendor, a fine-boned lady from Saurashtra who braves the cold in a shack, piled up in front with copies of the *Voice* or *Mirabella*, none of us have a name for each other. We gather for our business in the marketplace, buying, selling, scurrying in the cold. We try to survive ourselves.

I think of a line of old monks I saw in Eritrea a lifetime ago. They walked, single file, in the streets of Asmara, their big robes torn and eaten up as if the snouts of wild animals had poked through the fabric. Bits of animal hide from buffalo and wildebeest hung over their shoulders. To an Indian child who had stepped off the plane for a brief stopover at Asmara, the old men, five of them, walking stooped and smelly, had a holy stench to them. One of them had glanced downwards at my feet, at the bright red Clarks shoes amma had bought for me from somewhere near Picadilly Circus, London. That great city, with its gray river and Big Ben and Hyde Park where men on carboard crates cried out in rough voices, was a blur in my head. All I had were the shoes, covered now in the dust of Asmara. I knew that my once bright shoes were now almost the same color as the old man's loincloth. That is what the dust of the earth did, blurred us all over, all creatures of flesh. The old monk had glanced upwards then, and looked at me. As if seeing something there, a small person, illiterate in his ways, but of some interest. Or so I had felt with a sharp pleasure as I moved away from my mother's swishing silks as she walked just to my right.

En route from Khartoum to Bombay, for our yearly return to Kerala, we had stopped off in Asmara and were strolling, my parents, sisters, and I, towards a famous cemetery. It was 1962 and the civil war that was to tear that country apart was just smoldering. Asmara was a lovely city, filled with light and the red soil of the Horn of Africa. "It's filled with urns that the Italians left there. And cypresses. You'll love it," the woman at the little pension where we stayed for our day in town had smiled brightly. "Enjoy!"

The chauffeur in the blue car had driven us this far and then, as appa had preferred to walk, left us to our own devices and sat, nervously behind the wheel, biting at the raw end of a cigarette, staring at the young things in their knee-length skirts, tripping by on the sorts of stilettos that two years later were banned from all aircraft. The metal tips to the heels were ferocious and punched down through the fuselage.

We had come across the monks at the entrance to the cemetery. It was clear that, unlike the driver, they had no interest in the gray-walled garden filled with young mothers, breasts bulging through cotton and Lycra; lovers in frilled skirts and tight white pants. The old monks were walking farther and farther away. All the way to Addis Ababa, I thought, to their monasteries and stone houses. I would never see them again. Not even the man who had looked up at me for an instant. I could live in that gaze I thought, as he walked past, those eyes dark, hooded, rimmed with skin the very same color as my own. He was an old man, and something in his gait reminded me of my dearly loved grandfather who had recently died. As the old man turned past me, I saw his feet, bound with cloth, more naked, more open to the air than those of the old man on Broadway.

I take tea with Paula at Cafe 112 a few blocks from the discount store where I bought Adam four pairs of multicolored shorts with drawstrings. I let him pick them out. They have "Pacific Trail" written on them and, in much smaller letters at the back, "Assembled in the Dominican Republic." Under the neon lights of the store, I shut my eyes. I imagine the small hands of girl-women bent over the cutting board, light streaming through a broken wall, the pittance that is paid in daily wages barely enough for rice and fish.

"Third World women have good hands," a fat man once murmured on a plane, staring at me. "All the batteries in my Hong Kong factories are put together by young women." His own hands, pale and be-ringed, lay folded on his lap.

"Meena," Paula broke into my thoughts. "I have no idea what it is you're complaining about." "Complaining?" "Well, you showed me Adam's new shorts and then you went on about the difficulty of writing. If you write the poems, and you've convinced me it's a great thing you do, keep at it. Otherwise . . ."

She stopped to sip at her tea, leaving the thought unfinished. Paula has a shock of close-cut hair. Years ago she used to play the French horn. She doesn't anymore. I am fascinated by what it might mean to make music in that way, seriously, obsessively, and then stop. Paula's hearing is far more sensitive than mine, the buses with loud brakes, the screeching ambulances on Broadway trouble her greatly. Sometimes on summer nights the lads playing baseball at 2:00 A.M. on the broad flats of 106th near Riverside startle her awake. She travels to Pakistan as often as she can. We discuss time zones, why it is that coming by way of Kennedy International Airport, sleep vanishes the instant you hit a futon on the fourth floor of Broadway and 106th; what becomes of the faded ink on visa stamps a decade old: does it vaporize, pass into the tainted air?

I turn to Paula, shifting a little in my seat, suddenly uncomfortable:

"There's all this stuff I'm scared off by. I don't mean *People* magazine stuff, the secret sex life of Donna and Marla and the TV evangelist-of-the-week gone to seed. I don't mean what you don't wear on your sleeve, but fear about."

"About what?"

"Well it's the difference between us. You lived on Long Island all your life and so it's not a big deal for you to pack your silk dress and make off to Hong Kong one week or Rawalpindi the next. But right from childhood I had these plane rides, train rides, back and forth, forth and back."

I stop. She is digging into her scone with the chocolate bits on it, her perennial breakfast. Always there's a fragment, large enough for a turtle or rabbit to eat, that she leaves over at the edge of the plate. Now she looks up.

"Well live it, tell it, that's all I can say. Your personal life, it's yours, not anyone else's. I have no idea how writers speak about themselves in this way. All the musicians I know have incredibly private lives."

She runs her hand through her hair. It's been over three months since Ronald had a go at it. He's been away on location cutting Isabella Rosellini's locks, somewhere, south of a border. Paula's been trying for years to get me to try Ronald, but I'm loyal to Mathilda, at the Bon Temps, a few blocks from here. I would miss her terribly if I left.

Under the buzz of the hair dryer Mathilda and I swap stories of things that count: how often you need to dye black hair once it's started to gray; Asian mothers-in-law and their strictures about the right conduct of wifely duties; what happened in the internment camps during World War II, the last a subject Mathilda keeps returning to, speaking full tilt as she washes the soap out of my ears, her fingers wet, as if it's the only time she can turn to a topic so hurtful.

"Two thousand dollars, can you imagine that, offering us two thousand dollars all these years later as restitution. Let them put it back in their own closets, I say." She sighs deeply. "We were born in this country. Second generation, what does it take?"

Listening to her, I too wonder out loud, then add: "You know, I came here ten years ago, married, very pregnant." "How thin you are now." She smiles approvingly. "Mathilda, my youngest is four." "Yes, yes I know. Straight at the back? Yes?" "Whatever you think." She picks up her scissors and continues:

"My sister always complained. She's very bright and beautiful. You know, perfectly manicured and shod and well able to take care of herself. Know what? In her office, when they bring in flowers, carnations, gladioli, they turn to her. She's Asian, they say. Asian women are good at that. Let her arrange the flowers. Now my sister, not a word passes her lips. Know what? She takes the whole lot into her office and dumps them into the vase, any which way. And marches straight out. Pushes the vase onto the front desk. They like her long black hair. The fact she never opens her mouth. If it was me..."

It's like that, Mathilda, I want to say, but the hair dryer is going in my ears, and Matilda runs her careful comb through my shoulder-length hair. They don't know what to do with us, exotic, Asian, border-line black. As she stops for an instant, I lean forward and hold her sleeve. I want to explain myself to her.

"I'm a poet," I say through the throb of the hair dryer, as if that might help. She listens closely. All sorts of people come to her, secretaries, computer whizzes, born-again folk, professors, housewives, doctors. "And sometimes I write lines about the city, rough and ready things, garbage cans, sidewalks." She smiles a little, pushing aside a plastic box filled with curlers. Then as she picks up the heavy hair dryer I press on.

"Not so long ago, I was giving a reading, wearing a silk sari as I always do at these things. Really, what else should I wear? A man comes up to me after the reading, he was one of the poets there, and says, 'You really took my breath away.' I wait, back against the books. 'Yes, really, you look so...' He stops. 'Well, you know, dressed in a sari and all that. But your words are fierce. Where do they come from?' I laughed, Mathilda, holding onto my body with both my arms. I couldn't stop laughing. The poet was so bewildered he started to back away."

I did not tell Mathilda that, in dreams that night, I heard my own laughter fill the bookstore. And as I laughed the books in that tiny shop started tumbling over. More and more books, little books, fat books, thin books, tumbling over me. My body shaking with black laughter.

*

I was crossing Broadway at 112th Street. A sudden rumble and the manhole cover in front of Citibank tore loose, and burst into the air, fell with a great clatter. Small flames rushed out of the black hole. The seller of old books, the merchant of worn clothes, the winos on the bench on the island, ordinary folks crossing Broadway, all looked dazed for an instant. Who had ever seen flames burst from the ground like that? Some of the shopkeepers darted out, worried, and the man who kept the shoe shop on the side ran and called the firefighters, who arrived ten minutes later in their gleaming red machines and peered into the hole.

Later I heard that other manholes had burst open in flames, one on 114th Street, one was on 145th Street, in Marie's neighborhood. As we sat together in Caffe Pertutti, Marie told me that a man had been blown out of his own bathroom window with the fury of the gas explosion. His neighbor downstairs was almost blinded in his kitchen. The portions of the first man's body could not be put back together. Because it had happened in a black neighborhood, no one cared too much. What does life count for, anyway, on the other side of the invisible fault line? Marie and I wonder out loud.

With Walter, I frequently lunch at Pertutti. Our conversations help keep me going. This time round we speak of the rat man. "Walter, this guy came to visit from the Department of Infestation."

"Rats, Meena, surely you don't have rats?"

"No, it was a mouse really. Sometimes several little mice. The lady next door screams off-pitch at the slightest whiff of a mouse. I was worn out with all the excitement so I called up the City Bureau of Infestation. This guy came with bright blue eyes, early fifties I'd say, a gold chain round his neck. 'I have come from the Department of Infestation,' he said."

Walter was listening intently now.

"I can't bear it," I add. "It's all bursting in my head. The rat man."

"You should read the Rat Man. Do you have it?"

"No, you know I'm scared of Papa Freud."

"Well, let me bring it for you. No, I'm using it in this course I'm doing at NYU. There's a book about Freud and the Rat Man, let me bring it to you. Okay?"

"Okay. It's all prose. I feel so excited, like a child getting at prose. And illicit really. Don't tell. Promise. Cross your heart, et cetera."

"Of course I won't tell. Who should I tell that you're into prose these days?"

"Black leather, whips, slashes, crosses, urine." I laugh merrily into my wine. I do not look through the glass. I do not notice the old man, cardboard tied to his thighs, who approaches. He has lost his shelter outside Dynasty. He carries himself as best he can in the sudden cold, more cardboard stacked on his back.

It is warm in the cafe. Once, for the purpose of an essay I had to write, I made believe I had met Talal at Caffe Pertutti and conducted an elaborate conversation.

I needed to make up that memory, which didn't exist, a conversation that hadn't occurred, for that was the only way that Khartoum could come back to me. I needed his spirit to listen to mine so the lost years might rise up again like mist between us, so I could live in the here and now of America.

The essay was for the Asian Writers Symposium at Cornell University. The topic was broad enough: Writing, Ethnicity, Being "Other" in New York. All the stuff that drives you up the wall till you realize that you are the wall you are driven up and what's doing the driving is the world's whip which you have taken so hard into yourself that you think it's your own hand holding the thing that's doing the hurting.

And perhaps it is and perhaps you have to rip the skin off. And perhaps that's what Gandhi did, rip his skin off, faced with British colonialism, and since that couldn't be literally done, he made a bonfire of all the clothes made with textiles from Manchester and Bristol and all those English spinning mills, a huge heap smoldering. And all the citizens of Bombay rushed out with more mill-spun clothes to burn, and everyone took to wearing khadi as my grandparents did.

O God, if we burnt our clothes, what would we be? Me and the old man down by Dynasty? What would we be who are our outsides merely? But the whip is not only within. The world exists and the world is bloody cold.

There was blood on the old man's lips when I saw him next, blood crusted over where the frost had bitten in.

It is warm, though, in Caffe Pertutti for an imaginary meeting, warm enough for a meditation about the bits and pieces of the world I have lived in, loved, and left, and about the multiple leave-takings that tore me apart till I turned into a skin-flicking thing, a pressure point for poetry. Sometimes I am filled with longing for Khartoum, for the rich, baroque sounds of the Arabic I used to speak. But the memory refuses to enter me.

"It is like a black hole in your head," amma complained last summer as we stood in the kitchen in Tiruvella. Sarojini was stirring the rice pot. There were bloodred onions rolling over the floor just as there had been in Kozencheri when my grandmother Mariamma was alive, and she skinned herself thinking her finger an onion. I had stared in shock at the rich red blood.

O grandmother Mariamma, where are you now, except in me? In me and us and her—she who has your name, the little milky-skinned child I gave birth to, my Svati Mariam who will never see you, but might touch her great-grandmother at the edge of these pages, at the edge of the desire that is her mother, a woman obsessed, scraping away at memory, using the bald knife.

"Meena, be careful with the knife." Amma was watching me like a hawk circling a wet chicken. "Why is Khartoum like that for you? I simply can't understand it! Nothing, you remember nothing."

"Amma, I do remember but it doesn't feel like real memories. Do you know what I mean? Real, raw stuff. None of that. Perhaps it's just that I'm scared, having covered it over for so long."

"Scared?" She gazed at me with the lovely dark eyes she inherited from grandmother Kunju who died before I was born. Amma picked up the little bone-handled knife to deal with the onions. She kept her silence. "The first thing a girl should learn is when to keep her silence," I heard her voice coming back to me from a lifetime ago. It made a black space in my ear, a savagery I could not yet decipher.

After the conference, I spoke about trying to remember Khartoum, about making up memories, about real places and how sense fragments in New York City. I flew back with my friends Kimiko Hahn and Jessica Hagedorn in a tiny twelve-seater plane, which took us from the Ithaca airport to LaGuardia. Kimiko and I had grown close to each other in the days our children were still babies and we would sit in a pile of diapers and baby food and swap poems with each other. In the plane, Kimiko was a few seats away. I sat across the aisle from Jessica, I laughed with her, saying, "Dear Jessica, here is what we are, almost sick to the teeth in this tiny plane, tossed up and down and sideways, crossing over, dressing up and down, pure postcolonial things!"

And she in her bold way, her hair sticking up over her head in straight lines, the leather jacket tight over her shoulders, laughed: ''I am imagining an Asian TV program in which we are all cast. I shall set you, Meena, across from Vivan. Really, think of it!'' As she spoke I clutched my hands to the sides of the seat and started to describe to her, in midair as the plane started falling and the hot fluids rose to my lips, the old man I had seen at Dynasty, the one with all the clothing tied to him, who carried his cardboard house as best he could on his back.

12. *Real Places or How Sense Fragments: Thoughts on Ethnicity and the Writing of Poetry*

What does it mean to carry one's house on one's back? I face myself squarely, wash my hands free of ink and think: the old notions of exile, that high estate, are gone; smashed underfoot in the transit lounges, the supermarkets, the video parlors of the world. The voice tricks itself. History is maquillage. No homeland here.

But another voice replies as if heedless of the full frontal, shoulders-squared-over bit: over and over again you fabricate a homeland, a sheltering space in the head. You can never escape into the ceaseless present that surrounds you. What you need, in Frank O'Hara's words, is "Grace / to be born and live as variously as possible."

In America you have to explain yourself, constantly. It's the confessional thing. Who are you? Where are you from? What do you do? I try to reply.

As much as anything else I am a poet writing in America. But American poet? What sort? Surely not of the Robert Frost or Wallace Stevens variety? An Asian-American poet then? Clearly that sounds better. Poet *tout court*? Will that fit? No, not at all. There is very little I can be *tout court* in America except perhaps woman, mother. But even there, I wonder. Everything that comes to me is hyphenated. A woman poet, a woman poet of color, a South Indian woman poet who makes up lines in English, a postcolonial language, as she waits for the red lights to change on Broadway. A Third World woman poet, who takes as her right the inner city of Manhattan, making up poems about the hellhole of the subway line, the burnt-out blocks so close to home on the Upper West Side, finding there, news of the world.

News of the World

We must always return
to poems for news of the world
or perish for the lack

Strip it
block it with blood
the page is not enough
unless the sun rises in it

Old doctor Willi writes
crouched on a stoop
in Paterson, New Jersey.

I am torn by light

She cries into her own head.
The playing fields of death
are far from me. In Cambodia I carried
my mother's head in a sack
and ran three days and nights
through a rice field

Now I pick up vegetables
from old sacking and straighten
them on crates: tomatoes
burning plums, cabbages hard
as bone. I work in Manhattan.

The subway corrupts me
with scents the robed Muslims sell
with white magazines
with spittle and gum

I get lost underground

By Yankee Stadium
I stumble out
hands loaded down
fists clenched into balls

A man approaches
muck on his shirt
his head, a battering ram
he knows who I am

I stall:
the tracks flash
with a thousand suns.

O confusions of the heart! O thicknesses of the soul, the borders we cross tattooing us all over! Is there any here beyond this skin-flicking thing where we can breathe and sing? Yet our song must also be a politics, a perilous thing, crying out for a world where the head is held high in sunlight. So that one is not a walking wound merely, a demilitarized zone, a raw sodden trench marked out with barbed wire.

Frantz Fanon, that great, tormented man whose work I have long loved—I read first in Khartoum, then in India, each time with a shock of recognition—speaks of the dividing lines, the barracks, the barbed wire that exist in a colonized state, of the "zone of occult instability" to which we must come in our art, our culture of decolonization.

In America the barbed wire is taken into the heart, and the art of an Asian American grapples with a disorder in society, a violence. In our writing we need to evoke a chaos, a power co-equal to the injustices that surround us. A new baptism. Else even without knowing that we are buying in, we are bought in, brought in, our images magnified, bartered in the high places of capitalist chic. I think of Bulosan's powerful novel I am reading these days, *America Is in the Heart*.

Wallace Stevens is a poet I treasure. His lines often repeat for me in the mind's privacy. Somewhere he speaks of the imagination as a violence from within that presses against the actual, the violence from without. But Stevens's world is not mine. Aware of the symbolist aesthetic that nourished him, mindful too of the deadened eroticism, a big-built white man who works in a well-paid insurance job in Hartford, Connecticut, wearing "suitboot," as we say in Indian-English, to work and at home, I turn to him and say: we acknowledge your power but turn your insight around. It is our bodies that press against the actual of America, against the barbed

wires and internment camps and quotas and stereotypes of silent
women with long black hair sticking flowers in neat vases. We need
the truth of our bodies to reach what ethnicity means, what the imagination must work with. And to get to this real place we need
the bodily self, we need a speech that acknowledges rage, a postcolonial utterance that will voice this great land.

But my pain persists, my difficulty. A line of poetry from Whitman's "Song of Myself" keeps running through my head: "To be
in any form, what is that?"

I keep up the imaginary conversation in a real cafe. My spirit
resounds in vacant space. I touch the wiry bounding line of the imaginary.

"Suddenly as I sit here I feel the whole thing might shatter on
my head."

"Thing, what thing?"

"The whole bag of tricks, everything."

My listener leans forward: "Tricks?"

"Sure."

"I'm waiting!"

"Well..." I take a deep breath here. "Are you sure you want
to hear?"

"Of course, why else would I ask?"

I try to recall Khartoum. These days it is broken down by disease and warfare, the three towns that span the Nile turned almost
into a refugee camp. Food is incredibly expensive for ordinary people. Famine is endemic in large pockets of the country. I need to
evoke Khartoum so that my own mind, my memory is not like the
Aswan High Dam, covering up the landscape in tons of water.
Perhaps in this great city by the Hudson River where the whole
world swarms, I can map out a provisional self, speak to someone
who lived there when I did, and, by virtue of this imagined speech,
remember.

But is it memory I am talking about?

I am a little frightened, for if I do recall those years, where will
I put it? It? Them? How silly to speak as if years, a life, a fragmented
ethnicity might be arranged as blocks on a parquet floor, or a row
of toothbrushes in a tidy Upper West Side bathroom.

I turn to my new-found friend. I move his teacup a little to the side. He watches my fingers. In speaking to him I must try and be as clear as I can. Set out the steps. After all, there is only so much of the unknown the mind can tolerate. I take a deep breath:

"It's as if in all these years as a poet I had carried a simple shining geography around with me: a house with a courtyard where I grew up in Tiruvella. My mother's ancestral house with its garden, a single street in front that runs all the way to the old Mar Thoma Church, palm trees, a few buffaloes ambling in the heat. And near the courtyard where the vine is, a well with clear water. And near the well a guava tree with rich freckled fruit. And always the cries of playing children, or women bending over to thresh the rice. And this picture was something I would pick up and turn to the light and pick up and set out for myself in times of trouble, as if to say, ah, there, there it all was.

"And because it was, I am whole and entire. I do not need to think in order to be. I was a child there, and here I am, and though I cannot find the river that brought me here, yet I am because that was. And this stubborn, shining thing persisted for me. It has done so for so many years. You know it's in my poems too. In 'Poem by the Wellside' for instance. You've read that?"

He says nothing; asks:

"And now?"

"Now? How do you mean?"

"Well isn't that what all our conversation is about? How something has happened to you now?"

I feel uneasy. Almost as if the air has become harder to breathe, ever so slightly hurtful to the delicate membranes of the nose, the soft fleshy places of the mouth. I would like to get up and walk around, but how can I? After all the tables are quite close to each other and this is a cafe, a civilized meeting place, not a rough field by the dog pen in the lower depths of Riverside Park. I make do by pushing my chair back so that the wooden legs scrape against the white painted wall.

The pot of Earl Grey with the thin thread dangling from the rim of the pot is almost empty. My companion is drinking coffee. I sense that he is waiting for me, though his eyes are turned towards the plate glass window. From where he sits he can see past the menu hung on the window, past the potted rubber plant and down through the metal bars that shoot up, preventing passersby from toppling into the subway. I do not think he can see the newspaper kiosk with a young woman from Saurashtra inside it, her hair neatly pulled back with a clip. I do not think he can see the cardboard shelter the old man has set up, but I suspect he knows it's there.

"It was terrible. I got stuck once." Without meaning to, I repeat myself:

"I got stuck. I can still feel it here." I point at my chest, above the sari blouse I'm wearing.

"Right there, it caught me between the ribs. All the way down. One breast on each side."

I smile in lopsided fashion, my hand trembling slightly on the teacup I have picked up. The cup is empty now.

"What are you saying?"

"I was stuck on the train once. I dangled there, right in the middle, one foot in, one out, bisected by the rubber-padded metal. The doors closed on me. Clamped shut."

"I approach and then they close," I murmur under my breath.

Four young Latino men pushed and shoved and poked me free. How strong they were, and excited with the task. It was an easy enough job for them, with just the right element of controlled danger. Wonderful strong arms. It hurt though, for days afterwards, right down the middle.

"I felt I was cut down the middle. Bisected where the heart is. Bisected! Is that the right word?"

I continue, needing to explain myself. I do not want to lose my newfound friend. I am fearful lest he think me a little off. Off what? Where is the center after all? But I am sometimes nervous of what people think of poets, creators of that small despised art. The mad fruits of bourgeois privacy: is that what he'll think? He must hear me now. After all, this knowledge is for others too, all of us together. So I pick up a little of the torn fabric and try to lay it out. There are so many strands all running together in a bright snarl of life. I cannot unpick it, take it apart, strand by strand. That would lose the quick of things. My job is to evoke it all, altogether. For that is what my ethnicity requires, that is what America with its hotshot present tense compels me to.

But there is a real problem for me. What parts of my past can I hold onto when I enter this life? Must I dump it all? Can I bear to? I cannot forget that reading Emerson as a young woman in India I was fascinated by his notion of a perpetual present. Of the centuries as conspirators against the freedom of the soul. Where I come from there was nothing that was not touched by hierarchy and authority and the great weight of the centuries. It was only after I got here that I read the bitter, fierce words of Frederick Douglass and Harriet Jacobs, Toni Morrison and Audre Lorde, and stitched together that pain with the postcolonial heritage that is mine as an Indian woman, the sense of English I got from Sarojini Naidu in India in her struggle during the Nationalist years, or more recently Ngugi wa Thiong'o in Kenya.

There is a violence in the very language, American English, that we have to face, even as we work to make it ours, decolonize it so that it will express the truth of bodies beaten and banned. After all, for such as we are the territories are not free. The world is not open. That endless space, the emptiness of the American sublime is worse than a lie. It does ceaseless damage to the imagination. But it has taken me ten years in this country even to get to think it.

It was in America that I learnt all over again about the violence of racism and understood that a true poetry must be attentive to this. It must listen and hear. Our lines must be supple enough to figure out violence, vent it, and pass beyond.

The cafe is much hotter now. More cigarette smoke in the air, the lunchtime crowd arriving. My companion leans forward across the table. He is watching me closely. What I have written out I have not said to him. I think to myself: all he knows of me is the loss of the shining picture I began with. I track back to the subway line, the train doors slammed shut on my body.

"It had to be the F train I was stuck on. I was hurrying down after a book party at Gotham's, trying to get to Hunter in time for a meeting. It was April 3, I remember. The whole furor about Salman Rushdie had broken loose, the ayatollah's fatwah and all that. Rushdie had gone into hiding. We had arranged a meeting at Hunter that I was to chair. After the chitchat in the high room at Gotham's, after the wine and the sweet talk of poetry surrounded by photos of the great ones, Faulkner, Hemingway, Beckett, and a single shot of Bette Davis with those stunned, dilated eyes, I had fifteen minutes left. Fifteen minutes in which to make it to 68th and Park. Hence the rush and the F train. I was trying to take the F train. Does that sound right?"

"Yes?"

My listener is courteous still, but hesitant. As for me, I hardly know how to go on. Pondering the F train in that crowded cafe, my mind slips. There are many sorts of death for a writer I think. Not just literal loss of life. Forgetfulness of the body can also be a death.

If I live here and write mellifluous lines, careful, obscure lines about the landscape by the Hudson, trees and clouds and all that and forget my bodily self, our bodily selves? Or if I write dazzling, brilliant lines filled with conjuring tricks, all the sortilege of postmodernism and forget the body, what would that be like? Didn't Baldwin say somewhere that being a Negro was the gate he had to unlock before he could write about anything else? I think being an Asian American must be like that. Through that bodily gate the alphabets pour in. This is our life in letters.

We have been in the cafe for over half an hour. The woman from Eritrea—I reckon we are roughly the same age, she is part-time waitress, part-time student at Columbia—has come our way. She refills the cups. She sets down a fresh pot of hot water. I admire her delicacy, her business-like sense of the job at hand, taking orders, filling cups, all the while making sure that someone at a faraway table isn't beckoning, or a glass of water about to topple over. Seeing her careful, methodical hands arrange the cups, bring fresh paper napkins, for mine is all moist and almost shredded, I take heart. After all I have come this far. And now I have to think it, spell it out. I have to become what I am—face the unbidden force of an ethnicity, here, now in America. I touch my fingers to the metal teapot. The heat, fierce tho ugh it is, consoles me.

"That picture I spoke of? It's all shattered. Into tiny little bits. It doesn't work anymore, not even as a backdrop. In any case what is there to drop back: inside/outside, mind/body, East/West, I don't understand that stuff any more. What is, is all around. Here. Now."

I throw out my left arm in slightly exaggerated fashion and narrowly miss the chair behind me. He listens hard, leans back in his chair. I press on.

"The awful bit is I'm not clear how to go on. I have to figure out a new way, a way that I share with lots of others here. Otherwise I may as well dump it all down the drain, rhymed syllables and all."

I point to where the busboy is clearing away cups, slopping them in hasty fashion down the metal sink hidden behind the platters of delicacies, kiwi torte, Spanish confection, black cherry tarts, baklava. I persist:

"It worked for a while and quite beautifully. It was a usable past for me in poetry. It was a sure thing when it worked, an ethnicity evoked, a past that took the form of an ancestor, a grandmother figure as in all those poems in my book *House of a Thousand Doors*. She came to me in image after image, a female power allowing my mouth to open, allowing me to be in North America. But then—it was like getting stuck on the train and almost being cut down the middle—I realized with a brutal shock the real place I am in. I wanted to tear myself free from that past. It had sucked me back in a vortex I could no longer support.

"It's all exploded now into little bits: house, courtyard, well, guava tree, bowl, pitcher. Just words really like subway track, newspaper, bread, water. And as for courtyard, it's the bricked-in square at the back of the apartment building with 'Death Razor' scrawled on in bright red ink. The super's teenage son did it one hot summer night filled with impossible longings for Florida. And the letters won't wash off. As for me, what do I have? An ethnicity but no past? Kaput. Finito. Katham. End of her story!"

At this point I'm fit to weep. And perhaps he senses it. Because he doesn't say anything about my picture having been a lie, or sheer flimflam or anything like that. What does he say? What can he say?

I want to turn to him and ask, am I American now I have lost my shining picture? Now I have no home in the old way? Is America this terrible multiplicity at the heart? Having broken from the old quick step, the old one-two, is there nothing but this dazzling quickness, this perpetually shifting space shot through as silk is with iron in ancient forms of torture, innumerate, multiple anchorages, breathless exhilaration, the only home we have at the tail end of this century?

I sit here asking all these questions as my listener vanishes and I keep repeating onto paper, writing in electronic letters, a dazzling, unreal marginality in praise of the only territory I can find in an island city filled with brilliant towers and burnt-out blocks, Häagen Dazs and Frusen Gladje and vomit in the subway stops where the poor still sleep.

But as my shining past fractures, never to be reassembled, ethnicity enters. And with it a different sort of priority. Perhaps one that is more fitting. So I wear it as I descend the underground steps and feel this too is mine, this purgatory, this presence.

My ethnicity as an Indian American or, in broader terms, an Asian American, the gateway it seems to me now to a life in letters, depends upon, indeed requires, a resolute fracturing of sense: a splintering of older ways of being, ways of holding that might have made the mind think itself, intact, innocent, without presumption. Now it may well be, indeed it probably is the case that talk of wholeness and innocence and all that really doesn't make sense, or if it does only as a trope for the mind that casts back wherever it is and whenever for a beforeness that is integral in precisely the ways that only a past can be. After all it is in the very nature of a present time to invade, to confront, to seize. It is the present that bodies forth otherness.

But does this mean that faced with the multiple anchorages that ethnicity provides, learning from Japanese Americans, Chinese Americans, Filipino Americans, Mexican Americans, Jewish Americans, African Americans, Native Americans, and, yes, Indian Americans, I can juggle and toss and shift and slide, words, thoughts, actions, symbols, much as a poor conjurer I once saw in the half darkness of the Columbus Circle subway stop? Can I become just what I want? So is this the land of opportunity, the America of dreams?

I can make myself up and this is the enticement, the exhilaration, the compulsive energy of America. But only up to a point. And the point, the sticking point, is my dark female body. I may try the voice-over bit, the words-over bit, the textual pyrotechnic bit, but my body is here, now, and cannot be shed. No more than any other human being can shed her or his body and still live.

And this brings me to the next point about ethnicity in America. While indeed at times it comes into being as a fracturing of sense and a play of surfaces, valuable, viable, for after all the old nostalgias have gone, and a vivid multiplicity prevails, there is something else that underlies, gives the lie to the sortilege theory incipient in the American sense of the present: that each thing counts as much as anything else, that you pull off your sari and put on your jeans, paint your eyelashes at Bergdorf's and that's that. That's not that.

Ethnicity for such as I am comes into being as a pressure, a violence from within that resists such fracturing. It is and is not fictive. It rests on the unknown that seizes you from behind, in darkness. In place of the hierarchy and authority and decorum that I learnt as an Indian woman, in place of purity and pollution, right hand for this, left hand for that, we have an ethnicity that breeds in the perpetual present, that will never be wholly spelt out.

So that the deliberate play of poetry, the metamorphosis of images that we prize, throwing things up in the air and changing them, a dove out of an empty cup, cabbage from bootsoles, a comb out of a throat, charged images that discolor against the plainness of our daily lives, is only one small part of the story, a once shining truth all broken up and its bits and pieces turned into sequins on a conjurer's sleeve.

The bigger hunk of what needs to be told, where the bleeding footsoles are, where the body is, comes with rage, with the overt acknowledgment of the nature of injustice. The struggle for social justice, for human dignity, is for each of us. Like ethnicity, like the labor of poetry, it is larger than any single person, or any single voice. It transcends individualism. It is shaped by forces that well up out of us, chaotic, immensely powerful forces that disorder the brittle boundary lines we create, turn us towards a light, a truth, whose immensity, far from being mystical—in the sense of a pure thing far away, a distance shining—casts all our actions into relief, etches our lines into art.

13. Narrow Gate

*I*t's hard to pick one's way out of Manhattan with two little children, oddments of baggage and toys. But the roads glisten in the quick rain and out the cab window, the hurtle of life on 116th Street and Lenox Avenue, the shops where they sell hair from Tirupati in vast quantities, rough, black human hair for wigs, plastic flowers, silk bouquets, all washed in wind and rain, offer a foretaste, a glimpse, of the pleasures of sheer motion, to the migrant poised in the car, children clutching her, the metal body on wheels moving swiftly. And she is filled with hope that two days away, another street, other windows, other rain-drenched roofs will welcome her.

The old exilic notions are gone. In the blur of returning, in the back and forth of this crisscross life, it is the multiple anchorages that count, the holding game. Then, thirty-six hours after leaving Kennedy Airport, the small Indian Airlines plane circles over the seashore. From the plane window she sees the Arabian Sea foaming at the edges, the sharp green of the coconut palms, water glinting in the ponds, the red soil cut and shaped into spaces for a hundred thousand habitations. In the long circling fall of the plane, controlled by wingspan and engine power, she holds tight to her child's hand and breathes again, slowly, ever so slowly, as if beginning again, all over again. Then come the hot embraces, the four-hour car ride from the Trivandrum airport, past rubber plantations and paddy fields, past the signs of hammer and sickle raised in the clear air, and hundreds of red banners flying. At the stone gates to the house she almost stops breathing in excitement, and then, when the car stops, she helps the younger child out the door then walks ever so slowly to her father's bedroom. He lies there on the bed, half raising himself, waiting for her. Her mother stands behind, worn out with the travel in the car, watching them both. The little girl-child is worn out now, whimpering a little. Two sisters come out to embrace the children. They leave the small child with her mother, but lead the boy away, into the cool back bedroom, the veranda, the silent courtyards of childhood.

As I embraced my mother on arrival, I noticed the gathering gray in her hair, the lines on her forehead etched more firmly. Age, the distress at appa's illness, had done this to her. But all her daughters were in the house now, finally, and her two grandchildren too, and that gave her pleasure.

Anna, my middle sister who had returned to India at the age of thirteen, who had studied in Pune and Delhi and Paris, and now taught French, was at home. And with Anna had come her manuscripts of poetry, her canvases and oils. Elsa, my little sister, ten years younger, only eight when she had returned to India, was here too. She had also studied in Pune and Delhi and now was doing research in Indian history at Madras University, writing a master's thesis, examining the documents of the Nationalist movement and the special involvement of Kerala Christians. Her focus on family history was a great help to me. She was looking at what lay behind us, at what had made us the family we were. For the first time in a decade, the three sisters had all gathered in the Tiruvella house. We were all aware of the fragility of our father's life.

I wanted amma to speak to me about the past, and so often of an evening I would try to draw her towards the cool stone parapet that ran along the outer veranda. We could sit there, I thought, and breathe in the fragrance of the incense flowers, hear the birds cry out in the mango trees, and out of the distant gate catch glimpses of the dark buses that drove past on what was now the busy Kottayam–Mallapally road. Perhaps then she would talk to me, of her life, of our lives together. But it was so hard to get amma to stop moving. Her days were filled with a woman's work, keeping a household running. Sometimes I walked with her through the house as she measured out the rice for lunch, or checked to see whether the linen had been ironed, the mangoes well cut, the fishman paid off, the buttermilk cooled as it should in the icebox, the grandchildren well pleased, with lumps of jaggery or cupcakes in their fists. Once I held onto the edge of her sari as I had done so often as a child: "Come, please come with me," I coaxed. "Please, otherwise the guests will come or the children will call out and it'll be impossible."

She had learnt so well the constant necessity of turning away from oneself towards others, having just a few minutes to rub together to kindle a small fire for the mind to warm itself by, that she barely listened. Still, one afternoon, after a week of my efforts— something in my tone may have caught her attention, or perhaps it was just that she had half an hour or forty minutes at her disposal, a cool square of time that she could fold or open up as she pleased—amma was persuaded to sit with me on the the the stone parapet and stare out at the incense tree. She laughed a little, adjusting her palm against a glass of cool buttermilk she had brought with her from the kitchen.

"So what is all this, mol? What can I tell you?"

I instantly regretted my high-pitched flurry a day earlier, just as lunch was being served. Voice pitched too high, as if I had ridden the subway too long, I had burst out against the decorum of marriage my mother had brought me up with. Still, it gnawed at me. I had burst out with something like, "Really amma, admit it now, if you're a woman, in order to exist, you have to marry. You know that yourself. So how did you feel when your own marriage was arranged?"

Clearly my words lacked grace. There was no way for my mother even to conceive of being without marriage. She was gentle, though when she turned to me and reworded her earlier thoughts, which she had voiced and which I had tried to brush off: "Look at you now, a married woman with two children. How can you speak like this?"

"But, amma, think of the cruelty that occurs when women don't marry."

Inching my fingers towards her on the parapet, feeling the smooth stone under my fingertips and palms, I spoke of those close to us and added, "I think cousin Sugatha is the only person I know who was really made happy by an arranged marriage. At least she seemed happy then with her gold slippers and her Captain of the President's Guard and the band at her wedding, and elephants and crystal gifts and the innumerable children sprinkling rosewater outside the church while the children of the very poor stood outside."

''Meenamol, what has happened to you? I thought it was all going well for you in America with David?''

''I suppose it is, in a way, but that doesn't stop me from thinking, does it? Or thinking of how all those dreams of a man, just the right man with just the right blood and the right background and property, can hurt and tear a woman's skin. Amma, I never told you this, but those dreams of an arranged marriage almost destroyed me. I wanted David to carry me into that land, a house, an old family, property. 'No one in my family has owned property,' he said to me. 'We are Jews after the Holocaust.' Amma, can you imagine that?''

I laughed a little, then stopped, seeing her worn hand tremble on the glass of buttermilk.

''Let's talk a little while the children are playing,'' I said to her. ''Can we?''

She started to speak, halting now and then, as if unsure of her words. I wonder if it was in her mind how her own mother had refused countless offers of arranged marriages and waited till she had met Ilya. Grandmother Kunju had forged ahead in her own life, received an master's degree from Presidency College, Madras, worked as the National Secretary for the YWCA, worked in the Nationalist movement. But what kinds of pain had my grandmother known, refusing as she did the traditionally sanctioned dream of waiting for a man, a perfection no woman could be without? When she married it was relatively late in her life, to a man of her own choice. And my grandmother had never borne male offspring. But then her daughter, who had led a life sanctioned by culture and ceremony, agreeing to a man of her father's choice, at the right time, in the right place, she too had lacked male offspring.

As I sat beside amma on the parapet, it came to me, like a petticoat string that cuts into flesh, like a metallic piece in a too-tight brassiere: the only way I had been able to make my way back into this house, into this family, was by marrying and having children. Somewhere at the back of my mind when I had married David, the thought had risen, like a dim, somewhat suffocating mist: Yes, this is a man from another country, not what they would really want, but now you can go home, you can face your parents. How that knowledge, when I had finally faced it, hurt me. And all around me in Delhi, those days in the very late seventies, the women's movement was active. My friends, Madhu Kishwar and Ruth Vanita of *Manushi*, were in the forefront of organizing against the spate of bride burnings that were taking place. As adult women we were facing the reality of women in arranged marriages—housewives and government workers, college lecturers and doctors, all young women married in accordance with their parents' wishes—who were being burnt to death when their families of origin could not meet the demands for extra dowry. An exploding stove here, a burst can of kerosene there, matches that mysteriously caught flame when held to a dupatta or sari pallu.

Living in Delhi in those days amma had heard of the deaths and was deeply shocked. Sometimes she would have little arguments with appa who returned home tired from work.

"Dowry is a terrible sin, you know. Really. The bishops are taking a stand against it. The Metropolitan will make a statement soon, banning it. But will our people change?" He had listened quietly as he removed his shoes and settled down with a cup of tea. I wondered what was in his mind. And sometimes amma spoke to me.

"It's not poverty, you know that, child. It's all this craze for money that's sweeping ordinary lives. People want a fridge from here, a scooter from there, chiffon saris from the other place. Also it's in Delhi. I have never heard of such things in the south. This is a Punjabi thing. But those poor, poor girls." Her cousin who was sitting there nodded her head.

"But, amma," I had persisted, "you know, in your days there were wells. Women jumping into wells." My aunt gave me a little stare and stirred her tea. Almost exactly my mother's age, she was educated at an old established women's college in New England and had returned, as befit a young woman of her social background, to an arranged marriage. My aunt and my mother were great friends and I knew that they sometimes shared news of young men and women from "good families" of appropriate blood and property lines, all of marriageable age.

"Amma, shall we talk now?" I wanted to start our conversation again before we were interrupted.

"Yes, yes, of course, you were asking me," she said, feeling comfortable again, casting back to our conversation the night before while putting the children to bed.

"Last night, just as Adam and Svati were falling asleep, you asked me such a curious question. How I got to Allahabad. I got there because I married your appa. You know that. And he was working there in the government service. Why else would I go north? Why did you ask me?''

What could I say? Why indeed did I ask her; why did I need it explained to me as if I were a teenager again? So I could have it hot and clear in her own words, the age-old reasoning of women from which I wasn't exempt? One went places by marriage. A feminine form of transportation and sanctioned well by culture. How else should a woman go places?

Earlier, at certain fragile moments in my life, I had been filled with fear at alternate possibilities. Without attachments I would shuttle back and forth, clutching at the toilet bowls in numerous international airports, lilac toilet bowls, white, blue, pink, gray; clutching the sides of metallic escalators, weeping, weeping into my own eyes. A few more years like that and I would be my own Aswan High Dam, burying my past in my own waters and I would never speak again for I would have swallowed my tongue in all that salt.

It had been hard living as a single woman in Hyderabad and, meeting David, I had felt that marriage, and the crossing of yet another border, might stitch me back into the shared world. So why should it seem strange to me that amma should marry a man she had just met once? David and I had decided to marry three weeks after meeting and we had immediately started on the task of packing up my books and papers and lugging them to the post office on Nampally Road. A crude enterprise. Amma at least had had custom and ceremony on her side.

Hadn't the meeting with her future husband taken place in her own father's house, arranged by relatives? Hadn't she served him sweetmeats at that first meeting, head decorously covered with the fringe of her muslin sari? All the proper ceremonies had been observed. And surely there was nothing to regret. What followed was life, in all its roughness and irregularity and if it tore one up a little as it persisted, graying the hair at the temples, etching wrinkles into the fine skin of the forehead, bleaching expensive silks, what could be done? And amma had been married off, as she was starting to tell me, with high custom and ceremony.

In my own case the memory of a small improvised marriage in the Hyderabad courthouse, no family present, just three friends as witnesses and the countless faces staring in through the barred windows at the blonde foreigner I was marrying, still worked a bitterness in my mouth. How thin I had been at the time, how pinched with the difficulty of doing it all by myself. Yet David had taken the major responsibility, going back and forth to the courthouse to get the permission for the Special Marriage Act that we needed. At first the clerk of marriages had refused outright. Did my father know? Did my grandfather? Did I have permission? Mohammed Akhtar pursed his mouth, dug in his heels behind the huge metal desk. "No, no, no." It had taken the intervention of a lawyer to get us the common right. And gradually, in the face of our persistence, the clerk of marriages felt his will corroded by pity. Once he glimpsed us hand in hand, David and I, crossing the busy street to the Blue Diamond Restaurant where steaming Chinese food was served. I used to live on fried chicken livers in those days. It was the only way I could keep the tension down. My time to get married had come and the dangers had to be braved. Appa and amma were in Delhi at the time and wanted nothing to do with the whole business. So David and I had arranged our own wedding, small, strange, abrupt, it seemed to me at the time. But the best we could do in the circumstances. Afterwards, in sheer delight at the whole thing being over, relieved, exhilarated at the sudden freedom we had caught a bus to Osman Sagar, found a room in a guest house, and then bathed the next morning in the clear opal waters of the lake, along with a goatherd and his small flock. David had lifted me up in the water and spun me around in all that blueness. Three weeks later, appa and amma had provided a grand reception in the Lodi Garden house in Delhi, complete with shamiana and hundreds of guests.

But the marriage itself, the wedding day, had been very hard on me. I had felt all the old dreams of feminine innocence broken into splinters. I had dressed for the event in a perfectly ordinary brown and white cotton sari, but Chirantan, one of our witnesses, a colleague of mine, said "Meena, whatever the ceremonial loss, it's unthinkable you should marry in that color. Go, put on some red." So I had obeyed his Rajasthani instinct and wrapped myself in a red kanjeevaram my parents had given me as a graduation gift ten years earlier. What had passed through Chirantan's mind? Did he pity me? For he too was adventurous, having ventured into North America, searching out Saul Bellow, interviewing him, asking him about the Jewish sense of things. Did he know that my father-in-law-to-be was a rabbi?

Chirantan in those days was a big, bustling chap in his early thirties. He consulted an astrologer on a weekly basis: it was cheaper that way, and more precise too. The astrologer could add corrections to fate, figure out the stars on a more consistent basis. Chirantan also had a graduate student come to him all the way from Haryana, a gentleman who wore off-white turbans, and whose thoughts were gradually taking the form of a thesis: "The survivor in Saul Bellow's fiction." Once, for no discernible reason, meeting in the corridor, this gentleman and I discussed the Indic position on fate. "This the Jewish perspective does not permit," he argued. I suggested he read the Abraham-Isaac story. Ilya had told me that tale again and again when I was a child, I felt it was filled with nothing but fate, that inexorable power that tangles with us, dissolving even desire into the black waters of death.

When I returned for the marriage ceremony in the courthouse, dressed in red, Chirantan had signaled his approval. "There, there, just as its written, Meena, it's all already written." Two years later he was dead of a cancerous tumor in the knee. Hearing of his death in America, the pity of it overwhelmed me. I thought of Chirantan who had helped me through the narrow gate of marriage, his kindness at the time.

"My father, your Ilya, felt I had reached the right age. The right age is very important, you know." Amma cast a sidelong glance at her three daughters, crowding around her on the parapet. The cool wind brought the scent of jasmine that grew in clusters by the side of the steps, and the delicate, more elusive scent of box that had blossomed on the far side of the well. Grandmother Kunju had planted that bush, Elsa explained to me one morning. I had forgotten that. Amma's voice continued:

"College was over and it was the thing to do. Those days no one consulted girls very much and my father wanted it. He was busy and getting old. Everyone wanted to see me married. I didn't know anything about your appa except that he was working in Karachi. I hadn't even heard of the Meteorological Department! Imagine that, a whole department dealing with the weather!"

My sisters and I leant against our mother, laughing together. Quite gently now, we teased her for marrying a strange man, for not choosing her own mate. She enjoyed the teasing. After all, the man was our father, and where would we be without him? He was behind us somewhere on the veranda, walking with slow careful steps, holding his head and shoulders straight, breathing hard. After the heart attack the doctor had asked him to walk as much as he could in the shelter of the house. Nowadays appa never stepped out, unless it was into the car that would take him to hospital for his checkup. He was too weak. A slight exertion here or there, opening a window too hard, pulling out a heavy book, a jot too much wind, and his blood pressure would rise, and he could feel his head flooding with blackness. But with care, things might be stabilized. His pacing comforted us, his wife and three daughters, all together now under the same roof.

"The real go-between for the arrangement was Oomechayen, my distant cousin, you know. He used to walk back and forth between the families with all the relevant news." I thought of my thin, pale, aristocratic uncle, dressed always immaculately in starched clothes, a gold wristwatch prominently displayed on his thin forearm. Imagined him walking in the midday heat between Kozencheri and Tiruvella, muttering as the passing bullock carts splattered him with the soft stinky stuff that bullocks let slip to ease themselves as they trot, mounds and mounds of coiled black stuff. Imagined him flicking his umbrella, wiping his cheeks with a silk handkerchief, muttering long strings of English conjugations that he so delighted in.

"Oomechayen was quite keen on the marriage, you know. In any case it would have been the joining of his two families and it was his duty as the eldest son-in-law. Then appa's father was interested. The next step was for me to be taken to Oomechayen's house so they could look me over. They must have approved of me. But I still hadn't met the boy. He was in Karachi at the time. Yes, yes, when he came for the first time to see me, he stayed on for lunch, which two of my own aunts came and cooked. Chicken broiled with spices, payasam, just a Kerala lunch."

I was puzzled. Did she talk to him?

"He wasn't shy at all. I thought he wouldn't eat, given the circumstances, visiting a new house and all that. But he had a good lunch and filled his stomach. I sat at the table, too, you know. He stayed for a little while. Ilya was anxious till the final word of approval came from the boy. Oomechayen brought word the next morning and within a few weeks I was married."

"Within a few weeks?"

"Yes, yes. Appa had already had an interview for going to England, and veliappechan was keen that he marry before going. What
if he should meet one of those Madamas! The whole family would
be ruined. The only son and all that. So the marriage had to be quick;
in any case no one wants these things to drag on. Nowadays, of
course, if people arrange a marriage with a boy in America, it can
take months for the boy to come. And who can tell how he's been
living there? In our day, of course, those problems weren't there.
Before a boy went abroad to study he had to be settled."

She paused a little and looked out into the garden, squinting
into the sun. Appa too had stopped his regular pacing. He couldn't
carry it on for more than ten minutes. He had returned to rest in
the side bedroom where their two beds lay, separated now, after
his last illness, by the rosewood desk and chair. It was easier that
way to get up in the night, fetch water or medicine, or set up the
oxygen cylinders if need be.

Through the bright haze of afternoon sun I saw the children.
Amma waved to them. As Adam raised his hand to wave back, the
makeshift swing wobbled precariously. They were on the swing
now, both my children, cramped in sheer delight onto the piece of
jackfruit wood Raju had wedged with rope and hung from the low
lying branch of the incense tree.

The incense tree dominated the front garden. Its smooth knobbled roots were visible for at least twenty feet around the tree, edged
out in one direction, where the driveway curved around to the
porch. It was as if the roots of the tree, which was planted just before my grandfather's death, had never managed to dig into soil,
but remained there, a visible frailty, clutching the earth. Yet there
was immense strength in the coiled woody stuff. Sap ran through,
and clearly there was a staying power that balanced the tree with
its great hood of glossy leaves and delicate clusters of beige flowers. After the flowers came the fruit. Hard incense fruit. The fruit
was treasured, for out of it could come other incense trees whose
bark, when stripped and burnt, would permit ceremonial offerings
to be made, in churches and temples and in places where the dead
are honored.

Before Adam was born, amma had written to me of the first blossoms of that tree. It had taken almost two decades of flower. It was March in New York when I got her letter describing the thick leaves, the pale petals of the flower parted at the glistening stamens. "The first blossom after Ilya's death," she told me in the letter. I knew she was wishing me well with the birth. Thousands of miles away, in a small sublet apartment on the Upper West Side, its walls jammed with little curios and keepsakes belonging to an old lady who had headed south to Florida for the winter, I leant against an old couch, read her writing on the flimsy blue air letter form.

That evening David took me to his mother's house for supper. After the meal, as others cleared the plates, I sat on Toby's brown upholstered couch and listened to Beethoven's "Moonlight Sonata," a piece I had loved for many years, ever since hearing it played in the concert hall in Khartoum, the hands of the pianist imported from Brussels for the occasion, tripping over the scales as outside on the streets and flat white houses the desert moon rose.

But in the moonlight imagined in my head it wasn't that North African desert town that came to me, but a garden whose every inch I had known in childhood, and at the heart of the garden, a tree with shining leaves and dipping blossoms I had never seen. I saw Ilya's hands planting the tiny shoot, Bhaskaran watering it, the coiled bark thickening year after year till the time for blossoms had come.

I was eleven when Ilya died after those terrible months of heart pain. "The heart is a muscle," someone once told me, "it cramps like anything else." I could not bear to weep for him, when he died. A hand as dark as incense bark shoved the pain inside me: when it trickled out, from time to time, there was an acid taste to it, as if iron had mingled with stream water underground, out of sight. Listening to that tinkling music in a room high above the Hudson River, I felt the old pain rise. But I had no strength to hold it in. The tears dripped down my cheek onto the blue pinafore a friend in Paris had lent me. I shut my mouth with both hands for fear I would howl, as a hyena might, for my home, my native town, a great tree blossoming in moonlight.

Sometimes I feel things not physically there, but feel them anyway and they hint at a truth, even if it's hard to unpack till years later. So it was with the tears streaming out as I sat on Toby's couch. I felt the actual tears; as they streamed down I felt them taking my skin off, ever so gently, with them. It wasn't just my skin they took off. It was also the topsoil, a ruddy brown color it gets in Kerala during the rainy season. The soil parted, and out came a sticky child, its hands clamped together with blood. I placed my trembling palms on my belly and shut my eyes tight. I saw an old man's body dance in the light and fall away, dissolving, making an aura all around the half-born child. I saw the child's hands making fists. Then his wet bloody head emerged.

Now he sat there, a stone's throw away from me in Tiruvella, squished next to his sister on a swing under the green leaves. I could hear him shouting at her, into the wind.

"What is it? Should I stop?' Amma had caught a curious look on my face. "No, please, please go on." I didn't want amma's voice to stop.

My sister Elsa shifted on her knees and started laughing, boisterously. "You don't want us to hear your adventures!"

"No, of course I'll go on. A huge kotil was laid out for my marriage. Are you listening? Anna, Elsa, do you know the difference between a pandal and a kotil? A pandal has a flat roof, a kotil a sloping one. Both of course are thatched. A kotil was constructed. It ran from the old mango tree, remember where it was, over there."

"Yes, the tree Ilya knocked a nail into. It needed iron. The copper bracelets on it weren't working." I was impatient now.

She smiled at me. "My mother's sister, Amukochamma, arrived two weeks before the actual date. Also Ilya's sister, Chenagerileamachi. All the arrangements had to be made. It was the end of April 1947. The wedding was due to take place on May first. There was no water to be had. The well here was all dried up. The water had to be carried all the way from the Mar Thoma Church in Kuttapuzah in buckets and brass pitchers, and it was stored in urns in the kitchen and all the side verandas. A whole row of shining urns, imagine, on the veranda."

She raised her delicate hand and conjured up the invisible urns, filled with clear water in preparation for her wedding.

"The lunch was the usual sort." Amma's voice was going on. Behind her the crows were droning on in the guava tree.

"Usual. I don't know what that means." I laughed to hide my confusion. "Remember I was a child here, then slap-walap, it all went. I don't know about all the wedding stuff!"

*

For years, even when my life had taken me so very far away, I had had a fantasy of marriage. I saw myself married in the Mar Thoma Church down the road, feasting on all the savories and sweetmeats the finest cooks of Tiruvella could provide. I don't know quite where that longing had come from. After all, in those old days when Aswathy and I sat collecting silk and gold slippers, trying them on, curling out our toes to hobble over the cool verandas, our pavades tucked up so we wouldn't fall and shame ourselves, I was of a different opinion. I saw no benefit in marriage at all. The game rather bored me.

"Aaoiu, aiouo, kalyanithe pogeno?" Aswathy sang out in her lilting, high-pitched voice. She was quite clear about what she wanted. We shoved ourselves together under the roots of an old banyan that grew in her grandmother's yard and compared notes.

"I want lots of chappals, the silk kind you get in Seemati in Kottayam. And Benares silk and barfis with silver and gold on them. And shiny necklaces, ruby and diamonds." She prodded me in the side with her elbow. I was a little uncomfortable, though the games were sparked up when, pretending to be bride and groom, we tried on the chappals.

"But where would I put them, Aswathy?" I was worried about the huge number of chappals she wanted to collect. She giggled, not bothering to reply. "I want to have elephants too, at the marriage, a real brass band." Brass bands were all the rage. One had to travel as far south as Trivandrum to see a real one, and the instruments were polished, glinting, mixed up with shenai and mridangam too. After all, just to have trumpets and trombones would have been too absurd.

"Gold slippers. You wore gold slippers, didn't you?" Elsa challenged amma.

"I want to hear about the food. Let her go on," I interrupted, hoping I could restore myself. I felt all lopsided, unsure. The gold slippers were part of an impossible dream. Suddenly I felt tired. I longed for her voice go on and bathe me in the downpour of detail, all the fragrant solid things.

"There were three fish preparations: meen veyichede, meen patichade, meen varathade." The first is a Kerala delicacy, fish bathed in its own juices, moistened in a three-day marinade of tamarind and red chili. The second, normally made with tiny silvery fishes from the backwaters of the Arabian Sea, has mounds of coconut flesh, scraped into freckled bits, fried with turmeric and onions. The third involves a fleshy sea fish, swordfish or parrot fish, fried in a paste of ground spices and garnished with coriander.

"Then meats of course: both olothiede, curried, also a chicken. We had eriseri with lentils and ghee. Then papadam."

I imagined the rich gravy from the chicken, blended with yogurt, flowing into the vindaloo paste that basted the fiery lamb. Papadams, fried fit to pop, hoisted themselves over the edge of the banana leaf. The eriseri with lentils and vegetables was mellow, cooling, set in a little dish to the side.

"We also had cutlets and bread."

"European style?"

"Yes." She laughed, slightly embarrassed but also pleased at my remark.

"That was only for the guests, not for the housefolk. Of course we also had sambar, maure, kachimaure. All this and the meats and fishes had to be given to our friends and relatives, their servants and their families and friends.

"Yes, yes," she tossed her head. "We had lots of people to help. Manpower was not a problem in those days. Thoma and Bapu who had worked for Ilya when he was principal at the Mar Thoma Seminary came a whole month ahead. Bit by bit they started making all the arrangements. Of course my aunts and uncles oversaw it all. The house was overflowing."

"Where did people sit to eat?" Behind us, the large rooms filled with old wooden furniture, with teak and rosewood and mahogany, echoed in the silence. The children too were silent, off the swing now, picking at stones to make into a mound.

"The men sat in the kotil. Mats were laid out end to end, covering every inch of ground. Banana leaves were placed in rows on the mats. The women sat inside the house. In almost all the rooms the doors were flung wide open and the back courtyard too was filled with guests."

"Did people come from appa's side? Yes?"

"Bus loads of people. Who they were I still have no idea."

She was quiet for a minute. How bewildering it must have seemed as she washed her face, or sat at the edge of the mura to have her hair done, the aunt combing down the long black waves then poising them on the flat of her hand before tightening the heft. Did she murmur at all, my amma, did she ask, "All this, is all this about me?"

But the story was far from done and we wanted to hear more. In our impatience we pushed on. And amma was in the mood now to speak on. It was as if the past, released in her, was bubbling out. Curved around our mother on the old veranda, we were the very listeners she would have wanted. Once her own flesh rounded out, now broken free from her, we framed her words.

"Don't you want to hear what I wore?"

"You know I do." My voice seemed low, hoarse even to me.

"Of course, tell us, amma, tell us," Anna spoke. In spite of ourselves we were happy at the feast of silver and gold and brocade our mother would draw up for us, treasures of impossible weight, part of a forgotten story. Not one of us three sisters would enter that old world. But the imagination might draw us into it. The web of our mother's words warmed us as the chill monsoon wind started to blow.

"I wore gold. With pearls studded in. And a few rubies on rings and all that. But it was very simple, you know. My youngest aunt believed in a clear line of jewelry. Something simple and fine. I was in Tiruvella, so we had to send to Madras for the wedding clothing. I didn't choose the clothes, my aunt Sosakochamma did. Her husband was a professor of pathology at Madras Medical College in those days. She had time on her hands and was delighted to help. My own mother was dead, you know that."

She paused, looked at her hands. They lay quiet in her lap, clasped one in the other, a blue vein visible by the left wrist.

"I sent a blouse for size and she chose the saris. The sari I wore to church was white Benares tissue. The war was just over and the sari was considered very expensive in those days. With a brocade border and buttas. I had a silver tissue blouse to go with it. Yes, the chappals were quite lovely, a silver pair to match the brocade in the tissue sari. I had a gold pair as well. The manthrakodi was heavy gold brocade. We said that the boy's side need not bring it. Normally they do. They present it to the girl and she covers her head with it in church at the culmination of the marriage ceremony. But we said that they needn't. Who knows what their taste would be in these matters. And suppose it didn't please us? My aunts, your great-aunts you know, were a little nervous of the Kozencheri—

Raani people, your father's father's side. They were not as Western-
ized as we were and might go in for something rather gaudy. So
my youngest aunt chose the manthrakodi too."

I had seen the sari with the patterns of turquoise and blue and
sapphire let into the golden flowers that lit the pallu. I had run my
fingers over the little bumps in the brocade, set the fine silk to my
cheeks, and draping myself in it, I had stood in front of my grandmother's rosewood mirror. How dark the mirror had seemed with
the monsoon clouds passing through the bamboo grove, shutting
out the sun. I could hardly make out the contours of my own face,
or trace out my eyes, dark as amma's, that did the seeing. Only the
sari shone, as if the elaborate silk so many fingers had woven two
decades earlier had taken on a life of its own, shrinking my female
flesh that held itself upright within the coverture.

Normally the sari was kept wrapped up in muslin in my Kozencheri grandmother's rosewood chest. Grandmother Mariamma had
brought the chest with her as part of her dowry and now her only
daughter-in-law used it. The sari had lain in that chest, wrapped
up in elaborate tissues and lighter burdens of silks, studded with
coils of camphor that would help keep it from decay.

I wanted amma to take the sari out, let it see the common light
of day, let the breezes that blew in from the Arabian Sea waft over
it, let a little of the dust from the garden touch its golden creases.
Perhaps we could all sit there, in the sunlight, and look at it for a
minute or two, perhaps someday my little girl, born and bred on
the side streets of the upper west side of Manhattan would return
to this very house, this garden, to drape the brocade over her delicate brown hair and gaze into her great-grandmother's mirror. What
would that garment be for her? What would she see in that mirror?

"Well, in case you were wondering, I sold it."

Amma's voice butted into my daydream as we sat on the veranda ledge.

"Yes, of course it was gold tissue and fetched a good price. It
cost about five hundred rupees in those days. I sold it all two years
ago and got a lot of money. More than two thousand rupees."

"Without telling us, you sold it?" I leant forward, shocked.

"Yes, it was all discolored. A man came by to buy up gold and
silver brocade so I got him to weigh it all and sold it. I gave the
money to a missionary effort. I told appa, of course. It will build
a hospital or help towards a school in Nagaland."

Appa was beside us now. He had risen from his bed and returned to the veranda for some fresh air. He moved forward, slowly, anxious to put a word in.

"It was fine to sell it, but about that sari, I must tell you, her mother's people were all snobs. That's what they were. They wanted her to be covered in gold. Her father was a simple man. Only wore khadi. Even in church for her wedding that was what he wore."

"They were not snobs. You know that," amma retorted, bitten to the quick. "Why, they were even fond of you. Seven priests and the Metropolitan married us in the private chapel. There was incense and hours of prayers and you slipped the minu over my neck and there it hangs!"

She pointed at her throat. In the folds of her neck lay a chiseled gold thing, mangalsutra, icon of marriage. In rough weather, and her bond with him had led her through much of that, I often saw my mother's fine brown fingers twisting by her throat. And as her fingers tightened the gold thing disappeared into her fist.

My little sister Elsa leant forward quickly, her gestures precise as ever. She touched my mother on her trembling wrist. She wanted to set things right, get the story going again. As I got up to get my father some tea from the kitchen, I heard her ask about the wedding guests of forty-three years ago:

"There must have been Raani people too. Surely?"

Raani was in the hills, where my Kozencheri grandfather's brothers lived, all seven of them, with their fierce warlike brood. Almost without stop the Raani people spawned male heirs, then swooped down to get women for them. They were landowners in that rough red soil, infinitely fertile with coconut and areca nut. At night the Raani people sang hymns like everyone else, to God the Father, Jesus His son, and all the angels. The hymns turned into boisterous shouts, bordering on boxing songs or songs that are sung during the Onam boat races.

A week earlier, having just heard of appa's illness—several months after the crisis, word had got through by way of a baker's son who studied at Mar Thoma College across the paddy fields from us—the cousins descended on us. They came in jeeps packed to bursting with husbands, wives, children, even several grandmothers in their chatta and mundu, whose toothless mouths closed kindly over the fried bananas I served them, as they sat almost dozing in the assorted armchairs in the living room. The tiny male children raced around like wildfire, all over the kitchen, pulling at the cat's tails, trying to slam the geckos that were lazing in the kitchen heat into the flat of the walls. The young mothers, plump and well starched, watched over their daughters in starched frocks, and made sure husbands had enough to eat and drink. One or two came to help me in the kitchen, for they had chosen a moment to come when the two women who cooked for us, both named Aminey, who cooked for us were absent. Amma was far away, across the railway tracks at a prayer meeting.

Appa was tired, lay in bed, his blood pressure high. One of his Raani cousins, born almost the same day of 1921 he was, sat next to him, holding his hand lovingly, a grown man with glasses, weeping over his cousin-brother. I saw tears trickle down my father's eyes as I took the tea in. In the darkened bedroom they sat, the two men, silent now, having met for years only at funerals and baptisms. As young children they had spent summers together in Raani and Kozencheri. Pauloschayen had established a restaurant business on his return from years of work as an accountant in Dubai. He was modest, in spite of all the money he had amassed, and had plowed a large portion back into his plantations of rubber and coconut. Appa had studied, gone to England, joined the government service, his Kerala connections attenuated in all those years abroad, but still thick and dark as blood in a man's forearm. So he lay there, my father, propped up on pillows as I took in the tea, the tears on his face shining in the half light from the window.

Behind them, Pauloschayen's eldest son, probably around my age, sat quietly. He suffered from gout. The swollen legs had prevented him from traveling to supervise his restaurants and bakeries. He did what he could from home. My appa has no sons, only three daughters and I am the oldest. I am conscious of that often when I face my father. I must be to him a little of what a son might be, but how unequal I feel to that emotion that wells up in him at odd moments, especially after his illness, how useless I feel. Longing to be what my father would have wanted me to be, equal to his needs, to carry on his line, I wish for a moment what I have never wished before: that I might have been born male.

In the cool bedroom, I pulled a table up to the bedside and rested the teacups there. I arranged the plateful of Marie biscuits and the avalos unda and walked out. I left the three men alone in the quiet breeze that dipped the muslin curtains in the dim sunlight that fell on my father's face. I said nothing. In the living room, one of the Raani wives, just fresh out of Women's Christian College, Madras, was chucking her husband under the chin, popping a fried banana into his mouth. I stared at her.

Then I looked around for Elsa, my little sister. Where was she? I needed some support. She and Anna had refused to come out of the small side room that had been Ilya's study. The room was secure. To get into it, if the main door was locked, you had to pass through the master bedroom, and no visitors would do that casually. So they stayed there, letting me take care of the Raani people. Anna lived in Madras and taught French in a college. She wrote poetry. In her early thirties, she felt quite rightly that the Raani folk must surely regard her as odd, some sort of aberration, for not having married. It was a feeling I was familiar with, having felt that hot pang when, still unmarried, I had returned home many years ago to suffer under the gaze of gathered relatives.

Elsa, the youngest, was firm and clear. She had cropped her hair short in the new Madras style, wore jeans on most occasions, had little patience with arranged marriages, and said so quite openly. She was Anna's great friend and had obviously decided to keep her sister company in the inner room. Marriage was the stumbling block, the high threshold stone over which a woman might enter. And she would either walk or fall, bruising herself cruelly.

The Raani family had an elaborate system of connections, all readied in time for the marriage of a daughter—young men of suitable family background in Rourkela and Sagar, in Quatar and Lincoln (Nebraska) or even closer to home, in Vishakapatanam or Perumbavoor. The connections were established through an elaborate network of go-betweens and relatives and even neighbors aching to be in the family's good books. And at least at the outset the system had worked.

Each of the Raani daughters had been married off within a few months of graduating from high school or from college. After all, once a few months had passed while a marriageable young woman loitered between kitchen, drawing room, and the well side, anything might happen. Especially if she bound jasmine blossoms in her hair, or dried out her silks all alone by the hibiscus grove, fires might start crackling, tongues would wag, and not even the good

lord could prevent the consequences. Nothing but shame could en-
sue, household shame, female madness, death.

A week earlier Chackochen, a nephew, who had first received
the news of appa's illness, had been sent ahead to visit. A taciturn
man, he sat for an entire half hour in the living room, drinking his
coffee and saying absolutely nothing. His sister Nisha, a few years
older than I, had been married off fifteen years earlier to a man from
a good family and with a good job in a whiskey factory in Saskatchewan. But recently news had come of Nisha's husband's misdeeds,
his heavy drinking, and then of the beatings he inflicted on poor
Nisha, who had been forced to move in with the pastor of the evangelical church she regularly attended. The brother felt his sister's
shame, but what could he do? When amma inquired after Nisha,
his face grew tight.

"Who can say? In Canada, who can say?"

He could not forget he had approved the choice of Nisha's husband. Finally he softened, feeling how burdensome his silence was.
It was only appa, a man of few words, who had seemed to understand his relative's speechlessness.

"I've picked out three girls," Chackochen blurted out, referring
to his nephew who had just finished at IIT Bombay in electrical en-
gineering, "one after the other, all picked out, waiting for him."

"Good, good," appa murmured.

It was one of his easier days, when his asthma was not too
difficult and he was able to leave his bed and keep us company in
the living room. Chackochen's nephew had just been offered a job
in Delhi with BHEL and the thought of three girls, each dressed in
a bright silk sari, each with a college degree in hand, must surely
have been gratifying. Encouraged by his senior cousin, Chackochen
plunged in.

"And for the younger lad there's a girl I have in mind. It's not
a bad family but they fell on hard times and the mother trained as
a nurse. She went straight from Kuwait to Arkansas in America.
Of course, the girl may be a bit fat, I hear."

He leant forward slightly worried. It was a common perception
in Kerala that those who went westward grew fatter. It was the
general bonhomie, the good life in America. But on women weight
was no longer encouraged. Even the film stars in Kerala were fast
losing weight. The regular three hundred pounds, the old style of
beauty, much vaunted, much publicized through movies high and

low, was no longer considered desirable. It was rumored that even the actress who did the notorious *Avede Rathri,* which I had seen at the Lighthouse in Hyderabad, soft porn with its sequin-clad heroine, crawling on the floor, twitching all her parts, was considering losing a few pounds. Weight loss clinics and retreats using the ayurvedic formulations were springing up all over the state. "Kutianna," baby elephant, formerly an affectionate term for a lady of a certain girth, was no longer in currency.

"But who can tell?" Chackochen of the huge biceps and the catering business and the sister suffering in Saskatchewan, returned to the possibilities for his older nephew. "We still haven't set eyes on her, just photos. It's from photos and hearsay, all this."

"There are diets, everyone uses them these days. Why even the *Manorama* advertises one," amma pitched in, trying to show her concern, trying to show her Raani relative how within the bounds of reason his worries were.

"Well, we hope to settle it soon, both sons, perhaps a double wedding in Raani." He perked up at his own words.

This time, Chackochen had not come with the rest of the family. I walked through the rooms, making sure that food was on everyone's plate, that the children had not come to harm. Suddenly the doors blew open and amma entered, her arms laden with mangoes that the woman, in whose house the prayer meetings were held, had presented her. "There, there, give them to the grandchildren." And her eyes shining, she moved forward to embrace her relatives.

So she had arrived, my mother, gray hair flying out of her hairpins, arms laden with half-ripe mangoes, her white cotton sari with the blue flowers on it, drawn tight round her ample waist. The Raani daughters-in-law, her own age, fell upon her and embraced her. The eldest presented her with the elichi she had plucked with her own hands from the family plantation. "I shall treasure it," amma said firmly, slipping it into her silver paandaan that had lain empty awhile. In all the bustle at home, she had not had time to fill it.

That night, after the guests had left, and the children were asleep, something moved in me. I walked out of the bedroom, unbolted the large double doors, and entered the garden. As I raised my face into the night air, the stars wheeled in slow, languorous patterns that quickened as I gazed upwards, till dizzy with the pressure of that massive, frenetic light I stooped, and touched the knobbled roots of the incense tree.

It felt like something so old that it had no need any longer of the sorts of life we commonly trust, life filled with motion, volition, palpable heft. It felt like an iron slowness in the blood, elephant hide on an ancient temple wall. I sat on the ground, no longer conscious of the house behind me. I knelt, running both hands over the fine cracks in the earth near the incense roots. I touched my cheeks to the root cover. I felt a small ant crawl over my lips. I picked up a rough incense fruit, set it to my mouth, and tasted raw earth. I felt I needed the peace of a place where there was no more marrying, no more taking in marriage. And in bright moonlight, on the soil of my grandmother's garden, for a few moments I felt I had found it.

Returning to the house, I entered the drawing room and bolted the doors behind me, then walked over to the carved table and the silver box that rested on its surface. I pushed aside the elichi the Raani relatives had brought for amma and added to the box with the silver handle and the carvings of elephants and lotus blossoms, a rough dark fruit, the fruit of the incense tree on which my children had swung.

The next morning I stared past the swelling incense tree with its hard brown fruit, towards the gate. The front gate gave onto the Kottayam–Mallapally road and the buses were racing past. One, two, three, four. Children clambered up onto the ledge to watch them. The buses were racing towards the Tiruvella junction, right next to the old Syrian Christian Seminary where my parents had been married, where Ilya and grandmother Kunju were buried. Some of the buses would stop there, others would pause briefly in the traffic and race on. Now as the buses passed so swiftly with their bright red and green paint, with images of Lord Jesus or Lord Krishna painted on the front, the human faces that pressed out of the windows in a terrible crush, struggling to breathe, made a density of flesh that threatened to blow the metal frames apart, blow the painted gods into smithereens. Some of the travelers, the more intrepid ones, hugged the luggage racks on the roofs. One young man had cleverly roped himself on. Only his Hawaii chappals made of cheap pink plastic threatened to fall off, as the bus that bore him outraced the monsoon winds that swept off the Arabian Sea into our southern town.

II. Book of Childhood

Language shows clearly that memory is not an instrument for exploring the past but its theater. It is the medium of past experience, as the ground is the medium in which dead cities lie interred. He who seeks to approach his own buried past must conduct himself like a man digging. This confers the tone and bearing of genuine reminiscences. He must not be afraid to return again and again to the same matter; to scatter it as one scatters earth, to turn it over as one turns over soil. For the matter itself is only a deposit, a stratum which yields only to the most meticulous examination what constitutes the real treasure hidden within the earth: the images severed from all earlier associations, that stand— like precious fragments or torsos in a collector's gallery—in the prosaic rooms of our later understandings.

Walter Benjamin, *Berlin Chronicle*

14. *Dark Mirror*

What follows tells of trauma and memory, childhood and its forgotten past. A book contained within a book, held as darkness is held at the core of the jamun fruit.

I began this writing in New York City in the months immediately after September 11, 2001, and completed it, a lifetime away, in my mother's house in Tiruvella, a house swept by monsoon rains, scented by damp earth and wild jasmine. This is a book of slow, sometimes uncertain accretion that I have had to cut and polish into form. The destruction visited on the island where I make my home, a second home, tore open the skin of memory, made me start to write again. But to close this book I had to go back to India. I had to return to the house of childhood.

Sometimes I wrote by candlelight, for the power often fails in the monsoon season. Lightning strikes low and sheets of rain fill the air. Sometimes I wrote in the brilliant sunshine, in the aftermath of a storm at the edge of a garden, a green bowl flickering with tropical birds. Sometimes I wrote my way through nights that seemed akin to the darkness of childhood, a buried childhood which, in my own way, I have tried to recover.

But what of the book *Fault Lines* I wrote a decade ago? My aim is not to cross out what I first wrote but to deepen that writing, dig under it, even to the point of overturning one of the most cherished figures I created.

I have written in indigo ink. Trying through my own indirections to imagine the truth, for that is what art does.

If memory has finally brought me face to face with its dark mirror, with what for so very long I could not bear to hold in consciousness, with what I could never have chosen, then that too is part of what the imagination must clarify as sharp sunlight, over a southern landscape, after a monsoon storm.

We go back home and what do we find? When we go home, who lets us in?

Perhaps now, knowing what I do, the need to return that has haunted me will find absolution. In *A Berlin Chronicle* Walter Benjamin writes: "He who seeks to approach his own buried past must conduct himself like a man digging. . . . He must not be afraid to return again and again to the same matter; to scatter it as one scatters earth, to turn it over as one turns over soil."

If I have conducted myself like a woman digging, it is as a woman who has tried to understand that she must dirty her hands with mud and red earth and broken stones so that the splintered images of the past can shine through.

MA
New York City / Tiruvella
September 2001–October 2002

15. Notebook

When I was a child amma gave me a notebook. She passed through the curtain that separates the drawing room from the bedroom and set a rice paper notebook in my hand.

"Your grandmother Kunju had one just like it. She used to write in it each day. They say it is a good discipline."

Then amma shut her mouth so tight it made a mark on her forehead.

"Did you have a notebook?" I asked her. "Did you write in it?"

She shook her head hard.

My notebook was made of white rice paper, and on the front cover it had markings of the sun and the moon and the stars. On the back cover the artist had drawn rivers and bridges.

When I first got my notebook I kept it under my pillow, thinking I would write in it when the fancy took me. Sometimes I opened pages and to my surprise found them quite bare. Then I realised what had happened. I had written things down in my head for fear of putting them down in the notebook.

To help me get over the fear of things I could not write down, I had the idea of making a list of things I liked.

The idea for a list of things I liked was something I got from a book grandfather Kuruvilla read to me: *The Emperor Babur's Book About His Own Self.*

Under the heading "Pleasant Things of Hindustan" he made his scribe write down: masses of gold and silver; rains that make houses damp and wash them away; aandhi, darkener of the sky, wind that blows bearing so much dust that people are blinded, entirely.

*

I had never seen the darkness of an aandhi. But in Khartoum, at the age of five, I saw the haboob. Black umbrellas bore down from the Sahara, covering up the thin grass on the lawn, the leaves of the date palm, even the white egrets that made throaty cries, flying in from the Nile to strut beside the oleander bush. I stared out at high noon into the blackened sky and saw the whole of the visible world—tree, rooftop, sky—vanish in the blink of an eyelid.

Somehow the fact of the haboob reconciled me to the loss of an earlier life, the evidence of the senses lifted by distance, death, traumatic forgetfulness.

Mémoire, mémoire, que me veux tu?

I had to learn those lines by heart when I was a child and went to school in Khartoum, on the other side of the Arabian Sea. From outside the white painted classroom came the sound of gunshots, the acrid scent of tear gas, the noise of civil strife. As I stood by the school gates, I saw men dragging a body away. A man killed by police bullets, a poor man in a white gelabiya.

The air was very hot and there was a woman selling dates out of a wicker basket, black dates from desert trees and the brown humped shapes of the dom fruit. A dull brown fruit shaped like a cut head.

A head stocked with memory fragments.

That night on the terrace, as the whole family slept on mattresses side by side, I saw the stars huge as eyes in the brilliant blackness of the desert sky. In the neem tree I heard the red bird cry. It sounded so like the bird in the mango tree in the garden of the Tiruvella house. I shut my ears and tried to see that house again.

Memory needs nothing from me. Not the black waves on the shore, not the clouds that rise into infinity. It is a language without beginning, a mirror without a back where all that is crowds in, sky, stones, even the holes in the churchyard where my grandmother Kunju and grandfather Kuruvilla are laid side by side.

Memory knits us together then tears us apart. It is the first blessing and the last curse. It makes the sky and water burn. It turns me back into a four year old who squats at the wellside, not far from a bamboo grove, counting out stones.

Inside me is a spring of forgetfulness. Indigo water in which I dip my pen and write. I need to cut figures for a map, mark the fate of a generation forced far afield, thrust from native soil, reckoning nothing as foreign as our own selves: gnawing at history, swallowing geography.

16. *Writing in Fragments*

I write in fragments. The poet's craft has cut so deeply into my thinking that I am dependant on those bursts of rhythm and sense to steer me through the pages of prose, an uncertain passage at best.

I have had a year of writing dangerously. I cannot write when I sit square, athwart my body, in a simple chair. It is only when I start to lift myself up that it flows. Sometimes I fear that this book of childhood will be a series of field notes. My notebook is littered with scribbled prefatory notes: M4, M66, A train, B train, C train. Each of them moving vehicles, buses, trains in which I write, black tracks, indecipherable on paper.

I write as I enter the subway. The train jerks away from the platform and starts its race in darkness. On thoroughfares I hold my notebook and pen close to me as I scribble and start to cross. At Thirty-fifth and Fifth, right in front of the building where I teach, I am almost knocked down by some passing bicycles. Three of them come straight out of the mist. Men in long black cloaks, fast down Fifth Avenue, outside that stone building. One of them looks as if his clothing were smeared with salt, salt from the Arabian Sea I had crossed as a child.

I cannot write without being at the very edge of my life. I keep moving, here, there, everywhere I can in this island city. Even the little desk on which my writing instrument, a tiny computer of 2.9 pounds, is set has wheels. Little black wheels on rollers. It shifts and sways. Sometimes the parquet floor becomes a sea surface. When I stare down, hoping to see my feet so that they might anchor me, the air in the room seems filled with clouds. Clouds my father taught me to read, raising me high above his head into the clear light of the southern skies.

Sometimes at night I dream that my writing hand is cut off at the wrist. I cannot remember the circumstances, but the dream is in vivid color and my wrist hurts when I wake. I cradle my wrist, I massage it. I touch the bone to make sure it is still there. The pain is so real, I cannot doubt it. But what have I done to deserve such punishment? What secrets could my sentences reveal?

In Khartoum there came to be a shari'a law that was sometimes enforced. You could get your hand cut off at the wrist as punishment. For stealing what was not yours. I will take nothing but what is mine by right. The story of my childhood. Out of a reed that grows in my grandmother's garden I will make a *qalam*. I will set it to my palm. I will stain the waters and write.

Qalam is Arabic for pen. It is one of the first words I learnt in Khartoum at the age of five. Together with *hawa* for wind, *sucar* for sugar, *bint* for girl, and *ana sakna fi hai al-matar* for I live in Hai el Matar. Amma and appa made me learn that sentence in Arabic so that if I got lost someone, anyone, a kindly stranger could bring me home.

I pick up a book, Assia Djebar's *Fantasia*. Close to the very end, she tells of a Frenchman who saw a brown woman's hand lying in the dirt. He picked up the severed hand and tossed it aside, unable to touch it again. He recorded the incident in his journals.

And she, Assia, over a century later writes: "I seize on this living hand, hand of mutilation and of memory, and I attempt to bring it to the *qalam*." Over and over I murmur this line to myself. It calls up a sense I cannot hold in my mind, my memory.

I have a friend who teaches me Arabic.

Some words I have forgotten. Some I never knew. When I ask him he tells me that *hawa* means wind, air, weather.

He adds that it also means love, passion, desire, whim.

I think of what he has said. I stand at my window. Tall trees make a green blaze. Love returns in our life, as wind, as water, as touch.

And with love, a searing pain.

*

I can understand why, far away in the country of my birth, amma has cast the old leather suitcase filled with family photographs out onto the veranda for the monsoon sun and rain to attend to.

I understand, if that indeed is the right verb, without spelling anything out.

One photograph I have brought with me to New York. In it I see a small child in a white dress with tiny roses embroidered at the yoke and hem. Her face is squinted at the sun. In her hand she holds a bunch of wildflowers. There is a black rock behind her, a rock at the edge of the garden.

When I prise the photo out of its delicate hinges and flip it over, I see the date written carefully in lead pencil in amma's best hand. Four years after I was born. Five years after midcentury.

I walk in the park by the river. There is a faint smell of smoke in the air. Smoke from the southern tip of this island. On the cliffs I see a small figure in white waving at me. A dark child in white. Even at this distance I can tell that her feet are bare. She has wild-flowers in her hand. She runs away very fast. The wind blows hair into my eyes. I stoop, I touch the earth with my fingertips.

Again I see her at the cliff's edge, still in her white dress. She squats under a tree, she picks up small stones and swallows them. She keeps doing this, over and over again. She cannot stop.

Her belly swells, it hurts her. Each stone is a sentence coiled up, knotted with hard gum, something she cannot tell.

What am I stealing, except a truth I make for myself by writing, a truth that bursts in flashes from the place where it was locked up, in the keeping of those who are dead?

Why has it taken me so many years to get to this?

After I look at Djebar's book I write a single sentence in my notebook.

Write in fragments, the fragments will save you.

I try to hold onto this.

What I have learnt to remember is the wound I could not carry in memory. I must write it out if I am to go on living. There is no other way. A decade after *Fault Lines* I turn to flashes of remembrance, bits and pieces of memory, backlit, given at high intensity, so I can piece my life together again. After all, as a writer, what do I have but the raw materials of my own life?

*

When *Fault Lines* first came out many people wrote to me. Thank you for telling my story, my life is exactly like yours, one letter said. It did not matter that the writer was a young man, less than half my age. It was the tale of dislocation that had found an echo.

In 1997, the Advanced Placement English Language and Composition Examination came with an opening question asking students to "analyze how Meena Alexander uses language to convey her fractured identity." Then followed a long extract from *Fault Lines* beginning with "What would it mean for one such as I to pick up a mirror and try to see her face in it?"

Somehow that question unsettled me. It was not just seeing it on an exam paper, though I had always found exams nerve-racking. I recall one exam in Khartoum when I had a nose bleed just as I was trying to explain Pope's "Elegy for an Unfortunate Lady." I still wonder what the examiner made of the brown splotches on the page.

It was the question itself. Did it mean to imply that there was something unresolved about my days? Did the question mean to imply that my tale, such as it was, was necessarily incoherent?

I laughed it off; the unease stayed with me. I had the gnawing feeling that under the story of multiple places, of a life lived between languages and cultures, there was something more. That actual dislocation and exile, though true as it was, had served me as an emotional counter for a darker truth, bitter exfoliation of self, something that as yet I had no words for.

It began with a New York summer when I could not breathe properly. On the sidewalk I felt there were footsteps behind me, low breathings on the back of my neck. In the hidden places of my body a cold sweat broke out.

Worse, I felt my hands were about to be cut off and the knife blade would start to inch higher.

I shut my eyes and took deep breaths to fend off the images. Such phantasmic violence is hard to put into words. It's like watching a horror show in which the "I" is an unwilling participant. There was little I could do to regain a sense of ease. I went for yoga classes, I tried fast walking. It helped for a little bit but then the discomfort returned.

I felt it was sparked off by a piece of work I had agreed to do for a conference on Mary Shelley. I was to write a paper on her 1819 novella *Mathilda*. A taut slender work, it tells of a young woman who has turned into a pariah. She must die, pushed to the brink by her father's incestuous desire for her.

The father, returning after his long travels abroad, sees in his young and beautiful child, the exact copy of his dead wife. He wants his innocent daughter. He hovers at her door. He forces her into a realm shorn from words. No physical violation takes place, but the feverish limbo of the internal action Mary Shelley had penned drove me into a panic. I could not enter Butler Library, where I wanted to consult some books. Nor could I go near New York Public Library. The headaches were almost as bad as those I had endured when I suffered from malaria almost two decades earlier.

I saw a child in a white embroidered dress, threatening to break free of me. She was wild and furious. She was part of my flesh and yet had broken free. Watching her at the edge of a cliff, across the river or on the other side of the park as I crossed the street, I felt I would go mad.

Through the help of a friend I found a therapist, and that lasted two sessions. I could bear neither her lap dog nor the perfume she wore. But I needed help and found another therapist, a woman who seemed more ordinary, closer to the real world I was part of. I had a gut feeling she would see me through.

In her office, the very afternoon I was to read from a new book at the Barnes & Noble ten blocks or so up the road, I broke down. My lower back started its furious burn. I was a child pushed against a wall. A child in a white dress.

His arm was raised above his head to beat me.

I was stuck against the wall. Who? Whose arm?

He was tall. He was in a white kurta. I could not see his face. What I saw came to me as if flashes of lightning were breaking into darkness, tiny flashes, then great bolts that threatened to fell me.

I saw myself on the ground. At the same time I was weeping, at the edge of the therapist's couch. It was a high place in the hills. It looks like Switzerland but it's not, I said. It's beautiful, like wild grass in the cardamom hills of Kerala. I have fallen to the ground. He is there above me. All I can see are his legs and thighs. He is very close to me. I am so frightened.

I saw in flashes I was trembling and could not stop. Later, after I calmed down, I tried to explain: It was like a scene in *Frankenstein*, in the movie version, when the child is plucking flowers and the monster comes and finds her. Not a real place. It didn't look like a real place. They were all cutouts. All of them.

But what I felt was all too real. In the days and months ahead there were moments when I went into a tailspin and had to call my therapist on her cell phone to help me. I felt as if I were jerked helplessly upside down. As if I were a top being whirred at high speed, all my atoms flying apart. Pain afflicted my back. My torso was utterly numb. I had always believed in the truth of the body. What was my own body telling me now?

"They are feelings that you had that are coming back," my therapist said to me. "They are frightening, but you are not a child anymore. Go through the pain and it will release you."

Once hearing the panic in my voice, she asked me what had comforted me when I was a child. Holding onto trees, I told her. I had run away into the Tiruvella garden and climbed trees, the great branches had saved me.

"Then do that," she said, "hold onto a tree. "

I walked out into Fort Tryon Park. I found a flowering lilac, a tree that stood at the opening of the heather garden. It did not blossom in the hot season. It had four or five arms, knobby, dark brown. I went up to the tree. I did not care who saw me. I stood there, a grown woman, and held tight to the tree. I could feel my flesh again, clarified, sap and bark upholding me.

Calmer, I returned home, to cook and set out food, to read and write. But something had altered beyond recognition.

The details of abuse emerged slowly, always in flashes. His library with the theology books and books of Gandhi and Marx and Lenin. The teak desk where I had to lie down as he touched my body. The white wall where I pressed myself back trying to escape.

The scissors in the silk-lined box on his desk. As a child I had picked them up in rage, tried to hurt him back. This was the scariest to me. This was what I tried hardest to prevent memory from reaching.

Now it came clear, why I had always been frightened of kitchen knives, feeling they would rush into my hand, solder themselves to my palm till I was forced to hurt someone or turn on myself.

Why, I asked myself, would I rather cut off my own hand than remember what had made me pick up my grandfather Kuruvilla's scissors? What sort of choice was that? And now, I ask, what sense of shame prevented me?

Still, there was a molten rage, a power of self-preservation in my childhood self. Something I needed bit by bit to draw into my adult self to live, to make a new life.

What foundations did my house stand on? What sort of architect was I if the lowest beams were shredded? If the stones were mouldering, fit to fall apart. What was the worth of words?

A woman who did not know herself, how could I have written a book of my life and thought it true? I was tormented by the feeling that I had written a memoir that was not true.

Yet as I found the courage to read my book again, I discovered the truth of the imagination, she who plunges ahead in darkness with her torch of palmyra leaves, leading us through fear to a place where words cannot easily reach. I had written of Ilya and myself almost as one flesh, as indivisible. The attachment was so strong, we were of one substance. I could hardly feel the air on my own, breathe my own breath.

My mother, it seemed to me as I read my book again, was constantly averting her eyes, looking elsewhere, not seeing, not able to see.

And my father?

My father was the one person I could have told. But by 1997, when bits and pieces of my childhood were restored to me, my father, who had hung on for over a decade, was really dying.

I imagined us sitting at the teak table in the Tiruvella dining room. I would tell him, "Appa, Ilya hurt me sexually when I was a child. I could not bear to remember."

He would believe me, instantly. He would feel the rage I still could not trust myself to feel. He would struggle to get up. Walking would ease his thoughts. I saw him again as he was in my childhood, strong with black curly hair. He would yell at my maternal grandfather. Appa would carry me away from that house, drag my mother away too, swear at Ilya, "We will never enter this house again."

But my father, though he retained that extraordinary mental clarity he had till the end, was so weak he could not get out of his bed. I sat by his side and felt a great tenderness for him wash over me. I knew I would not tell him. Each breath cost him. The knowledge that he would believe me, that he would have wept with me was enough. The following August my father died. I was not there when they bore his body out of the house, down the same steps they had carried Ilya. His body was in the morgue behind the hospital waiting for me, waiting for burial. In a glass case, I saw his delicate bones whittled down, the white silk shirt and the dhoti they had set him in.

When I went to see the grave they had readied for him in the small churchyard, I found the only comfort I could. I leapt into the red soil of his grave and sat there for a moment, touching its sides, returned to native soil.

Later I was able, bit by bit, to feel rage at an old man, my grandfather who had torn my innocent childhood, cut my woman's life so that desire for me was ever after etched in with the sharpened stick of pain and always in my mind was Lavinia, she who I had seen on the stage at Stratford a lifetime ago, hands cut off, tongue torn out, forced to set a twig to her teeth to spell out the name of the man who had violated her.

In my notebooks from that era of my life I see the lines I have copied over and over from Shakespeare's play: "*Sorrow concealed, like to an oven stopp'd, / Doth burn the heart to cinders where it is.*"

Sorrow concealed. I ponder the phrase. How slowly I learn to breach the firewall of my own heart.

How could I not have known what happened to me?

The question has haunted me. The short answer is, of course I knew, I simply could not bear to remember. I picked through any books I could find on trauma and trauma theory. I taught myself to accept that there is knowledge that is too much for the nervous system to bear, that disappears underground, but sparks up through fault lines. I learnt again that the body remembers when consciousness is numbed, that there is an instinctual truth of the body all the laws of the world combined cannot legislate away.

Slowly, I learnt to absorb this difficult truth into myself.

Slowly, I turned to the Book of Childhood I kept starting over and over again. I touched the soil of my self, a field with its necessary knowledge, harsh, shining, buried in bits and pieces.

As I remembered Ilya, as I wrote him into being, I saw the child that I was, the child who set herself the harsh task of forgetting. To learn to forget is as hard as to learn to remember.

The girl child and the woman flow together. Will the hand that was cut off become part of my body again? How slowly I pick up the *qalam*.

It is evening in Manhattan. I sit and have coffee with Assia Djebar in her flat near Washington Square, and she speaks to me of the sounds of planes, the harsh fires of September 11. Of the refugee camp in Jenin that has been torn down by Israeli tanks. We speak of the young suicide bombers in Israel.

I tell her about the carnage in Gujarat. Unspeakable things: the rape of innocent women, a pregnant woman, belly slit open by a sword, an unborn child, heart still beating, raised on a sword tip. Evil in Gandhi's land.

Later, as we sit on the sidewalk at MacDougal Street, in a tiny Algerian restaurant, we sip our lemonade. In the night air scented by lime trees, I tell her how much her book *Fantasia* has helped me.

And she takes my hand, and after we have eaten she leads me into a tiny shop filled with young men hunched over, playing chess.

"Look, Meena," she says in happiness, "you and I are the only two women here."

We stand at the glass case and stare at the chess set of jade with prancing horses and elephants, and another that the owner has just bought, set in the front of the display, a chess set made of alabaster, in the shape of burning towers.

Do you know that chess is Indian in origin, I say to Assia. It was played sometimes with slaves. And I start to tell her the story of Draupadi in the *Mahabharata,* turned into a pawn by five brothers in the banquet hall of shame.

17. *Khartoum Journal*

*P*ast and present mingle within me. Sometimes I cannot tell the child from the woman. Emotions cluster and rise, sand grouse on a bare field I saw as a child at the edge of the river Nile.

In Khartoum, not far from the Nile, a mirage rises off the road. As appa drives his Hillman roadster, I see a camel. Instead of one there are two, and the man on the camel has a twin, just behind him. The scarlet fez cap doubles on the road soundlessly.

The flat black road becomes a mirror. Someday I know, appa, amma, and I, we will drive through. To the other side. Into another life, where the days go on and the monsoon skies part for moons streaked with indigo.

Someday I know, but not now.

In the backseat of the car, my nose starts to trickle. Sticking my head out the window and breathing in the scent of the acacia trees doesn't help. The scent of the blossoms makes my nostrils twitch. I don't want amma and appa to notice what is happening to me.

There is a Cadillac on the other side of the road. Its windows have tiny curtains made of white mesh. Inside the backseats are the wives and daughters of the Mahdi.

I can see a girl, pulling back the curtains, staring at me. She wears a red velvet dress with a bow at the neck. I would be embarrassed to wear a dress like that.

She is just my age, and she is unveiled. She stares at me. Her cheeks are dark and round.

"O look," amma cries. "The speed at which they drive. It's the silly driver."

Appa swerves, avoiding the Cadillac. It has chrome fins and ruby lights.

My head jerks against the backseat and blood starts up. Like one of the tributaries of the Nile, all the way in Upper Egypt.

I pull out the handkerchief amma has tucked into my cotton dress. The delicate linen square I tug out of my pocket is white, mango leaf and heron's beak stitched in ivory silk, from my lost grandmother's almirah. Amma brought it with her from Tiruvella.

The handkerchief she tucked into my pocket was meant to be an heirloom. Perhaps even part of my dowry. I know that someday, like any girl, I will marry.

But why did amma tuck this into my pocket?

Did she mean it to get stained with blood?

Linen with embroidery and cutwork is not the best thing for absorbing blood. But it's too late to call out. I have already stuffed it under my nose, poked it with my little finger into the offending nostril.

I feel the harder I push it in, the less I will bleed. But it takes a long while, my head against the leather seat, wind in my hair, for the bleeding to stop. All the while appa is driving fast toward the bridge that will take us over the river.

The Blue Nile and the White Nile meet here. Where the two rivers meet is a line. Not straight but jagged. Sometimes it is a shadow line.

Each thing moves under its own skin.

Under the skin of water there are rocks, silt, fish, corals, a carving of a tiny girl from Abu Simbel, cut in red granite, her eyes shut, palms folded.

When the Aswan High Dam was built, they came with flat boats and raised up statues of granite, alabaster, iron ore, jewels of silver and platinum, and the finest mica mirrors. Materials dug into tombs or laid out on the surface of the earth, beckoning eternity.

The White Nile is sluggish, packed with silt. The Blue Nile is brisk, with a pallor like the underside of a dove. During a picnic a dove came and perched on my wrist. It started cooing in my ear.

I feel as if I were in a dream, my whole body floating like my cotton dress, the one with half-moons printed on it. I want to grow up and become a painter, like Marc Chagall. I have seen his paintings in a book in school. I want to make one called "Girl with Dove by the Banks of the Nile." And the picture, though set by the Nile, will be filled with the sky and trees and stones of my native village. Stones by the wellside in my lost grandmother's garden. A little pile of stones, moist with well water.

I feel a little jerk in my body when that thought comes to me about my native village. I lean out of the car and see the waters reddish, looping over as if the waves had mouths and tongues they were forced to swallow.

I put my head out, the hanky balled under my nose. I feel the waves are saying something to me. But they are so intent on swallowing their tongues; I cannot understand what they say. The waters on the other side are bright with little zingy lines that go up and down as if a boy were fishing, pulling his line in and out. The color of the water is blue green, like a butterfly's wing.

"Marya, lean back," amma cries, "don't daydream with your head stuck out."

I can hardly hear her words, for we are approaching the bridge.

"Who can drive if you stick your head out?" appa calls. "It's a narrow bridge. It's not safe. A passing car and whoop. Remember the Cadillac?"

He grins at me in the mirror and makes a quick gesture with his hand. Plash! Striking it into an imaginary wall.

Appa loves tennis, squash, that sort of thing. When he was young he used to watch my Kozencheri veliappechan train at kabbadi. He stood hopping on one foot, then the other at the edge of the sandpit while my muscular veliappechan, his body rubbed over with mustard oil, strained at the arms and thighs of his opponents.

I do not want my head to fall off. Quickly, I tuck it into my neck. I will do as the turtle does in her pit of earth. I lean back and listen to amma singing.

Amma loves to sing, and since she is the only one in our family with any sort of voice, appa always encourages her. Her repertoire consists mostly of hymns she learnt in church and oddments of English folk songs taught in school. I think my grandmother Kunju also taught her songs like "My Bonnie Lies over the Ocean."

Or perhaps it was my grandmother's best friend, an English-woman. I know of Sabrina Walton-Jones from photographs in a faded green album, and a bit of a letter amma once read me. She read only half of the letter to me. The rest she folded up and covered with her sari so I could not see. I cannot imagine what it's like to have an Englishwoman as your best friend. In the British school I go to, I am the only child who is not white. Amma and appa send me there because they want me to learn English and because they feel I need company. Being tutored at home by Mrs. McDermott doesn't give me what I need. That's what I heard amma saying to appa.

Sometimes at school, the little white children take turns to pinch me.

One of them, Sally, pinches very hard. I thought she wanted to be my friend, when she came so close. At first she stroked my arm. I watched the white of her hand against my arm, it felt like a shadow. My little hairs bristled. Then picking up her thumb and forefinger she started pinching.

At first I thought it was a game. But it hurt, almost as the red ants hurt. She seemed to like what she was doing. Ouch ouch, I pulled my arm away.

"Why did you do that?"

"I just wanted to see if it would show. There, it doesn't, does it? It won't matter to you, will it, Marya? It won't show."

I wanted to spit in her face. I was filled with envy too, the way she smoothed down her skirts and skipped away. I stood in the middle of the school yard, near the roundabout painted green.

I hung upside down, my head in the air, as one of the boys in his blue uniform raced in the dust, making it go faster and faster. Over the edge of the roundabout as the air trembled and the great bells of the cathedral Gordon built, before he was beheaded by the Mahdi's men, rang out. Flies settled on the acacia trees, and the air of the northern desert lit up with streaks of brilliant pink and phosphorescent white.

I liked hanging upside down in the air like that. Everything that touched me was flowing, each thing that might have been hard: wall, lamppost, desk, hand, turned into the elements of its own dissolution. Not that as a child I would have put it into those words, but the truth of a flowing world entered me.

Perhaps it all began as a coverup for pain. But perhaps there was more there, the instinct that makes the butterfly flit to its nest to mate and perish, that leads the salmon up the black rocks, over the rushing stream, to spawn and die.

Later we would enter the cathedral for our religious instruction class. Sing the Lord's Prayer. I would sit in a pew behind Sally, who pinched me so hard, and pretend I did not care.

But I could sniff the incense from the high church ceremonies, watch out of the sandstone door as the boy with goats and a bundle of sticks, his cheeks scarred, his eyes so bright, gazed in.

In the car, as we drive over the bridge, amma takes it upon herself to sing a mournful hymn. Her high voice fills the car as she sings. I can tell that appa is not displeased. After all he has suggested this to her. He knows she cannot satisfy him with the Hindi film songs he craves, Lata Mangeshkar crooning in her nightingale mask, so he settles for what he can have.

As he drives I see his face in the mirror. Appa has an odd look on his face, like a little boy who has swallowed a whole lump of jaggery. The sweetness fills his mouth, but he tries to keep a stiff air, lest someone suspect him. I feel the words make no sense for him at all. If he had his way he would beat time with his hands against the sides of a mridangam.

But amma has the right mournful air to her. Her hands clasp and unclasp as she sings:

> Rock of ages cleft for me
> Let me hide myself in thee
> Let the water and the blood
> That from thy riven side do flow
> Be of sin the double cure . . .

As I listen to her, my eyes fill with angry tears and I cannot tell why. By now, the tires of the car are grinding over the metal surface of the bridge. We are somewhere in the middle, cast over water. Almost the whole of the hanky that once belonged to my amma's amma is stained. I hold it away from my nose and look at it. There is just a tiny bit of white left, at the corners. In some parts the blood has started to clot on the threads. The embroidered mango leaf is mud brown, the heron's beak almost black. The stain has seeped into the inmost threads.

And all the while amma goes on singing, on and on as we drive over the Nile River.

Sometimes I think that it is because of her voice that I could never leave amma behind. That she is in me as a shadow sticks to its substance. I thought this even in my darkest moments, when I stared into the well imagining what it would be like to leap in, join the shadow girl in there.

Or when I started eating stones. A practice that seemed, at certain moments in my life, as familiar as combing my hair or pulling on a cotton petticoat.

But that gets me to a part of my story that is so very hard. A tale with no head to it, no feet, only a stump of a thing. So I have to keep beginning, again and again, as if I were facing a mirror in a white painted room, and in that mirror a girl cut in red granite, lifted out of the floodwaters of the Nile, her hands and feet cut off, and where her head should be the lonely voice of an Indian woman as a small sedan grates on a metal bridge, over a dark river.

Other arms and legs and mouths reach out to succour me, help me through the portals of memory.

And now I think that amma's cry flows into the voice of my Kozencheri veliappachen. Appa's father, who rubbed English words together to make tiny fires, who sang in a deep-throated voice in Malayalam, our mother tongue, under lamplight in a centuries-old house. Later, in a fit of modernization he tore it down to build a villa with running water and electricity.

He had a hoarse, grumpy voice, but he sang his evening prayers as if he had touched the very edge of time and his heart were breaking. Was it because he feared he had whittled away all his ancestral wealth in a useless chit fund? Was it because he feared the Com-munists were coming to get him?

Or was it something entirely simpler, a love and fear more piercing, something to do with the way a small boy at the edge of a river will cry out for a hand to hold and shiver, knowing there is no hand to hold his and that the river, quicker and deeper than his own will, must flow on through the banyan trees, into the ceaseless sky?

Pathiravil athi pathi e
Anantha graham
Peru nadi e

Lines I might translate roughly as:

In the middle of the night,
in darkest cover
God's grace is a great river

18. *Our First Dead*

Our first dead open the door for us. We walk through that dark door to live our lives. Grandfather Kuruvilla was my first dead, and amma and I came from across the sea to be at his side.

How old was I at grandfather Kuruvilla's death?

Ten, eleven? It was June, the heart of summer. The trees were burning with their burden of fruit and sun. He took a long time dying and amma became very tired. Once she fainted from exhaustion. She and I had flown back from Khartoum so that he could die in peace. At least that's how amma put it to me. The phrase had an awful, sonorous tinge to it and felt to me like something she had learnt from the boarding school for Syrian Christian girls, where she had been sent at the age of seven so that grandmother Kunju could concentrate on her political work.

I was not new to death. Once in the reeds at the rim of the Nile, where appa took us for a drive in his Hillman—we often drove with the windows down to catch the evening breeze—I caught sight of a body with the hand curled up, a dark hand extending out of a white gelabiya, the whole of the dead man compacted into the bruise his hand made. A white egret pecked at the man's head as if the heavy curls were dark fruit dropped down into dirt. No blood was visible, just the tired stain at the edge of the gelabiya, under the sleeve.

Amma put her starched linen handkerchief over her mouth and crossed herself. Appa just murmured "poor bugger" and got amma to light him a cigarette that he kept puffing as we drove towards the Grand Hotel.

There was great excitement at the Grand. They were preparing to film the movie *Khartoum,* and Omar Sharif had arrived ahead of time from Cairo. It was rumoured that he was taking the air on the balcony. In preparation for the filming, many of the regular guests had been moved onto the steamer *Metamma,* docked just across the road from the Grand. I felt a shiver of excitement on my thighs as I sat sipping my iced lemonade, my feet crossed demurely in what I held to be correct ladylike fashion. What if the devastating Omar Sharif were suddenly to appear? Once I thought I caught the flash of a white smoking jacket, a handsome head tossed back. There was a buzz in the air by the balcony. Was that him? The waiter thought so. No one else was sure.

Later as we drove back past the river, darkness had unpacked itself over the water's edge and very little was visible. That night in my dreams I saw the dead man's hand. All I could see was the dark brown hand that clutched the metal trellis of the balcony where Omar Sharif stood, a cigar stuck in his mouth. In my dream the actor decked out in his gelabiya turned to walk away, tripped over the cold wrist, and went flying.

What follows sent me flying and I have made it up as I could, mixing memory and dream. There is no other way I could do it. One word stands out. *Sinking* was the word that Uncle Itty used in the letter he wrote to us. The letter lay, a flimsy blue aerogramme, in the metal box in the stone post office the British had built in Khartoum. Mail was never delivered at home, and it had to be picked up when one could. Inside the box lay odds and ends of letters and airmail copies of the London *Economist* appa subscribed to. On this particular day all we had was a letter from my uncle Itty. It lay flat and dry inside. Appachen is *sinking,* old heart trouble, my uncle wrote. Then came the telegram summoning us, and amma and I were forced to catch the first flight back.

Memory is a red bird perched in a bush, a bush with roots swirling in a current of water that bears both the scent of the fallen flowers and the song that seems to have no source.

Returning makes a turmoil of its own.

Will the red-tiled roof look the same after the storm? Will the rosewood chest in the drawing room still stand a little askew from the wall? Will grandfather Kuruvilla still be alive, his breath hoarse, alive and waiting for me? Will he put out his gnarled hand and touch me? I am at the edge of puberty and feel a mixture of emotions I find hard to tolerate. I feel I want nothing more to do with my grandfather and cannot understand why.

In the Tiruvella house when amma and I arrived everything seemed, at first, to be much as it had been when we left it a summer ago. Ayah scraping snails off the kitchen steps each dawn, the cook wielding a huge spoon blackened with jaggery, Cousin Sosa in yet another new set of silk garments, pink pearls brought all the way from Tokyo clinging to her neck. But somehow I could not summon up my usual jealousy.

Cousin Koshy, who was back from boarding school, played endless games of rummy with me. The leaves glittered on the mango tree. And grandfather Kuruvilla changed utterly, lay propped up in a rosewood bed so visitors could see. He was often delirious, pumped full of morphine. Amma was exhausted with the whole ritual of visitors and doctors and her father's illness. Sometimes she would throw up even the little *kanji* she was able to take in. That was when Uncle Itty decided that a time away for R&R was essential.

Just one day, he pleaded with amma, and finally one afternoon when grandfather was on an upswing, well enough to sit up and sip tea and receive visitors, Uncle Itty drove us off to the Kochi.

We approached the island in a painted boat, complete with two betel-chewing boatmen. It was a miracle we did not slide into the sea. We had banana leaves filled with roasted fish, fresh coconuts to slice and drink from, carafes of rosemilk, and sweetmeats wrapped in silver, a damask tablecloth, mats, wooden clogs that my grandfather Koruth needed to walk through the sands, my uncle Itty with his cheroot, my grandmother Mariamma holding her own palmyra fan.

The fan was made of leaves of palmyra and stitched with velvet ribbon. It cast a shadow, a winged thing. In the rocking boat, it kept the sun from my grandmother Mariamma's face.

Time opens up in my face like a trapdoor. Am I confusing this outing with an earlier picnic, a time when we floated in a boat over the waters of Kochi bay on a day of the sun's eclipse and appa's parents were with us too? I cannot tell anymore. Perhaps the two boats have melted into one, so hot that sea we floated in. Everything goes very slow.

I see Cousin Koshy in his khaki shorts and Aunt Amu clutching a cheap romance novel to her chest, gently snoring as the scent of sweat and Chanel No 5 poured out of her.

Under Aunt Amu's legs, packed in the wicker basket in oddments of cotton and felt, were the bits of smoked glass that were readied for our use. An eclipse of the sun was foretold, and a tiny island in the bay was just the right place to catch it.

"There is rock, right by the lighthouse," Uncle Itty told us.

"We can climb up there and see the dark sliver of the sun. Imagine that, children, catching darkness visible."

He was a learned man, my uncle, a barrister by training, and all kinds of phrases slipped into his speech. The only person who might have competed with him was grandfather Kuruvilla. But he was not with us. He was in the great house with the walled garden, ill with a heart condition, not sure if he wanted to die.

Neither was appa with us. In my time in Tiruvella I grew used to having a father who was far away in a desert town by the Nile. Often amma and I lived with him in the cooler months, when we slept on a stone terrace and needed the covering of blankets and even the thick *razai* amma had brought with her from India. In May, when the hot winds peeled off the belly of dry earth, amma packed me up and fled.

"It's oven hot, we were not meant to live here," she would say, leaving appa alone to manage his life. And she brought me back to a land where the monsoon winds bound us in a rain so heady that sometimes, for days on end, there was no breach in the sheets of silvery liquid that shrouded us, our clothing clotted on ropes that ayah wound round and round the back veranda. Even the chickens and drenched ducks from the kitchen garden scrambled into the grain cellar in search of shelter.

Where was my home? It was hard for me to figure out.

Leaning over the edge of the rocking boat, staring down into the flat and glassy waters, I wondered if appa, who was on the far side of the Arabian Sea, was thinking of me.

Was he driving his Hillman roadster to work, a silver thermos filled with coffee by him? Was a haboob approaching him? Did swirls of dust rise and cover the windscreen, the edge of the road, the white palace of the Mahdi?

Where was Khartoum? I could not tell. What was real was the cold water of the Arabian Sea and the edge of the boat that smelt damp and fishy. When I trailed my hand in the water I felt a tremble of delight, a sudden cold that turned my fingers into the silver color of flying fish.

"Have you seen flying fish?" I yelled out at Koshy over his sleeping mother's head. Kozencheri veliappechan woke up from his doze, and rubbed his eyes and stared at me.

"Silly Meena, how can fish fly?"

Koshy shook his head. He looked unhappy.

"Why don't you check the *Encyclopedia Brittanica?*" Uncle Itty pitched in to help. My cousin had a sulky look. I turned to him.

"They were silvery. Like new paise, you know the kind that veliappechan sometimes gives us."

"With wings?"

"How else could they fly? Wings double up as fins. They can swim in the sky and fly in the sea."

"The other way, silly." He shook me by the elbow.

"Like what?"

"Fly in the sky and swim in the sea, you mean."

I wasn't going to give up on the flying fish. I had seen them with my own eyes.

I shook my head so hard my braids started spinning, making a black blossom. One of the braids flicked the sleeping Amu on her cheek.

"Stop it you, wild girl!" Koshy yelled.

Suddenly both boatmen cried out as the boat thudded against grit. My grandmother Mariamma leaned over and, with the edge of the silken fan, tapped me ever so gently on the knee. When I started stirring, she blew into my eyes, as if a grandmother's breath might make me see.

As she led me out of the boat, we made a four-legged thing, a very old woman and a young child, her son's daughter, a girl fleeing an old man's death. A girl who would be forced to search out water and air for living alphabets:

that tell of fish flying in the southern skies
birds crawling backwards out of nests

stones starred with saliva
reams of white paper
grey intercontinental landing strips, a no-man's zone of
    transit lounges, no woman's either. Where cups of coffee in
    styrofoam cups are bought dear, and riceballs leave a sweet
    aftertaste on the tongue, summoning up the everlasting
    palimpsest of desire.
Migrations of sense that take a lifetime to decipher.

19. *Home at the Edge of the World*

Sometimes words flee from me. And I fall through a dark door, into a zone where consonants and vowels vanish, when syntax bends into broken hooks, like so many pieces of jagged metal.

I feel at such times as if I were walking in between the tracks of languages, much as one might walk between the rails of a train line and touch the stone beneath, bloody dirt over which the lines of transport are laid.

Sometimes I have felt that I was translating from a place of no words—translate in the early sense, of transporting across a border.

An art of negativity, translation seems to me akin to the labor of poetic composition in precisely this: it reaches beneath the hold of a given syntax, beneath the rocks and stones and trees of discernable place to make sense.

There is a zone of radical illiteracy out of which we translate our selves in order to appear, to be in place. A zone to which words do not attach, a realm syntax flees.

Zone that cannot recognise the moorings of place, sensuous densities of location, coordinates of compass and map.

I need to go there in order to make my poems.

I think of it as a dark doorway that lets me in: slides shut, then ruts open again.

I fell through that door as a child.

Returning to India from Khartoum, amma and I landed in Bombay Airport. My newfound Arabic vanished in the hot winds. Hindi, which I had known since earliest childhood, was ringing in my ears.

When I opened my mouth, no sounds came, nothing.

I could hear amma saying something to me in Malayalam, but all that came was the swirl of emotion, a sense that I was plunged into a space where words did not attach, where a mother's hands could not rescue.

Zone of radical illiteracy out of which I write, translating myself through borders, recovering the chart of a given syntax, the palpable limits of place, to be rendered legible through poetry which fashions an immaterial dwelling yet leaves within itself traces of all that is nervous, stoic, edgy. The skin turned inside out.

Is this what Walter Benjamin evokes when he alludes to the "interior" as the "asylum of art"? In *Arcades Project* Benjamin muses: "To dwell means to leave traces. In the interior these are accentuated."

The interior of the house of language, fitful, flashing.

And under the house of language, a fiery muteness, this zone of radical illiteracy.

Where we go when words cannot yet happen, where a terrible counter-memory wells up.

Home for me is bound up with a migrant's memory and the way that poetry, even as it draws the shining threads of the imaginary through the crannies of everyday life, permits a dwelling at the edge of the world.

I use that last phrase since the sensuous density of location, the hold of a loved place can scarcely be taken for granted. The making up of home and, indeed, locality, given the shifting, multiple worlds we inhabit, might best be considered part and parcel of an art of negativity, praise songs for what remains when the taken-for-grantedness of things falls away.

And I speak as someone who even as she writes in English thinks through the rhythms of many other languages: Malayalam, Hindi, Arabic, French. So that the strut and play of words, the chiselled order of lines permits a sense crystallized through the seizures of dislocation.

I think of the poet in the twenty-first century as a woman standing in a dark doorway.

She is a homemaker, but an odd one.

She hovers in a dark doorway. She needs to be there at the threshold to find a balance, to maintain a home at the edge of the world.

She puts out both her hands. They will help her hold on, help her find her way.

She has to invent a language marked by many tongues.

As for the script in which she writes, it binds her into visibility, fronting public space, marking danger, marking desire.

Behind her in the darkness of her home and through her pour languages no one she knows will ever read or write.

They etch a *corps perdu*. Subtle, vital, unseizable body.
Source of all translations.

20. *Shadow Work*

*I*n the drawing room of the Tiruvella house where amma still lives, close to the carved windows that look out onto the courtyard is a small teak table. On the table stands a heavy black telephone that rings loudly enough to wake even the owl that perches in the back veranda. Sitting in New York I dial the string of numbers. I hear the little clicks and splutters as the phone connects, then starts to ring.

I hear amma pick it up and set it to her ear.

"Ah Meena," she murmurs. "I knew it was you."

She sounds relieved to hear me. I can tell she is lonely. She asks me what I am cooking these days.

"Salads," I say, "it's so warm here."

It always surprises her that I can cut up spinach without cooking it and not fear damage to my intestines. "You should at least steam the head of spinach," she admonishes me. "We would never dream of eating things raw like that."

I cut into our food conversation.

"I am going away for three weeks, to a château in Switzerland."

"Why on earth?"

"They invited me and I need a break."

I cannot tell her that memories have been flashing in on me at the oddest moments, flickering flames that threaten to eat me up. I do not tell her that I have been visiting a therapist on Central Park West who sits me down on her couch, helps me to remember what is too hard to bear.

Quickly, before amma can object, I ask her to write down a phone number for the Château de Lavigny.

Then suddenly my voice dips.

"What happened to grandmother Kunju?"

"Happened?"

"Yes, I mean her death." I ask this quite bluntly, then add, "It's for something I am writing."

Her breath comes in gasps on the phone.

"It's for something I am writing," I repeat in case she hadn't heard. I hold on tight to the phone as her breathing returns to its normal pitch.

I fear amma still thinks of my writing as a useless profession. Years ago she told me that women who wrote did so because they had nothing better to do. "It's like hanging your dirty laundry outside the house for all to see. Nothing more than that." She said this in a fine clear voice. Trained in classical vocal music and also in the Anglican hymns her mother favoured, she has a lovely speaking and singing voice. At the age of seven amma was sent off to a boarding school run by two Scottish Presbyterian sisters, the Misses Nicholson. So that grandmother Kunju could devote herself to her political work, to her travel and organising for the Indian nationalist cause.

Now I hear amma say: "Your grandmother Kunju died in 1944."

"How old was she?" I ask.

"Your grandmother was exactly a month short of her fiftieth birthday."

My mother speaks very softly into the phone, as if she were whispering to a child. Her calm words send a jolt through me. As if I have touched a live wire in the wall and received a jagged shot of electricity. Not harsh enough to burn but sufficient to remember.

This is exactly my age, give or take a few months. Now in midlife, childhood is playing havoc with me.

I stare through my window and see the waters of the Hudson River. I feel I am falling through the surface into the river of my childhood. The ash trees turn into sharp green blades of paddy. Slowly a car is driving through the trees toward the river. It is a metallic silver color. Staring at it restores me.

I need to change the pace of our talk, adjust the balance of the ancestral scales. I cannot forget that my mother is still waiting for what I might say.

My mind flashes to a pair of ancient scales. Ilya once took me to a temple courtyard in Tiruvananthapuram. We were on a visit to the Arabian Sea. How old was I, four perhaps four and a half? In the courtyard, poised on a stone pedestal were scales that reached into the sky. Ilya explained that the scales were used to measure the weight of kings. In one scale the rajah would squat. In the other they piled up gold, precious stones, bananas, papayas, the sweetest coconuts. Sometimes they would sneak out the heaviest palm leaf manuscript they could find. Or the burdensome Malayalam dictionary.

Ilya lifted me up, so high my skirts flashed in sunlight. He set me in the scales. As they lilted precipitously, he leaned into the other side, pressing hard with his hands, so they would balance.

Is his ghost still there, to push me into air?

Suddenly I need amma as I have never needed her. Her voice will settle me back into my torn, scuffed skin. I am the girl who fled her skin, I want to cry to her. But she cannot hear me.

As amma goes on about the high price of sugar in the market-place, the rising costs of rice and dal, a ritual portion of our weekly conversation, I think, who can measure the burden of flesh, whether that of a child or a king? Who can weigh the evidence of the senses?

Something else cuts into my thoughts and I interrupt her, quite rudely breaking into our conversation, tearing the decorum of our weekly back and forth, a fine line of words across the waters and the landmasses, marking the borders of belonging.

"And Ilya, when did he die?"

I realise she is displeased that I have returned to the topic of death. But I am still there and she needs to answer me.

"He died in June."

"When in June?"

"It was the year you turned eleven. June of 1962," she adds slowly, calculating backwards. Like me, she sometimes has trouble with numbers. Then suddenly she was quiet.

"You are calling on his death day; you realise that don't you?"

"June thirteenth," I murmured.

It was light where I stood, dark where she was on the other side of the planet. We were both silent for a little while. Then, because she has learnt how to survive, let some things lapse into silence, she went on briskly.

"Believe it or not, Meena, your ancestral house has not been properly whitewashed for so many years. Even though you are in constant *globetrot*," she pronounced the word slowly and carefully, "someday the house will be yours."

I understood from the way she spoke that she needed money for a paint job and did not want to ask me directly. After all, it is the role of a daughter to understand these unspoken things. All the years that my father was ill, it was hard to paint the walls. He was very sensitive to flecks of paint, motes of dust. His lungs were so fragile, scarcely managing the intake and output of precious breath.

That night, in the simple room in which I sleep and write, I pull out my cheque book, then hesitate. I mean to write out the cheque but put it off till the morning. I sleep badly in my nest of white sheets. A dream comes to me.

When it is time to sign my name as I would normally, on the bottom right, I start scrawling all over the cheque in tiny letters. Letters so minute that they could only be read with the use of a magnifying glass. Letters making sentences in the languages that, as a child, I had once set down in my ricepaper notebook, the sentences of my childhood hooked and snarled in the secret hand that bears witness but cannot reveal.

Over the neat letters where I have written *One hundred and one dollars payable to Mrs. Mary Alexander,* I have set down at top speed, in black jewels, the illegible story of my life. A Book of Childhood. Of memory and forgetting that no one will read.

Later amma takes the cheque to the little State Bank of India that stands next to the banyan tree. The bank is on the Kottyam–Mallapally Road where the buses pass, crammed with souls, fit to burst, the road I had written about so many years ago trying to close *Fault Lines*. The bank manager steps out of his little Plexiglass compartment and says, "What sort of cheque is this, kochamma?" He shakes out a white cotton handkerchief and wipes his face. It is very hot, just before the monsoons. He faces her.

"It is most curious, kochamma. I cannot read an amount, nor even your daughter's signature. You know it's always been quite unstable and now it is illegible entirely. Obviously it is worthless, we cannot tender any money for it."

As amma steps out of the one-room bank, wild parrots in the banyan trees start flapping their wings. I hear them screech. Suddenly the world is full of wild parrots.

What shall I write when I sit at my desk at Lavigny? What can I hope to reach in the shelter of memory? One line will be enough. A single line to catch the glory of stubble fields, trees, a red bird in a green tree. An image, or even a single letter of the alphabet, something rare and glowing.

At Lavigny, ever so slowly, I start my sentences.

Amma was an only child and the death of her mother passed into me as sunlight on a lake filled with waves.

The sunlight turns the water crimson, then subsides as foam glistens and the colors beneath darken, as silk does when it is drawn under the heft of cloth. I was water and she was shadow I swallowed. She was the blood in me and the indigo. I longed to hear about her, but amma was loathe to talk. I do have her birth date and her death date. Born in Calicut, in the princely state of Cochin, in 1894. Died in Tiruvella, three years before Indian independence, in 1944.

The death of grandmother Kunju affected amma greatly. It was as if she were forced to wear a sari with a hole burnt into it. The kind of hole that flares up when a careless dhobi lets a coal drop from his hot iron and it sears the delicate cloth. And wearing the sari with the hole, amma had to dip and pirouette, tug hard at her pleats so the burnt black part would never, ever show.

Once I asked amma straight out why grandmother Kunju had to die. Amma had taught me it was rude to turn your back when someone is speaking to you. Though she prided herself on being the soul of politeness, just then, ever so sharply she turned her back on me. I saw her broad back, wrapped in a pink sari, bump into things in our drawing room. A silver candlestick that had belonged to grandmother Kunju, a rosewood table which held a porcelain bowl filled with water.

In the water floated jasmine flowers. They pitched about as amma knocked into the table. A few drops of water splashed out. Later the maid came by with her soft cloth, washed so many times it was a dull brown color. She had to rub the table hard, so a stain wouldn't form.

Amma was sixteen when she got a telegram summoning her home from college. She stood in her cotton sari with the flowery border drawn tight around her waist, her head folded down on her neck, her eyes fixed

*to the ground, refusing to enter the house of death. She would not put
her foot on the lowest of the stone steps. Those steps are dappled with the
shade of palmyra leaves, lined with pots filled with mauve petunias,
petals streaked with jet.*

*"I refused to put my foot on the steps. I refused to enter the house in
which my mother died. Can you understand that?" That was all she
would say to me. As she spoke I saw my grandmother, utterly weightless, a feather torn from a gull's back, floating over the threshold of the
house in which I was raised. A house with a red tiled roof, dark tiles of
the floors, white walls upholding the chiselled teak of the ceiling, and in
the sandy courtyard, a mulberry tree my grandmother planted. In the
rainy season it filled with tiny red fruit and, sometimes, silkworms
crawl there.*

Château de Lavigny is an eighteenth-century mansion with courtyard and stables. I have a room in the annex, which is set apart
from the main house. The annex is built like a carriage house, with
rooms over an archway next to the stables. The room itself is simple, white walls, a bed, a chair, a desk. The low window on the
right gives onto the outer gateway, and the cobbles of the drive
make glinting circles of stone beneath the gas lamps. The traffic, in
and out of the château, odd bicyclist or car, passes under this room.

I realise that the place where I write is nothing so much as a wish,
a breath, four white walls upheld over an archway into the interior.
I have set the writing desk close to the window on the left so that as
I sit I have a clear view onto the courtyard. The chandeliers and mirrors and lacquer work are barred from my gaze by thick walls, but
I can see the rose garden, the white patio chairs, and one of the other
writers, a man in a blue shirt who comes and goes, notebook in
hand. Behind him is the glinting surface of Lac Leman. Later when
I meet Robert, he tells me that Lac Leman is where T. S. Eliot came
to recover from his nervous breakdown. Somewhere on other side
of the lake, closer to Geneva.

There are six of us here, writers, each embarked on her or his mission. I had written on my application that I would be working on
new poems. The Book of Childhood seemed much too hard to spell
out. As I start to write my bits and pieces, I soon realize that I am
searching for the grandmother who died before I was born. Why do
I need her so much? Do I feel that finding her will help me make
sense of what happened in my buried childhood? Sometimes I feel

as if my life is flowing into hers. I want to shake her hard and cry, why, Grandmother, why did you die so soon? I want to stop her in her tracks.

Why don't I realise that to find her I will have to cross an impossible border?

At Lavigny, over and over again I sit and write fragments, stitch and unstitch sentences that seek to link my childhood to her death, a shadow work that leaves me breathless.

When I was a child, amma had a special dress of shadow work made for me in the Mindamadam. In Malayalam, Mindamadum means "House of No Speaking Nuns."

Mindathe is "Do Not Speak," as in "Marya mol, shsshsh shsh, mindathe." Madum is "a house where nuns live."

It was a dress I knew by-heart. By-heart means I loved that dress so much I knew each tuck in the soft silk, each ruffle at the sleeve, fine folds in the sash, petulant dip of the Peter Pan collar as it rode on my collarbones. Cut to precise measurements, it fit my body perfectly. It was made of the softest muslins and silks, and held in place by a series of petticoats. Eyes closed I touched each whispering layer of muslin, each tight pink rosebud and jasper leaf knotted in silk. Above the topmost layer, on the underside of the silk was the delicate tracery of shadow-work butterflies. Humayun in all his glory, riding his white charger, could not have been prouder of his brocade suit than I was of my shadow-work dress.

I knew about Humayun because grandfather told me of Humayun's father's conquests, his victory march: Humayun lying ill with a fever no one could cure, Emperor Babur circling his child's bed thrice crying, "Fever, fever, leave him, come to me," muttering like a medicine man, till the fever rose and covered the emperor's flesh.

I do not think amma knew anything about Emperor Babur or Humayun. All her concern was with Rahelamma, the young novice who was so skilled at shadow work."Yes, Rahelamma decided you would like butterflies," amma said. "I told her that you and your cousin chased butterflies." She said this with a little smile.

Shadow work was and is still prized for its delicacy. The silk was worked in under the fabric so that only a trace of the color showed through the limpid surface. Very few people were good at shadow work. Making the silk slip under the fabric, teasing the threads into just the right shape, a mango leaf, rosebud, or butterfly was no easy matter.

In shadow work, the embroidery is done with great care on the under-
side of the fabric. The missing parts are hidden under the skin of cotton
or silk. All that is missing casts a shadow. And sometimes the shadow is
considered lovelier than the thing itself. I was hopeless at embroidery,
and my grandmother Mariamma, who lived in the fortress-like new
house twelve miles away, my pale-skinned, gray-eyed grandmother, was
the only one who had even bothered to make me try to learn.

Perhaps amma felt that the nuns in the Mindamadum with their
devotion to silent stitching might inspire me. It still surprises me how
determined she was that my willfulness must be cast out, cleansed
through a regime of prayer and watchfulness.

Amma was getting an assortment of dresses cut for me, for soon we
would have to cross the black waters, go to a desert town in North
Africa, where appa had been sent by the Indian government.

On the way down the drive, as I sat in the car next to amma, smoke from
the garden fire made me cough. She gave me her linen handkerchief to
hold over my nose. The handkerchief was white on white. Linen embroi-
dered with the pattern of mango leaf. The handkerchief had to be held up
to the light to see the pattern. Or felt with the fingertip.

"It belonged to your grandmother Kunju," amma whispered.
"Someday it will be yours." She watched me run my finger over the
mango leaf embroidered in ivory."The finest things are like that," she
murmured, "invisible. Except when they stain."

At Lavigny, on a shelf near the writing desk I find a postcard in a
frame. Dark red walls, mottled table and chair, and through the
window, trees, lake, and sky. Almost as if it were painted from my
room, or one very like it, the colors altered, a figure half-visible in
the doorway.

I feel this is something that Bonnard has done. I love his work.
Who else has that deep, vulnerable red, brushed to a patina? Yet I
have never seen this image before. I pick up the frame and prise
open the back. It is the only way to be sure. A cheap frame and the
two metal strips that hold the backing come off easily enough in my
hands. I turn over the card:

Exposition Bonnard, Fondation Pierre Gianadda, *Fenêtre*
ouverte sur la Seine a Vernonnet, vers 1912, Huile sur toile,
74–113 cm, Musée des Beaux-Arts, Nice.

So it was Bonnard, his work in mechanical reproduction. I set it under the bright halogen lamp they have given me. Even in this mass-produced form, the brushstrokes of the master painter are visible, in the woodwork of the window, the hollowing out of the clouds, the trees that front the water. No, not a lake, as outside my window, rather a river. In Bonnard's painting there is a desk and, on its mottled surface, a book or a binder. It seems to me that, just for a brief space, the figure in the doorway has turned away from his work. I set up the postcard on my writing desk and let it remain.

How would Bonnard paint my grandmother Kunju?

Would she sit on a chair, her hands in her lap? Would she be a figure, backlit at the edge of a doorway? Would she be a dark nude floating in a bathtub, something Bonnard has never done before? I somehow feel he would have painted her in red, with a red scarf, a red sari, with a pair of rubies glittering in her ears. When Bonnard painted red, what was he thinking of?

Red, the color of stone quarried from deep inside the earth, the gorge I knew as a child, molten rock, fire.

Bonnard took that color and put it on the walls of the house of flesh. In that way, through his adherence to things, near at hand and common, he was able to illuminate what it means to stay in place.

So much of my life has been motion and flight, the tactics of self-evasion. When I think of one face, one figure I layer it over with what it is not.

Even now I need courage to enter the interior of the Tiruvella house, where amma sits on a rosewood chair that had once belonged to her mother. I need courage to pass into the bedroom with its rosewood mirror and then move through the dark door of grandfather Kuruvilla's library.

I turn back to the image I have set up at the edge of my writing desk, the postcard struck from Bonnard's painting. With my fingers I touch the red of his walls, repeated in the garment the figure is covered in, except for a blue shawl.

The red that you would expect to find at the edge of the inferno, where there is a slight cooling off of lava so human beings can plant their crops and harvest them and forge kitchen utensils and fall in love and drop into hate and paint and write and stumble at the feet of great mountains.

*

There was a portrait of grandmother Kunju in an inner room of the great house. It was made two years before she died. It hung on a raw stretch of wall, across from the mirror rimmed in gold she was given as part of her dowry. In the portrait her eyes are luminous, and she is gazing into the photographer's lens. Her hair is curly, drawn back on her head. A simple clasp of pearls shaped like the prow of a boat holds up her pallu.

The background is painted in so that in the manner of those times, no horizon appears, and grandmother Kunju appears in the frame, unmoored to rock or root or stone.

How shall I put it? There was a lightness about her that sent me soaring. When I was a child, sometimes I would go into that room next to the bamboo grove and squat and stare at the portrait.

Sometimes I heard her say words to me, words I could not write in any of the languages I was forced to learn to read and write: Malayalam, Hindi, Sanskrit, English. Sometimes I fell into the cracks between the languages, and the very best I could do was dream. I would stare into the pool in the garden with the single blue lotus on it. The petals of the lotus were a vivid blue.

It seems to me now that my inner life is akin to a species of shadow work, the real stuff of consciousness hidden under a transparent surface, as a bird beak or rosebud or leaf is tucked under the surface of silk, drawn out by the quick needle.

A dream state can suck me in, making it hard to draw straight lines, tell right from left, up from down, setting impediments to the links one needs to be in the real world.

I tell myself that it is entirely natural to hide from pain. Hence this dream state. The shock to the nervous system, the betrayal of childhood love is not something one recovers from easily. I needed to believe, to trust, in order to survive as a child. I needed not to remember.

Yet what makes it possible to survive also exacts a price, a smokiness of vision that covers over the wound, still bloody.

"One never paints violently enough," Bonnard wrote in his journal, quoting Delacroix. What did he mean?

My mind moved to grandfather Kuruvilla. Why did he expose me to the violence in his head? Sometimes when he touched me a strange light came into his eyes. Why did he use my flesh, my soul instead of canvas or paper? Why did he paint on me so violently?

Afterwards he would set me on his knee, speak of the horrors of Partition. What was the old man doing?

He was born a little over a decade after Bonnard. He was seventy years old when I came into the world. By then the bloodshed of Partition was part of our national memory.

I cannot bear the thought of my grandfather. I want to find my grandmother, the woman I never knew. At Lavigny I am haunted by the idea of Mont Blanc. It seems to me as elusive as my dead grandmother.

I walk through the stubble fields hoping to catch a glimpse of a snow-covered mass. Once, following instructions from Christine, who works as the administrator and chef extraordinaire, I stroll through the cut fields, through a sudden swell of almond trees with their hard green fruit.

I come upon a little sign: *parc de l'Avenir* it says in big letters, and behind it are swings, a seesaw, a slide, all set up for small children.

I keep walking and see an electric pole with a big sign saying Danger. I glance up beyond it and stand struck at what has opened up, mountains rising to the edge of the lake, a terrain of stone and cloud.

"Mont Blanc is all white," Christine had assured me, but not one of the mountains I see is just white. They all have scrapings of stone and bits of cloud stuck to them.

I keep walking and enter orchards with pears and apples, and piles of wooden crates with the name J. P. Perrot. I am enclosed by the trees and their green darkness, as if the mountains never existed.

Sometimes the only way to catch the impress of a lost body is through notations, musical, specular, entirely iridescent.

Notations that nothing catch, nothing render back except the trail itself, the desire for the impassable sustaining us, longing sheer as for a heap of stone invisible behind the banks of mist. A great white mountain.

Sometimes in my room I tilt the mirror around, hoping to catch a reflection of what I cannot see.

Clouds fill the mirror. Once the cloud bank is perfectly shaped, in the rough V of the mountain. Then, as I stare the clouds start to drift apart.

*

In dreams, the world is very small. It's a pebble streaked with jet, held in a rosewood mirror. Flecks of color rush under its skin. Held to the light, it gleams as a jamun might. A fruit perfectly rounded, flecked with indigo. I have heard ayah say that when children swallow things, bits of bone, buttons, stones, they come right out. I splash my hands with well water, run my thumb over the stone, hold it up to the sunlight. I set it on my tongue, close my lips, and swallow.

My dress is covered with mud from the wellside. I clasp the extra stones I have collected in my skirt, and when I let go, streaks of mud run down the pleats, staining the delicate embroidery.

I look all around but no one is in sight, not grandfather Kuruvilla, not Bhaskaran the cowherd, not ayah. Slowly, barefoot, I return to the wellside. I decide I will splash well water all over my face and throat.

The silvery bucket at the wellside is almost empty. There is just the tiniest layer of water inside, enough to touch to my forehead. Nothing more. I put my hand out and touch the stone rim of the well. The parapet is as high as my waist.

I stand on tiptoe. I lean over harder, hurting my ribs, till I am balanced flat as a heavy pole over the well's mouth, just my toes anchoring me to the ground. I squint, then open my eyes. There is a slight mist over the base of the well, a green halo over the water. A well frog leaps up, sharp green, the color of a new mango leaf. It bites the air and vanishes. Something quivers at the mouth of the well, a dark child's face.

I open my mouth, but no sounds come. A parrot swoops down from the guava tree and circles overhead squawking.

The shutters were wide open in the small room at the northernmost end of the house, and the floor was flooded with light. The walls had not changed. They were indigo stained, the color of bitter bark. I put my hands out and sought out the mirror. I rushed into the house, damp with well water. I had to see myself.

The rosewood mirror had come as part of grandmother Kunju's dowry. It was tall enough so a grown woman could stand and twirl her sari around, gather up the pleats, swoop them over her shoulder into waves of jade and enamel.

I pulled up my dress. I ran my fingers over my ribs, over the bumps of my nipples. A creature with a bared chest, neck cut off by the crinkle of cloth. There were tiny black flecks around the base of the mirror where the silvering had worn off. Something caught my eye. A swatch of white.

Grandfather Kuruvilla standing with his sleeve on the window bars. His hand was on the window and he was holding on to the bars and holding so tight that his knuckles were cut in stone.

I must have struck it with my elbow, for the mirror rocked on its pedestal. The bamboo grove started drifting, and through the green depth of bamboo leaf and stone wall, the silent sky began to flow.

I stared at the sodden lump of cloth that had covered me, and I gave it a little nudge with my toe. Away it spun under the wooden cupboard that held my dead grandmother's clothing.

In her heyday, grandmother Kunju cared little for her clothing. She lay down in the middle of dusty Main Street, coaxed other women to come lie down with her. They knotted their saris together to make one human chain, and they chanted, "Bharat Zindabad"—"Down with the British Raj"—and other such slogans.

The voices of the women rose up like fragrance from the crevices of the earth, like attar of the earth when the first rains fall. Their voices turned into cries of circling herons over the paddy fields by the riverbank. Their voices turned into the rough grunts of elephants at mating time: "This is our Land, let us rule it." They were followers of Gandhi and the police didn't dare touch them.

In my dreams grandmother Kunju had gone on the Salt March with Gandhi, had walked with Sarojini Naidu and kept walking even as the men dropped like flies under the charge of police with rough, blunt sticks called lathis. Under the fallen nationalists, the dirt spills like smoke.

There is smoke in grandmother's mirror. A child stares in, a girl with high cheekbones, a broad brow, a fine ridged nose, and a chin with a tiny dip to it. Dark child with two plaits pulled so tight they seem to be made of polished bone. She is dressed in a fine silk dress with delicate embroidery at the collar and waist.

Her back is to the teak almirah that holds her missing grandmother's clothes, the elaborate silk saris, the pashmina shawls, the brocades, all of which grandmother gave up wearing when she joined the freedom movement. The child knows that her grandmother joined Gandhi's freedom call, the injunction to wear only khadi.

One night, along with her friends, grandmother Kunju scooped up so many of her silks and tossed them onto the bonfire that was lit on the maidan. Cloth that was woven in the textile mills of Manchester and

Lancashire, that was bleeding the economy, tiny squares of linen and silk, foreign-made chiffons, European paisley brought back to spice up the wardrobe, crackled and leapt into flame.

The child imagines the flames behind her, glowing in the mirror. But as she turns her head, she sees that the glow is coming from outside the window.

There are wild grasses in the garden. From time to time the gardeners set fires, wild grasses, nettles, and the long-stalked thistles.

The child rushes out into the bamboo patch. The bamboos whistle in the monsoon wind, there are holes in the ground between the bamboo roots where the snakes can dip their long tails, crawl through the holes made by the paddy rats. The bamboo leaves are silver with smoke.

Quickly, before she can change her mind, she undoes the tight sash on her silk dress. She leans her shoulders back almost as if she were a classical dancer. She unhooks the tiny hooks at the back. It is hard without ayah's help.

At the base of the dress is a tear that the tailor mended the other day. It came when she crawled in the orchid patch with her silk dress on. Now she tugs hard and the dress is over her armpits. She feels the silk creak a little as if the threads were tired. She feels the wind on her bare chest as the dress rolls off. She crumples the dress into a tiny ball. How slight silk is when it crumples. She sighs a little as she stares at the dress, then tosses it into the fire. She watches the silk float and land at the edge of the burning patch, catches a whiff of something acrid as the long streaks of flame start to eat into the shadow work.

21. Lyric in a Time of Violence

*T*he girl who eats stones, swallows them so that she can live. She comes to me at a time of difficulty.

She comes as if to say, so long as one lives there is no escape.

Time has touched her. She is a woman now, just as I am.

There is a slight shimmer of grey at her temples. She has grown wings, large wings, but she keeps them folded.

In dreams I see her, wings folded, as she crouches by the stones at Liberty Street, at the foot of the burning towers.

She is dressed in a blood red sari, and at times she tears apart the sari, tears the blouse and strips to her skin to show me the heart beating underneath.

Noke, noke, she flaps her wings so that I can learn to look and see, so I can write elegies for those who died the day the towers burst into flames, and for those who were killed in another country, in the aftermath.

Sometimes I think inside me is a girl child who refuses to die. She has become a dark metamorphic creature.

She has grown wings, wears bloody clothing, and keeps pace with me.

The sky is very blue on the morning of September 11, utterly bright and clear, one of the those September mornings when it feels as if light might flow through your body.

I wake up early, as I often do to write. Just returned from Lavigny, I am getting back into my New York skin, learning the sounds and smells of the apartment again. The bits of prose I wrote in Lavigny have come to nothing. I set them away in a drawer and try to settle into preparing for class.

A little after 8 A.M., I pick up the phone and call amma. Sometimes it feels as if my life is punctuated by these phone calls. When I listen to her, space is stitched together, migration turns true. Her voice at the other end restores, abrades.

For the first time in so many years, she has gone on a journey. During the time that appa was ill, it was impossible for her to leave him and travel away. She has boarded a plane, flying north from Kochi, into the city of Chennai to visit my younger sister.

Amma asks how I am settling back in, how the children are doing. I feel a sense of fulfilment, sipping my morning tea. For months now I have helped her, step by step. Asking her to buy a new suitcase, set our family documents in a neighbour's safe, get another chowkidar for the house she is leaving behind for a short while.

I put the phone down, stretch out my legs, and imagine my mother in my sister's garden in Tambaram, the deer that saunter in, the aging peacock that struts in through the tangled vines.

Then the phone rings sharply. Once, twice.

"Turn on the TV, Mom. Right now."

Adam's voice is pitched with some emotion I cannot identify. At his insistence, I turn on the TV.

The twin towers fill the screen. They are something I have taken for granted, those twin towers I see from Fifth Avenue when I go to work. I have often wondered what it would be like to live in such a tall building of steel and glass, though I know people only work there. Once when I went I had to have my photo ID taken, and I held tight onto it, as a marker of something, what I could not tell.

Now on the screen I see a tower with a ball of fire exploding through it.

First a streak of fire that a plane made as it rammed through, then flames and smoke and the slow black implosion of the building. I keep watching till it collapses on the screen. I cannot bear it anymore. There are thousands of all-too-ordinary people working in those towers. Down below is the plaza where my daughter, Svati, now a teenager, went for a dance performance just two nights ago, and close by is the pier where Adam hung out when he was at Stuyvesant High School. I think of the pier and the blue waters of the estuary, which now on TV look as if they are on fire too.

*

I force myself to leave the apartment, to walk outside. I feel as if I am walking outside of my own body.

Fort Washington Avenue is so very still. I walk toward the park.

I see two women who are cleaning up, leaves, debris, odds and ends. They wear blue T-shirts. The sky is very clear, the leaves on this northern end of Manhattan, a deep green. A perfect fall day.

One woman says: "I saw the slip of a moon, tiny, like that."

She points at the sky.

"It was a sign, surely. I have never seen a moon like that so early. In the afternoon for sure, but in the morning? Never."

The other woman nods. We are all searching for signs.

A man stands by a huge truck that has a parrot sign on it, Parrot Hauling. He has a parrot on his arm, plume perfect as if it flew off the side of the truck. He is listening to the radio.

"Do you know what today is?" he asks.

I shake my head.

"Nine eleven," he says, "Nine one one. Get it? What other day could it be? September 11, 2001."

I keep walking till I reach the stone parapets by the highway and the river. I have never seen George Washington Bridge like this, no traffic, absolutely nothing except a police car, its lights flashing in the clear light of day.

Approaching I see a man with a dog. He works in the Bronx courthouse, he tells me, and has walked over the bridge. All the traffic over bridges is stopped, he says, all the subways are closed.

I start to worry for Svati, who goes to the Bronx High School of Science. I return home but cannot reach her on the phone. The lines are overloaded. Cell phones are dead. Finally I reach her and she tells me that she is at the home of friend near the school and that she will walk back, over the 181st Street Bridge. I call up my cousin who lives nearby so he and his wife will come with me to pick her up. I am shaking inside and feel faint.

Ella, a friend who lives on Bleecker Street, calls.

"I saw both towers fall," she says. "It was a terrible thing, Meena. I saw them burst and fall from my balcony. And I saw them on my TV screen. One and the other, at the very same time. What is happening to us? What?" As I listen to her, I hold tight to the phone for fear I will drop it.

In the afternoon I wait by the bridge with other anxious people. The city uptown is an odd state of disarray. There are police, people milling about not knowing what to do. I run forward, seeing my child walk slowly, tired from her trek, over the bridge. I rush to embrace her and tears fill my eyes. She is a little awkward seeing me like that. Her friends, all girls of fifteen, are laughing, trying to make sense of the day. Laughter covers over their fear. They had thought they might have to bed down in the school but then finally were allowed to leave.

Walking back with Svati on Overlook Terrace we meet the super's son, who has walked home from Wall Street. His white shirt is stained with sweat.

"I saw a man leap as I was running," he says. "And another. A woman too. Yes, a woman jumped. She was filled with fire."

My child is with me as she hears this; she has walked safely over the bridge. She listens, her eyes moist.

In the evening as she is drinking warm milk, Svati tells me of announcements that were made over the public address system in the school to inform the children of the events. Children who had parents at the World Trade Center were encouraged to call them. Some of the children were weeping.

"There was such a long line at the phone, Mama," she said. "I couldn't have reached you just then, and in any case I knew you were at home. You told me you were going to stay home and write."

Then she tells me about her drama class. The semester has just begun and they are all new in class. It is composed mainly of white Jewish children. A girl leans over to her and says, "So are you Middle Eastern?"

"No," my daughter says. "Why would you ask me that?"

"Because you have that olive color."

"My skin was screaming at me, Mama," my beautiful girl child says, her face puckering up, tears prickling her eyes.

"They were all staring at me. All the kids in class."

There is rage in her and grief. Together we sit on the couch and watch the details of the devastation in this island city we love. Those in flight and those dead. The mounds of burning wood and plaster and glass and steel.

Students send me emails. Zohra from Afghanistan, who has spent bits and pieces of her childhood in other countries.

"Like typical New Yorkers," she says, "we tried to be brave."

But after hearing that the Pentagon was hit there was panic at the

Graduate Center. Zohra tells me all this, two days later, with great calm. In the company of others she decided to walk home to Brooklyn.

At night I speak to Adam again. I tell him that Stuyvesant has been turned into a triage center for the wounded. One of Svati's friends tells her that as they were fleeing the school, the wounded were being borne in on stretchers. This stays in my mind, makes a mark there.

Adam wants to return home immediately. He is in his senior year at Brown University and wants to catch the train back from Providence. I tell him to be careful, to wait a few days. Just the other day three Indians were taken off the Boston train in handcuffs. They were utterly innocent, but they were taken for terrorists. Adam is six foot two. A handsome young man, he has cultivated a mop of dark curly hair. I tell him to get a haircut, to be safe. I do not want him to be picked up. Then suddenly I catch myself short, anxious that my maternal fears will puncture the fabric of our lives. But that fabric has darkened, shrunk a little. It is has shredded in places.

Two days later it is Thursday. At the end of spring a friend and I had dreamt up a course we wanted to call Translated Lives: Postcolonial Texts. But Francesca is still in Paris, for her father is ill. Our course is on migration, crossing borders, what it means to make a habitation with words. In preparation I was reading some trauma theory and postcolonial texts, performances as well as poetry.

I pick up my papers and prepare to go to the university. I need to make a space to think and feel and grieve with my students. The timing of this week's reading seems uncanny: the topics are trauma, memory, war. I pack Theresa Cha's *Dictée*, a text that has enormous resonance for me, into my bag, also Cathy Caruth's *Unclaimed Experience*, which I had brought home to read again. As well as the thin Xerox of that fierce, lovely essay by Toni Morrison, "The Site of Memory," a defense of fragments.

What does it mean to fashion a self in the face of a violent world? I try to pack the truth of my life into what I will tell my students. Slowly I make my way to work.

On Broadway, as I make for the university, an acquaintance says, "Be careful."

"Why?" I ask.

"Because you have dark skin, they might think you are an Arab," she says. I laugh this off, but my skin starts to feel tight and parched.

The university is next to the Empire State Building, which was evacuated. There were ninety bomb scares in Manhattan, all of them false.

A smoke haze covers the far downtown end of Fifth Avenue, where the twin towers used to be. I think I see twisted metal sticking up. Smoke drifts uptown. The underground parking garages are filled with acrid smoke, the sweet scent of burning flesh and twisted metal and wood.

At the university, one of my students breaks out weeping and I try to comfort her. Another says she has been weeping off and on and doesn't know why. Why? Why, she asks.

Everyone looks dazed. A colleague comes up, his eyes red. "I was there," he says, "and saw the towers explode. I was in divorce court at the time. I ran for my life."

Yesterday they handed out smoke masks to people in our building. Today the wind from the site of devastation is milder. We have a community meeting to discuss evacuation procedures. A man says: "I know that patriotism is in short supply at the Graduate Center, but isn't this the moment to put up an American flag?" All the flags that were there have blown into the barbed wire of the scaffolding. The perpetual scaffolding we have for building improvement.

At night on Fort Washington Avenue, when I return home the leaves are black in the trees. The street lamps burn outside the shrine of Mother Cabrini.

Now there is a mountain in my dreams. Not Mont Blanc. This is a mountain of twisted metal parts and rubble and human bodies. Fire pours out of it. In my dream I see body parts, a hand, a thigh, a torn lip, twisted in. I wake up in the middle of the night to try to call amma, to reassure her that we are alive, but the phone lines are still dead.

The next night it rains. The rain mixed with mud makes the rescue work very hard. There is a mountain of metal, the debris of the towers. Fearful that lightning would strike, the rescue workers had to be very careful. My girl child wants to stay at home on the weekend. In this green bowl at the northern edge of the island.

*

I do not know what else to say just now, I write in my journal.

I write to myself so that time will not stop short.

The devastation is enormous, mounds of rubble and metal and glass and innocent lives blown to tiny bits. It rains and the leaves are very green. Elsewhere by Ground Zero rain mixes with ash and makes the rescue work very difficult. This is our floating life, this peril, this sweet island with its southern tip burning.

When I was a child I saw the sea burn.

How often I have thought that sentence but with no page to set it on, no place to make it mine. As I sit and write, my words fly off the page. I think of geese lumbering into the wind. Or paper kites grown men have held in their hands, stretched taut over wind, over water, lit by the half darkness. But the darkness turns into barbed wire. In reaching for the past I am forced to crawl through it.

Barbed wire grips fences, scaffoldings, beams. You cannot toss barbed wire into the skies and have it hold. Who would have thought that you could have jets holding innocent passengers hurled into tall towers that flame?

What did Nagarjuna mean when he wrote: "If fire is lit in water, who can extinguish it?" At the time he was living on an island, and he wrote his aphorisms on rock.

There was rock under the tall towers that flamed on this island where I live. After the planes hit the towers on that terrible day in September and the towers burst into flames and fell, rock started to burn in all its crevices too, a slow burn through the veins of the earth where gases leaked out and caught fire, and wires and fuselage and plastics and metal and bone and hair started to mass and fuse in a sortilege that this island of Manhattan had never seen before.

Tor of destruction that made even the clouds weep. Two days after September 11, clouds amassed in the sky in New York City and then it started to rain.

The leaves were very green outside my window. Leaves of linden and birch and, in the distance, across a stone wall, the Hudson River. The garden between the two apartment blocks was still sweet, at the edge of autumn, overgrown, plants gone to seed.

At night I dreamt of a flash of fire, a plane with fire from its wings, bursting apart the bricks, then vanishing in a puff of smoke. This keeps repeating. The plane is not coming through our building yet, but rather through the one next to ours, a building exactly like this, with which we share a garden. In the dream I am floating, above my own body. I wake up, sit bolt upright in shock as I start to remember.

I cannot keep up prose anymore. I turn to my first love, poetry. I do not want to write about childhood. I do not want to be swallowed up in the past with so much molten and flowing. I need to bear witness to what is now, and the poem will allow me to do what I can.

I make tiny notes on scraps of paper. I feel the lyric poem will allow me to catch the edginess of things, the sharp nervosity, the flaming, falling buildings.

I must work back from the pressure of the present into the past, for that is the only way I will reach into the real. And when someone questions me about this I say: in all my work, place is layered on place to make a palimpsest of sense. That is the kind of art I make. Yet the very indices of place have been altered by traumatic awareness.

It seems to me that the lyric poem is a form of extreme silence, which is protected from the world. To make a lyric poem I have to enter into a dream state. But at the same time, almost by virtue of that disconnect, it becomes a very intense location to reflect on the world.

The day I went to the university to teach my class, I started the first of a cycle of three elegies for the dead. I called them "Aftermath," "Invisible City," and, the last, "Pitfire." I used couplets making twelve lines for each poem, and somehow the form helped me to crystallize and think through without fear. Here are the first two poems; they need to stand side by side:

<u>Aftermath</u>

There is an uncommon light in the sky
Pale petals are scored into stone.

I want to write of the linden tree
That stoops at the edge of the river

But its leaves are filled with insects
With wings the color of dry blood.

At the far side of the river Hudson
By the southern tip of our island

A mountain soars, a torrent of sentences
Syllables of flame stitch the rubble

An eye, a lip, a cut hand blooms
Sweet and bitter smoke stains the sky.

New York City, September 13–18, 2001

Invisible City

Sweet and bitter smoke stains the air
The verb *stains*, has a thread torn out

I step out to the linden grove
Bruised trees are the color of sand.

Something uncoils and blows at my feet
Sliver of mist? Bolt of beatitude?

A scrap of what was once called sky?
I murmur words that come to me

Tall towers, twin towers I used to see.
A bloody seam of sense drops free.

By Liberty Street, on a knot of rubble
In altered light, I see a bird cry.

New York City, October 17–November 3, 2001

While making my poems I kept walking down to Ground Zero, as close as I could get, making returns, a pilgrimage, the site a graveyard for thousands, filled with the stench of burning flesh and wires.

On one trip, as I walked past Liberty Street I was struck by the extreme youth of the soldier guarding the perimeter, a young lad freckled, fresh faced. Behind him the shell of Tower 2, against which an ancient patriarch was getting photographed. Small children screaming in delight at pigeons, a rescue worker holding his hands to this own throat, face sunk with exhaustion, his gas mask at his hip.

I made a third poem as part of this cycle and called it "Pitfire." Nine months later I was invited to read my elegies at the Hunter College graduation. In Radio City Music Hall, a place I had never set foot in before, I stood at a lectern and read my poems. The bagpipers of the New York City Fire Department had just played their haunting notes for the dead. My voice was clear but I could feel the waves of suffering in their music.

I turned to face the bagpipers, who were still on stage as I read "Pitfire," a poem I had written in such loneliness, never dreaming that I would one day read it aloud, return it in sound and breath to the part of the world it came from.

Pitfire

In altered light I hear a bird cry.
By the pit, tor of metal, strut of death.

Bird song yet. *Liturgie de cristal.*
Flesh in fiery pieces, mute sediments of love.

Shall a soul visit her mutilated parts?
How much shall a body be home?

Under these burnt balconies of air,
Autumnal duty that greets us.

At night, a clarinet solo I put on:
Bird song pitched to a gorge, a net of cries.

Later a voice caught on a line:
"See we've touched the bird's throat."

New York City, November 20–December 5, 2001

The poem needs to be sharp, as clear and facetted as broken glass. It must pick up the multitudinous cries of the world that we are.

Later in the month of September, I started another poem. I called it "Kabir Sings in the City of Burning Towers." I need to tell the story behind it.

There was a meeting of the newly established Asian/Asian-American Research Institute. I had been asked to serve on the governing board, and the board members were to meet at the Graduate Center. As I recall it, the first meeting was set for barely a week after September 11, but that was postponed and we met in October.

It was the sort of gathering to which I would wear a sari without thinking twice, but now something nagged at me. Two of my South Asian students had encountered trouble wearing salwar kameez, men yelling, one throwing a paper bag with an empty bottle inside. A friend of mine called from Boston. She told me how a man had yelled and spat at her. There was a pall of suspicion extending over Arabs and beyond to South Asians, brown people who looked like they could be Arabs.

I wanted to pick my battles. In all the grief and torment of a city under seige I wanted some control over the small things of life. With what it was like on the street, it made no sense to deliberately stick out. My daughter told me that the cousin of an Irani friend of hers, a young woman with long black hair, had endured a man in the subway who brandished scissors and cut off some of her hair. Immigrants were being swept up and put in detention with no charges lodged against them.

I decided to save my energies for writing, and I was writing a great deal of poetry.

I rolled up my sari in a manner that would not crease it, set it carefully in a plastic bag that I lodged in the center of my bookbag. In the fourth floor ladies' room I slipped out of my slacks and put on my sari. I watched the silk fall to the tiled floor and stared at my face in the mirror.

How dark I looked, unmistakably Indian. I needed to think through my fear. Later when I reentered that fourth floor ladies' room and looked in the mirror, I heard Kabir, the medieval poet saint who I love, singing to me in secret. He was giving me courage to live my life.

Kabir Sings in a City of Burning Towers

What a shame
they scared you so
you plucked your sari off,
crushed it into a ball

then spread it
on the toilet floor.
Sparks from the towers
fled through the weave of silk.

With your black hair
and sun dark skin
you're just a child of earth.
Kabir the weaver sings:

O men and dogs
in times of grief
our rolling earth
grows small.

I had written my poems quickly, to survive. But after writing there came a time of fragmentation, being torn apart in so many directions: the fear on this island, the condition of our lives, not knowing what could strike next, fire, pestilence—that bitty white powder filled with anthrax spores. A floor of the building where I teach was shut down for awhile. Meanwhile, on the other side of the globe in Afghanistan, the terrible bombardment by the United States, stones ground down, children starving, women in burkhas fleeing. Both are places real. I live in one, I reach out to the other. Disjoined in space, they coexist in time, in a molten present.

As a child I had lived at the borders of war. Moving back and forth across the Indian Ocean, between Kerala and Khartoum in the Sudan. In Sudan there was a civil war raging. On the way to India we often stopped in Aden, in what is now Yemen. There were British Tommies on the rocks and Yemeni freedom fighters hidden by the broken walls. More recently in India, in the last few years there has been the rise of a fascist Hindu movement, and terrible ethnic violence has scarred Gujarat. Then too there has been the escalation on the border with Pakistan and the fear of war. All this has been part of my personal history and has left a mark on my writing.

How can these violent versions of the real that cut into memory be translated into art?

Art in a time of trauma, a necessary translation, "fragments of a vessel," writes Walter Benjamin, "to be glued together."

But what if the paste shows, the seams, the fractures?

In a city blown up at its southern tip, the work of art must use the frame of the real, translating a script almost illegible, a code of traumatic recovery.

It seems to me that in its rhythms the poem, the artwork, can incorporate scansion of the actual, the broken steps, the pauses, the blunt silences, the brutal explosions. So that what is pieced together is a work that exists as an object in the world but also, in its fearful consonance, its shimmering stretch, allows the world entry.

I think of it as a recasting that permits our lives to be given back to us, fragile, precarious.

22. Stone-Eating Girl

Sometimes the zone of dream is so close I can taste and smell things that are not there. I can even smell them burning. At such times I need help from the stone-eating girl. She flies in on her wings of bone. She perches on a windowsill and watches. So it was that after the ash from the towers settled into the earth, I whispered the line I had written months earlier in my notebook. In the darkness of a Manhattan night, I turned on a small lamp and started again the story of how as a child I crossed the Indian Ocean.

When I was a child I saw the sea burn.

I stood on deck, my hands clenched over the railings. Up and down, side to side, all around the sea was aflame. The waves made little sparks that flitted over the sea surface. The clouds were so lazy, floating in the pink sky. I thought I could see a flying fish with its silver, darting wings. And then another behind it, a bright shadow. Their wings touched, making a dark lace that the crimson sea splashed.

Amma and I had walked up the gangplank in Bombay harbor, and minutes later, it seemed, our ship in a jangle of voices broke free of solid land. I stood on tiptoe next to amma, tall as her elbow, as she pulled out a little white handkerchief edged with Brussels lace that had belonged to her dead mother and wiped her eyes.

"We're off," she whispered, "we've left nadu behind."

Afloat on the Arabian Sea, I searched for a dip in water, a dart of darkness, something that might turn into a tunnel so I could slip back into the Tiruvella house lost to me.

Beyond the deck the waters rose, crisp and slashed and crimson, the wind rested and the waters turned to molten silk that bobbed and wrinkled.

I could have stood there forever staring at the sea, my head filled with voices.

But amma was bearing down on me. She put out her hand to draw me back, but I shook my head hard and stood there, my eyes filled with the sea.

The sea was darker now, in patches, as if the fire had cooled, making ash out of its own mysterious substance.

"Didn't you hear me?"

Amma's hand was on my elbow, pulling me.

I knew she would not give up. I belonged to her. I was her only child. I shut my eyes. I wanted the sea to be painted on the inside of my eyelids so I could take it with me. I tried to hold my breath, but I felt it come out in spurts.

I prayed for strength to leap into the sea, become a water child, an amphibious thing, a silver flying fish. Schools of them had flapped and slipped by in the sea a few days after we set out from Bombay harbour, darting glistening things, at ease in air and water, midway creatures, beholden to no one.

"Go with God," grandfather Kuruvilla had said when he blessed me on parting.

Surely this was God, this flaming sea.

"Aaoiu, enda devame." I heard amma draw in her breath as she stared at the sea. Her hand tightened on my shoulder. We were travelling by sea during the Suez Canal trouble, and often ships were burnt by bombs dropped onto the waters.

But this was sun that turned the sea the color of molten brass and made the air rise in peaks of magenta and scarlet. Not bombs but the sea itself as the sun played on it.

Amma drew me into a lounge of sofa and chairs.

"Sit down, mol. Here is a birthday present for you." She laid a flat brown package on the table. I picked it up and pulled apart the brown packing paper.

Children's Coloring Book, it said in big letters and, under that, the intials CLS for Christian Literature Society.

It had shiny covers in red and green. It was wider than my two hands placed side by side. Wider than my grandmother Mariamma's palmyra fan, the one she used on hot days when the earth grew sticky and damp and the sky turned the color of elephant hide.

I flipped open the book and ever so slowly stared at the first picture.

It was done in bold black hand, almost like a woodcut. It showed a very old man. He looked oddly familiar. I felt I had known him all of my natural life.

I put out my hand and the paper felt cold, as if it had been whirred about in a storm. I ran my finger over the old man's robe. It was bent under him as he worked his way over heavy rocks. His beard was flung to one side by the wind. He had a long strong nose and over his shoulders was a funny sack.

I glanced up quickly at amma and saw that she was content now that I had actually opened the gift.

"Ilya thought you would like the book," amma said as she turned away. "He thought it would help you learn the Bible verses by heart."

When I put out my finger to touch what I saw, my finger felt funny, as if a dragon had rubbed my skin all over with its gossamer wing.

My finger did what it was meant to do, tracing that old man's body, from his feet covered in rough sandals made of skins, up past his knees, to that bent head.

Down below the picture, in bold print, someone had written out these lines:

AND GOD SAID: TAKE NOW THY SON THINE ONLY ISAAC WHOM THOU LOVEST AND GET THEE INTO THE LAND OF MORIAH; AND OFFER HIM THERE FOR A BURNT OFFERING UPON ONE OF THE MOUNTAINS WHICH I WILL TELL THEE OF. GENESIS 22:2

I looked more closely at the sack. It quivered under my eyes. I could not bring myself to touch it.

I could see now that what I had thought was a sack was really a child, about my age, flung over Abraham's shoulder. The boy's back was humped like a tortoise.

The old man had a staff in one hand, and its tip was pointed firmly at the sun. In his other hand he held a burning brand. There was a knife stuck in his waist band. His foot was firmly on the lowest rock of the mountain.

And Isaac, his body down to his father's shoulder, was staring up at me. I felt something bubbling up in me. I wanted to tear Isaac off the page and fling him upright. Yell in his ear, "Run away, silly boy. Why lie there like a heap of ash?"

Amma had told me that Sarah, his mother, was seventy when Isaac was born. So if Abraham was seventy-five, grandfather Kuruvilla's age, how quick could he run? Surely Isaac could escape? And why didn't Sarah go out there to help her only child, her Isaac? She should have stood up and yelled at the patriarch, brandished her rolling pin.

I sat there, staring at the book, trying to imagine the missing Sarah. I dressed her in a blue sari, the color that the girl who was Virgin Mary wore in our Christmas pageant.

I made her run as best she could, up the side of Moriah Mountain to help her only child.

That night, in the cabin I shared with amma, I lay on the bottom bunk and opened up the coloring book again. The lamplight was soft on the book, on the white sheets, on the green blankets that the attendant had folded up and hung over the edge of the bed. I waited till I thought amma was asleep, and then I pulled out the crayons I had brought with me. My hand curled around the orange crayon. It was bright as a love apple fruit. Shining and hard. I picked it up and set it to the page. I had meant to color in the sun but instead, without knowing it, my hand moved to the tunic Isaac was wearing.

I colored it in, the brilliant glowing colors of night fires, of blood that lay under the woodcutter's axe. I colored in the wood on his back till those brands started burning and Isaac, with huge dark eyes staring into mine, turned into a burnt offering.

I must have made an odd sound because amma leaned over the edge of the bunk and saw me. She slipped down quick and quiet and held me in her arms. I buried my neck in the space between her breasts. I could smell the mix of talcum powder and sweat and Chanel No 5 she had dabbed on specially for my birthday.

"What is it? Tell me, child. Tell me."

But my eyes were filled with tears and no words came out of my mouth. I held out my right hand, the orange crayon stuck to it, making a wound.

She stared at it, her eyes straying to Isaac's body with the harsh, tearing lines across it. She put out her hand and gently eased my fist open.

"There, you're not sick, are you, child? Here, open up your hand. You're trembling."

Her hand was cold as she prised my fingers apart, one by one, and freed me of the orange pencil. Then she started to sing.

In the lamplight amma's hands had a life of their own, and as she sang they fluttered, two brown birds tied to her body. I could see her in the mirror behind me, I could see me small and squat in my white dress, staring at her. The sheets were all about me making a nest. And behind me was the porthole filled with indigo water. Dark water with a ripple of moonlight.

After amma was asleep she came to me, a child my size and shape. I knew instantly who she was. The stone-eating girl. She flew in through the open porthole. Her skin was as dark as a jamun fruit. She had a pair of wings that grew through her shoulder blades.

They looked just like chicken wings but were brown streaked with gold and strong enough to let her blow in through the porthole.

She squatted next to me in a pool of light and I felt her skin with my fingers and knew that she had a little bump by the back of her knee just like I did.

With cracking sounds like knuckles make, fretting under skin, she broke off her wings and set them at my feet.

I knew she would not mind if I touched her broken wings.

When she opened her mouth no words came, just sharp hot sounds like stones rattling. She had picked up stones from the wellside and popped them into her mouth. She swallowed the stones even though it hurt her insides.

The stones made words for things she couldn't say.

The girl with wings had no mother or father or grandfather or cousin. She was fierce and free.

The sun was her father, the moon was her mother, the stars were her brothers and sisters.

The stone-eating girl squatted right by me and made me look out the porthole. I saw the midnight waters of the great sea on which we were afloat. But right under the porthole I saw a patch of something. It looked just like an oil slick.

Noke noke, look look, the stone-eating girl tapped on my shoulders to make me look. But I turned my eyes away. I did not want to see the dark shadow at the edge of the boat. I was relieved when a wave came in through the open porthole.

Later, I looked out in search of an oil slick. Amma had pointed out the oil slicks to me. The S. S. Jehangir had to be careful because of bombs that could be dropped on oil tankers.

But this was neither an oil slick nor a crater made by a bomb. It was dark sea shape, an old man mountain with a child tied to his back.

And the child, its tunic fluttering like a girl's skirt, was staring up at me.

I had seen Moriah Mountain. On special feast days the children put on a pageant in Tiruvella's village church. One Sunday the pageant needed a mountain, and Bhaskaran the cowherd was persuaded to bring piles of wood from the jackfruit tree that was cut down by the wellside. He stacked the wood in the courtyard of the church and covered the rough triangle with old cloth. This was Mount Moriah, against which the scene of the sacrifice of Isaac was to be acted.

During the pageant, when ayah's youngest son was tied to an old man's back and old man Kariap started plodding toward the rickety mountain, I bit my lip so hard it started to bleed. I could not bear to hear the screams of the little child when the knife ayah had borrowed from our kitchen was polished.

Only when I saw the crude mask of God slip from the face of the headwaiter in the local restaurant did I let go of my ears and thrust my elbow hard into Cousin Sosa's knee. "Meena, you're a crybaby," she hissed.

Suddenly, to wild clapping and the burst of song, little Mohan shot free of his dirty binding clothes and ran toward his mother. As ayah lifted him up she was trembling with pride.

That night as grandfather Kuruvilla read out the sacrifice of Isaac from the Bible, the story of an aged father who was willing to kill his young son in response to God's command, I buried my head in ayah's sleeve and drank in the stale sweat from her armpit. It comforted me, flesh that I could hold onto. If grandmother Kunju had not died so soon and I could still talk to her, would she help me understand the cruelty of that story? And what of Sarah, Isaac's mother? Why didn't she rush out and wave her fists at Abraham and cry out: You foolish, impenitent old man! Time for you to lie still in your grave. Lie utterly still covered by a heap of stones. For you there is no escape.

23. *Dictionary of Desire*

As grandfather Kuruvilla lay dying, everything fled from my head: house, garden, red hills, blue sky. He lay on his bed and the veins in his heart grew hard. His arteries were clogged with sea salt.

He grew delirious:

Mahatma Gandhi save our nation! Lord Mountbatten, let my people go!
Burn the wild grass at the garden's edge!
Kunju, Kunju where are you, why did you fly from me?
Jesus, take this cup from me.

His mouth grew dry. They fed him coconut water in a silver spoon, pumped morphine into his veins.

I wanted him to die.

Breath rattled in his throat. Dry seeds in a green pod, a tiny mongoose striped electric white, striking the ancient cobra.

They laid him out on the bench set out in the wild grass behind his library, stripped his clothes off, poured water over his chest. The ribs beat against each other. The skin fizzled like a live thing. His nails were yellow on his feet, his head was large, almost bald with all the pain he had gone through. They did not trim his nails. His stomach was sunken and down below I stared, shut my eyes.

They carried him into the house, laid him on the rosewood bed. The candles at his head and feet made pools of light. I bent over, saw the sun gleaming. The moon tilted in the dark sky behind the well.

The coffin, when they carried it down the steps, tilted and threatened to hang in the air. One of the men carrying it had one leg shorter than the other, no not Chandran. Someone else. A stout man in a fine white dhoti, who almost slipped. I was standing by one of the pillars of the veranda. I saw the black box—all night I had heard them hammering at it, stitching in the silk lining with little pins— tremble and slip.

When they hoisted the coffin down the red road that leads to the front gate, under the branches of the incense tree, I clambered into the branches. I let the leaves brush over me. I hung upside down like a night owl.

Then I opened my eyes so huge the sun would pour into me, make me not see. It has taken a lifetime to stare into the burnt hole in myself, to learn to see.

Forty days after he was buried, the Tiruvella house was cleaned with water. A ritual of passage. Streams of water poured out of the buckets borne by Bhaskaran the cowherd and by men whose faces I can no longer see. Buckets drawn from the well by the bitter lemon tree, buckets filled with water from a tap amma had installed by the outer wall of the house.

Water blossomed over the tiled floor, kissed the legs of the writing desk in the library. Mud poured over the threshold. An ancient woman, with snowy locks and skin falling off her bones, crawled through the mud, her white sari splattered with roses of filth: grandmother Kunju's cousin. She waved at me.

The moveable parts of the household, rosewood mirrors that grandmother Kunju had received as part of her dowry, the teak boxes inlaid with ivory, the pewter pitchers, the metal trunks, had all been carried out and stood on the wild grass by the bamboo grove. A household without walls, furniture burnt by sunlight.

Barefoot I stepped into grandfather's library. I saw a bookshelf lined with dusty cloth-covered books and, propped in front, a framed picture: all that Gandhi, grandfather Kuruvilla's mentor, had possessed at the time of his death. A pair of bent wire spectacles, wooden clogs, a simple charka, a folded dhoti. Next to the picture was a book flat on its back. As I picked it up a yellowed slip of paper fell out. It was in a clear upright hand I recognised as belonging to my grandmother Kunju. A note she made to her self, household reminders:

Soap for washing 10 annas
Kitchen rag 5 annas
A pot of jaggery (to be taken to Sumati's house)

On the flyleaf, in the same clear hand as the note, was grandfather's name.

From the desk I picked up a pen and stared at it. *"Pena,"* I whispered, using the Malayalam word. Had my grandmother Kunju used that pen too?

I let the pen rest on my palm. I was twelve years old, my grandfather was buried. I set my notebook on my thighs and started writing. First I wrote words in English, the language of my common use, the language I loved. I made a string of words in my best hand so that ever after I would be able to read it:

> *Girl   Book   Stone   Tree*

There were spaces between each of the words. I was glad I could not hear amma, that she would not call me. I stared at the words I had made. Soon other words rushed in, and barely thinking, I put down words in Malayalam, my mother tongue, the language of my dreams, and under it a string of words in Arabic, translating the first two, and then in French, which became for me a language of visible accomplishment. At home only my father and I could read French.

As I wrote I became someone else, not a girl whose grandfather had just died, a girl whose mother was in mourning. The writing freed me. I imagined the stone-eating girl I had seen long ago, listening to me as I read out the words.

> | *Girl* | *Book* | *Stone* | *Tree* |
> |---|---|---|---|
> | *Penne* | *Pusthakam* | *Kalu* | *Maram* |
> | *Bint* | *Kitab* | *Hajar* | *Shajara* |
> | *Fille* | *Livre* | *Pierre* | *Arbre* |

In bits and pieces, without connectives, relying on the blank spaces between the words to set up an ethereal terrain, I composed a dictionary of desire.

I wrote in clear upright hand, conscious that the page next to it had been torn out and bore the jagged markings of rice paper that has been mutilated.

I had torn out that page, on a hot night on a ship when I was five years old and amma and I were crossing the Arabian Sea. I had crumbled up the page in my fingers, sticky with salt spray, and flung the white, shapeless thing into the waves.

Just as I did in grandfather's study, after I finished writing I shut my eyes tight. Then I shut the notebook. The paper made a quiet thud, rice paper knocking against itself.

It was the very last entry I would make in my notebook of white rice paper, my first notebook, a notebook with cardboard covers marked with the sun and the moon and the stars.

I heard amma calling me. How long she had been calling I could not tell for I had an ability to block things out when I was writing.

But now I heard her loud and clear, calling from the front room to come and help her shift grandmother Kunju's mirror.

"Come, mol, come quick," she cried. "I do not want Bhaskaran the cowherd to move this mirror. It was something your grandmother received as part of her dowry. Only the women of the house must touch it."

I set the book back on the shelf and walked out quickly, into the wild grass by the bamboo grove. I saw my mother shooing away the servants, her body bent with the weight of a great mirror she had covered with the rim of her sari. The top portion of that ancient glass was covered with a fine film of cotton, but the lower part reflected all that fell into the hold of light, stones, trees, clouds, and even my own feet as I stood there, arms outstretched, ready to help her.

I still do not know how it happened. But as it passed between us, grandmother's mirror slipped and broke on black granite, the silver of its face shattered into a thousand and one pieces.

And each of those fragments, some still buried in red soil, will tell its own tale.

24. *Book of Childhood*

*T*here was a dark door to grandfather's library.

Made of wood from the jackfruit tree. Varnished the color of burnt leaf.

Breath stops when I think of that door.

A child in a white dress walked in the door, a while later a child walked out. Her eyes were burnt holes for the sun to shine through.

I do not like to say I.

I do not like to say I picked up my skirts and skipped into that doorway. For then I would be forced to say: sometime later I came out. Memory knows but knowing cannot remember.

She not I. Not I, not I.

What happened in grandfather Kuruvilla's library me makes float.

No before, no after.

No up, down, down, up.

Who will save me?

Who will save Meena mol?

Will fishing nets turn parachutes, sail homeward?

She doesn't walk on water like Jesus or Gandhi, she's suspended on it, eyes shut, flesh dressed in a pink costume, a circus girl.

Bones poking up through skin.

How could I speak to Cousin Koshy?

I felt as if I were pressing my bumpy nose against glass, staring in the way Cousin Koshy and I stared at the blowfish, an ugly thing with prickles out in the Kochi aquarium.

Cousin Koshy and I leapt up and down, yelled, put our fingers in our ears and made rude faces till ayah stopped us.

But the fish didn't hear. It was quite apart in its glass cage, floating in that odd, prickly body.

I walked slowly out of the library. Dress mussed up and wet.

I felt grandfather Kuruvilla's hand on my thigh. His hand was dark, with flecked hairs at the wrist.

The hairs were pure white like the cabbage butterfly's wings.

I floated toward the kitchen. Held onto the door and stared in. I could not cross into the kitchen, let go of the door, let my feet touch the dark red tiles of the kitchen.

I wanted to hide inside your sari, amma, let the soft pleats drape about me, make me vanish. Deep inside your sari, no one could touch me.

There you were, hand bound in a white kitchen towel, stirring the pot filled with sliced guavas and figs.

Slowly, slowly you stirred, adding the rosewater and the crushed almonds. Your hand moved in the moist air, a phantom thing, wrist and fingers covered in cotton to stop the bubbling fruit from splattering.

Amma, I cried, but no sounds came out of my mouth.

Amma, noke, noke, nyan a, nyan a.

Look, look, it's I, it's I.

"Sh sh, Meena. Sh sh. Can't you see what I am doing? Do you want the hot fruit to splatter?"

Day after day I crouched by the wellside, forcing myself to stare at the sun. When the sun was bright in the palm tree that stood by the well, the clouds around blew so swift, it hurt to breathe.

I made my eyes huge so the sun could pour through. I knew this could make me blind.

Blind like the old man cast out from the circus, who sat under the banyan tree. All through the day he crouched under the tree, and the parrots leapt and cried above him, made droppings. People put rice in his bowl, threw a few paise his way.

Sometimes parrot droppings landed in his rice bowl. Sometimes the coins fell on his bandaged feet.

"Does he have leprosy?"

Ayah shook her head.

"Is that why his legs are bandaged?"

"Perhaps he has a cut that doesn't heal," Ayah said. "Perhaps he has no money to buy chappals."

I repeated all this to grandfather Kuruvilla as he sat in his rattan chair with the great arms. The arms were as long as his legs would reach. Grandmother Kunju's father had bought the chair from the British Resident. Sometimes when he was at rest, sipping a cup of buttermilk with mint, grandfather Kuruvilla raised his legs, set them on the arms. His dhoti made a white flag that covered the chair.

"We must get the poor man some chappals," grandfather said. Bhaskaran the cowherd heard him shout, "Go get chappals, measure them."

When Bhaskaran brought back chappals with tyre tread under them, heavy leather on top, grandfather made him run back, exchange them for lighter chappals with leather soles.

"Come, mol, we'll pay a visit to the banyan tree."

We knelt by the old man. His eyes were filled with sores. His legs lay stiff in white bandages. Grandfather laid the chappals by him.

"For you, to walk with."

The old man stared ahead. He put out his hand. It had scars on it, the size of coins. As if bubbles of coconut oil had splattered, burnt the skin. Grandfather took the hand, held it.

The old man did not flinch.

That night grandfather drew me onto his knee. He told me about Jesus walking on water.

"The disciples who were in a boat saw Jesus. At first they could not tell his body apart from the mist and the rain. His robes were flowing like dark water. The fish of the sea tumbled and danced, phosphorescent streaks in the sky. The feet of the Lord were not visible.

"Do not tell others," Jesus commanded. "I have not yet ascended into heaven."

"Why a secret?"

"Others wouldn't understand. It was between them only. Some things are like that."

Grandfather passed his hand gently over my head. Then touched the hem of my dress, ran his thumb lightly over the embroidered hem. I could not help shivering a little.

"It was Partition time. India and Pakistan were splitting apart. Imagine that, child, one country torn into two. Like taking a knife and cutting a body in half. Thank God you were born after all that.

"When the trains came from Pakistan they were piled high with corpses. Sometimes a child cried out under the pile of clothing. Those who were searching for living souls scurried under the arms and legs and soiled blankets, trying to prise them out.

"Once there was a baby killed by a knife wound, its mouth still fixed to the amma's breast. A rosy mouth and head. The amma had covered her own head with rags. She didn't want the light to touch her own eyes. She didn't want to see."

I buried my face in my arms. I don't think grandfather noticed.

"Did grandmother Kunju see Gandhi?"

He nodded and turned away. I saw his fists clench on the table.

"Gandhi wanted to walk from one end of India to the other, a padayatra. One must walk on foot over the earth's surface, to know it is sacred; touch the ground with one's feet. Gandhi walked into refugee camps. The mothers who had seen so much killing had eyes like bits of slate. They crouched over empty cooking pots. There were small children drinking water from the gutters. Piles of waste and scraps of food side by side."

As grandfather went on talking I heard another voice in my ears. It sounded like the stone-eating girl.

She had spat out the stones in her stomach and her voice was free. Like shot silk her voice flowed through his words.

"The parrots were wild. They flew down from the banyan trees and pecked the children in the refugee camp. The parents were tired, several had already fainted. They could not stop the birds.

"When the birds heard Gandhi's footsteps—by this time he was a old man, worn out with his suffering—they swirled back up into the skies, swore never to hurt children again. Swore only to eat mango and chikoo.

"That's why parrots infest our chikoo trees. They chatter at dawn in the mango and chikoo trees telling of days in the refugee camps when they saw Gandhi.

"Gandhi's feet were bleeding with the dryness and the heat. A

woman bent and washed his feet. A woman like Marya Magdalene.
A fallen woman."

As grandfather spoke I saw the well, a girl with her spiky hair
floating in the indigo waters. A wellfrog nipping at her cheek.

Grandfather did not look at me. He went on.

"Gandhi swore he wouldn't eat till the great violence of the
British was eased. Till they left us to govern ourselves.

"We must govern ourselves. Self-governance. That's why I fast
on some days, do not take food."

Then he made me lean forward, touch the edge of his khadi dhoti.

"Feel it, Meena. This cloth is like sea salt. It is common, made
by ordinary hands, available to all. To this day I will not wear
mill cloth."

He raised me up in his arms so I could touch the spinning wheel
he had used in the days he was a follower of Gandhi and lived in
Sabermati ashram.

"To see Gandhi walk over the dusty roads, his white clothes flying, that was a vision. People came out of their house and brought
rice and dal and water for us. It was the start of the Salt March."

Three seas wrap us round on the southern shore. The Arabian Sea,
the Indian Ocean, the Bay of Bengal. That night in my bed I dreamt
of Jesus and Gandhi. They were walking on the three seas at such
great speed, they floated over the skin of water.

Gandhi was in light clothing, Jesus in dark. Arms linked, they
strolled through the waves. Sometimes they laughed and talked.
Sometimes they wept. Sometimes they were surrounded by silence.
Silence shone around them.

All about them boats were capsizing. Tiny fishing boats that set
out at dawn from the Cape, nets empty, caked with salt.

On the shore ammas and babies waited. The babies were hungry.
They sucked their fists and wailed. In my dream a baby was held by
an old woman. Her white hair blew. Wind conspired with the mist to
cover over the baby's throat and face, turning it into a headless thing.

They stood on the shore watching the empty fishing boats return.

There was a headless baby Jesus. To see him I had to make a special
trip with ayah to the St. Anthanasius Church on the other side of the
main road. I loved to touch the smooth wood in the Virgin's sari,
feel the black almond of her eyes, then move to the creased bubbly

wood next to her neck and the stump where someone cut off the baby's head.

How sad the Virgin's eyes were. And the baby? Who could tell? He had lost his head. The wood was worn smooth around his neck. Just a puddle of flesh there, like a real baby.

"They didn't cut it off, silly. Can you imagine Christians like us cutting off the baby Jesus' head?"

"Then what?"

"Then what. Foolish Meena mol, it fell off."

I didn't believe ayah. I found a better argument. Why get the baby's head and not the Virgin's?

"Because the wood was damp. You know how babies get wet all the time. Well, it's the same with baby Jesus. Look."

Ayah took my fingers, made me feel the tiny wormholes in the wood of the neck.

Sometimes amma had to go to St. Athanasius' for a funeral or baptism. Some of our own cousins had married into the Jacobite Church, so there were chances for us to visit.

Once I asked amma why the Virgin's baby was so old he lost his head.

"Don't worry about things like that, Meena," amma replied. There was a clarity in her voice that made me believe her.

"Jesus being God can't really be made into a statue or picture. And his having a head or not is beside the point."

Then amma's face took on a stern look as if she were repeating something she had learnt by heart.

"In our Mar Thoma Church we have no images of God. You're old enough to understand all this. It was your great-great-great-great-grandfather who was the radical reformer."

She shut her eyes and breathed heavily, unsure about how many "great"s she should stumble over. Her BA in Indian history from Madras University offered little help.

"Abraham Malpan, our ancestor from your grandfather Kuruvilla's side, bolted the doors of the church to the Patriarch visiting from Antioch. So that our people would not worship graven images, he took all the icons he could find, Virgins, childs."

She paused at the last word, worried in case I was overly affected by the headless baby and would not take what she was saying in the right spirit. She sighed a little, determined to go.

"He took Virgins, childs, horsemen, etcetera and threw them into the Pamba River."

Then amma drew her sari tight about her, made a pouty face as she did when faced with something she didn't care for. Her hands trembled a little as they held onto the sari's edge and this surprised me.

Was amma frightened by all this?

I closed my eyes and imagined the tiny head broken off baby Jesus floating in the black water. Now all that was left was a neck on squat shoulders, attached to a plump torso riddled with wormholes; he sat draped in his morose Virgin amma's sari. I made up lines, writing myself into the scene. Scribbled the whole thing in my notebook.

A squat, little quatrain.

Meena mol, who saw a Headless Baby
in Mar Athanasius' Church.
What is your name?
How do you do? Who are you?

I knew they were not lines of real poetry. Like the poems of Kumaran Asan. Like the English poem that grandmother Kunju knew by heart concerning a girl called Lucy Gray, who strolled to the middle of a bridge and vanished. Pouf, that was it! A few footprints on the bridge, then nothing.

A thought kept crawling through my head. Like a water snake in a well curled over itself, tail stuck in its jaw. I wrote it down to save myself from thinking it over and over again: *Meena mol, what is your name? Who are you?*

I was the girl who fell through a dark door.

Crawled on hands and knees through the orchid patch. Tore her silk dress of delicate shadow work on sharp stones, sticks, buried her head in the scarred roots of the orchids, dug deeper, found a big rat hole and stuck in her head till she could scarcely breathe.

I turned myself into a headless thing.

There were droplets of blood on my arms and thighs, from thorns and torn stalks, tiny jewels of disaster.

I let the droplets of fresh blood hang there on all the brown skin.

The orchids were rosy with butterflies.

I would have given anything to turn into a butterfly: copulate and die, become nothing but the rushing of wing, freed of my wet, dirt-covered body.

But thoughts I had of vanishing fled into moist air.

Closer and closer he edged, my cousin Koshy, net cobbled together with bits of mosquito netting, its bamboo rod held at an impossible angle.

Cousin Koshy and I had by-hearted butterfly names from a book Uncle Itty had brought home. I kept the butterfly names in my head when after years of home tutors, I was put into school for three months and made to learn the perfections of penmanship, the details of dictation.

> *Shobha is a good girl.*
> *Sunil is a good boy.*
> *Sunil weighs ninety pounds.*
> *What do you think Shobha eats?*

When such inanities came my way, I stared out of the school window and mused on the slow scrawl of butterflies in the afternoon sky, fleeing sweet-scented bushes as Cousin Koshy, resolute as a scribe, moved; his net cobbled together with bits of mesh the cook had provided, his hand etching syllables of a script no one would ever decipher as butterflies with the loveliest of names, Blue Morpho, Sleepy Orange, Cloudless Sulphur, moved high, higher, perpetually out of reach.

Koshy and I had grown up together. Together we would stoop and blow into the tiny holes in the earth, a huff and a puff and out it came, the dark and squiggling *kuriaana*.

I had learnt the phrase "A huff and a puff" from the Three Pigs' story that amma read to me over and over at my request, when we were far from ayah and she had to put me to bed. The phrase stayed with me. I shivered when I heard the Wolf's threat: "A huff and a puff and I'll blow your house in!"

"Meena, where O where, Meena? I know you are hidden somewhere," Koshy cried out in a soft voice, as if he knew I was scared. "Come help me catch butterflies."

Face streaked with dirt, I poked my head out of the earth. I liked it that Cousin Koshy needed my help for the impossible task of butterfly-catching.

Three months and two inches taller than me, stout in the beam and sturdy of soul, my cousin did not know how much I relied on him.

Unlike me, he knew exactly who he was and where he came from. And when he wasn't in boarding school in Bangalore, or home with me for the long summers, he lived with his parents in a white house by the sea.

It turns into dream. Each afternoon the house by the sea shone as if water had risen in great waves through it. Sunlight and sand swept onto the veranda and flowed into the inner rooms, the walls painted a cool alabaster color.

There was a small pool of water in the courtyard fringed by ferns and orchids, and a mulberry tree as in grandfather Kuruvilla's house, with tiny sleeping silkworms. Inside, the new house Uncle Itty and Aunt Amu had built at great cost had ceiling fans the color of dried palmyra leaves, and they moved with a slow creak-creak sound; there were water faucets the molten color of iron, instead of the brass vessels with spouts we used in our grandparents' house; gleaming power points for all the electrical fixtures, and shades of Venetian glass on the lamps that Uncle Itty had imported from Europe.

There was no telephone. No one had telephones. Instead there was the man on horseback who rode across the sands with messages for Uncle Itty. When he wasn't riding across sand on the black horse Sundar, the horseman was in the stables, reaching up for buckets, warm water to scrub the horses with.

I loved to visit the house by the sea. All afternoon Koshy and I would braid the tall reeds that grew at the edge of the sands on the southern shore. It hurt our hands but we persevered. We drew the reeds together, matted them tight as we had watched the gardener do in the lower garden by the pepper vines on Kozencheri veliappechan's property. When we finished braiding the reeds with all their speckles of bloodthirsty brown, we wiped our sore hands and peered in and out of the make-believe house, flapping our arms like wild geese.

"You can't catch me, boo hoo hoo!" I yelled.

"A huff and a puff!" he cried, my Cousin Koshy.

The sea wind blew our hair in our faces. We came out, faces

smeared with wet sand and hair, laughing. Two wild creatures at the sea's edge.

"Come Meena, come Koshy," Aunt Amu called out from a great distance. Her voice was sifted by the wind, the syllables fading as seaweed in sunlight.

"It's teatime. I have sweet rolls and figs for you."

She waited patiently as we raced past the man on horseback galloping into the distance where the buildings of the town rose. We stamped the sand off our feet, washed out hands and face with Pears Soap that sat in the tiny ivory-colored bowl, fluted in a shell shape. After tea, I wanted to be alone, I wanted to be quiet. I wondered if the horseman would race back with a letter for us from appa.

Appa had travelled to Bombay, then caught a ship to cross the waters and reach Africa. I squinted across the waters. I knew that centuries ago sailors had come to our land from as far away as Europe and Arabia and Africa. They carried gold, silver, coral, malabathrum in the hollow ribs of their ships. They carried peacocks and birds of rare plumage, monkeys, pythons, alligators. What was malabathrum? I decided to ask Cousin Koshy. He would have learnt about it in boarding school, he would know.

I closed my eyes and imagined appa in his neatly tailored pinstripe shirt on the decks of a white ship. The ship was sailing across the Indian Ocean. There were waves of bright indigo rising on the prow of the ship. Appa's figure grew tiny, he was holding his hand above his head to screen his face from the sun's heat. He was trying at the same time to wave to us, amma and me. He knew we were visiting the white house by the sea.

Those far from us, being in no place at all, see us ever present on the curved surface of the globe, in the mind's eye. Still, for my part, I could not bear appa so far away and all alone, so I moved to the other side of the porch. From this side I could see the rock with the red and white stripes of the lighthouse and, a little beyond it, a tiny mound in the pale gray of the ocean, an island filled with mist.

The island of the broken palace I had heard of since I was very little. Kalu Island filled with wild goats and vines and old women, it was said, who wander about half naked.

"Not that any one cares," Aunt Amu had assured me, "they are so very old and so it doesn't matter. They wander around collecting twigs and dry grasses for fires. Some of them sleep in the holes in the walls and on the floors of the emptied out rooms of the ruined palace."

"Meena mol, I'll take you and this young man for a picnic," Uncle Itty promised. "When you've had enough of your adventures," and he laughed, a great laugh that was almost like a cough, the smoke from his perpetual cheroot scenting the air. I shifted around on the porch uneasily. My feet felt like two bits of heavy lead, my arms more weighty than granite. I wanted to live in one place forever. I did not want to go anywhere and have adventures.

Then I heard a high-pitched voice. "Meena, Meena!" It was Cousin Koshy. He was calling me to the little house on the sands, the waves would soon tear down. The wind in my hair, I raced out to him.

Already I had many houses in my life, but I loved best our house of reeds, an offering to the sea, white sands flattened around it, herons in the polished sands, elegant as dancers, picking up their pointed claws, running water so delicate a breath could have clouded it.

25. *Indigo Ink*

A dream clung to me like a clot of blood. It hardened into stone and I wanted to etch the map of my life into it: the west coast of India, the east coast of Africa, the Indian Ocean with its foamy points of waves.

But the dream faded into pallor, white on white embossed onto a handloomed handkerchief, the square starched and ironed and folded into a child's pocket.

In the heat of midsummer the child has a nosebleed and the handkerchief is pulled out hastily, used to blot the blood, then crushed back into the pocket.

The stain that penetrates the embossed patterning never quite vanishes. The fabric seems changed forever.

Who can dip it in blue, hang it on the line in the heat of a Kerala day, so the color will revive, so butterflies swarm to the ivory-colored square, soft with the well water it was first washed in? What mercy there?

Closing the book of childhood I feel the dream dissolve into the dark waters that surround the island of Manhattan, passing away with the burnt fragments of flesh, mess of plastics and papers, torn wood and wire and stone. And above us all, in the north winds, the souls of the dead, wings tipped with fire, still whirling.

In my dream there is a house with two rooms. One and the other. Just large enough to hold what they must, two or three people, a mat on the floor, a chair, a simple wooden bed. The rooms are dark in spite of opening onto a veranda that runs the length of the house. The windows are painted green, shuttered, bungalow style.

Someone calls from the other room. A woman with white hair, curly, drawn back in a bun. Strands blow about her neck. Her face is turned from me. Something leaps in my ribs when I hear her voice.

"*Quick, he is going. Quick, come quick.*"

I enter the room. He lies on his side, his eyes huge in his head. I kneel by his side. I hardly recognise him. I do not know what comes over me.

"Bless me," I whisper.

I do not know where these words come from. But it's all I want from him. His eyes are huge, shining in his emaciated flesh. His clothes are white and shimmer. I want to get this over with before mother enters.

Bless me, Grandfather.

With great effort he passes his hand over my head. I feel his fingertips, dry breath, a light breeze over bleached paddy stalks in the hilly region where he was born.

Now he lies on his back, breathing heavily. The shutters over the window stir a little. In the dream I wear a cotton sari. A sari washed over so many times the threads are frayed. At times the cloth feels damp, at times the cloth is hot and dry as an iron. My legs are shaking.

My right hand is closed over something hot and hard.

A stone prised free from the ground where I was born. Shaped like a ear, it fits perfectly into my palm. My sweat makes the stone moist.

The dream repeats. Again there are two rooms, each rather dark, and a brilliant veranda. A small modest house I have seen before. I cannot be in both rooms at the same time, but feel I need to.

As I kneel on the cold floor, he reaches out to me.

I force myself to bend to kiss him and his lips find my forehead, right by the hairline. He is warm with the fever inside him. His lips brush my skin, my hair as if a life depended on it.

I pull myself away just as amma enters the room. Her sari is pulled tight about her waist. She has an anxious look. I can see that the powder she set to her cheeks is fading. Her skin shows through. She pretends she doesn't see me.

She makes straight for the figure on the bed.

Something funny happens in the dream as amma reaches him. I am no longer by the bed. I am flat on the earth, between the two tracks of a train line. The tracks run through a red gorge with steep sides. The spokes of the metal wheels grind closer, the sunlight on the parallel tracks make me blind. My eyes are holes.

Everything shakes. A screen of light made up of tiny particles moves as if during a ritual dance of warriors, silk threads were chopped into fragments in the breeze. I have a dim awareness that I will see only what I can hold, a fraction at a time, as if the morsels of the visible were cut with a silver sword: a bit of the red tiled floor, the corner of a wooden pallet, elbow, wrist, curve of dark throat that gleams and vanishes.

The bed starts to dissolve as if the atoms that composed it, the wood, the white sheets, even the flesh and blood of the emaciated man were all blown by a great wind, the boundaries of form sifting.

Things clarify. A man tall and gaunt, ready to die, wrapped in white muslin.

"Marya, Mary mol," I hear him cry out.

"You'll be a doctor. You will work in the service of India.

"You will do as Gandhi taught us, minister to the people.

"You'll cross the black waters.

"You will be a *yatrakari*, journey far away, as far as the Red Sea and the Thames, the Mississippi but always return to this land."

I see his hand flicker, dark as my own but with all the veins rising.

Suddenly I am no longer a woman of twenty-five.

I become a girl child, somewhat tall for her age, wearing a silk dress with tiny pink roses embroidered on the yoke. Grandfather grips my wrist and the dress turns damp.

His wrist has hairs on it, white with age, the color of pale butterfly wings.

When Cousin Koshy visited grandfather Kuruvilla's house, we used to catch cabbage butterflies, and on lazy Sunday afternoons we'd pin them to the corkboard the cook gave us. How bored we were on Sunday afternoons, after church, after the endless social rounds of luncheon and tea. But the mercy of associations, an amnesia of sorts, dark river water over which butterflies float, will not blot out what comes.

I struggle hard. I feel my wrist turn numb as I try to prise my flesh and bones loose of grandfather's grip.

Just then she enters. "Help me, help me," I plead. Using both her hands, she unlocks his fingers from their iron hold. But it takes up all her strength. The sari falls off her head. She has no face.

The dream starts to fade in response to a hurt I cannot name, my body the two wings of the black monarch butterfly, stretched over a crack in the earth.

The small house with the two rooms, the old woman with white hair who summons a young thing in a plain cotton sari, hair tied back, myself in this dream incarnation, all dissolve.

Mere moving accidents.

But why is grandfather dying in such a small house when he was laid out in the great house with the ravaged gardens I used to call home? And why a woman whose face I must not see?

What am I to her? Or she to me?

But perhaps dreams are not meant to be questioned like that, in a crude blunt way.

They rise in us, waves on an indigo sea, keeping us to a love that is always already there for those gone on, through hurt and harm, invisible presences that make us what we are.

What we are is flesh and bone, skin and blood and all the distances in between that mark the fierce palimpsest of need.

What we are is not readily tellable. We have instincts of loss, instincts of homecoming, a hovering tender thing, what a mother can do for a child passing her hand over that child's mouth, back, thighs. But something is altered beyond remedy.

I think of the sari made of pink silk worn by the warrior and poet the Rani of Kodamangalam as she set off to battle. On the sari were inscribed the names of the seventy saints and seventy-seven holy women and men who could protect her and her just cause.

When the Rani passed through fire the sari melted into her skin, so that even as she rode out of battle on her elephant and the conch shells blew to celebrate victory, the whole world could see that the warrior queen had changed in some way.

"Look at her hands," a child cried.

"Look at her breasts where the sari pallu rides up," a man yelled.

Grown women rubbed their lips and stared.

The letters inscribed in indigo ink on the sari she had worn for protection were burnt indelibly into her skin.

What allowed her to live out her life, made her what she was, was graphed in curving syllables over her woman's body.

But no one could read that script. The markings were bright as hairs in the elephant's tail, dots of pollen on the humming bird's claw, but no one could decipher them.

To be haunted by the illegible is the fate of those who have passed through fire and children who have been hurt beyond visible measure.

I have written what I could through the rips and tears in the dress I once wore, a shield for a small child's soul, silk stitched with shadow work in delicate rose, violet, and green.

Acknowledgments

FIGURE OF EIGHT

Before me on a wooden table are two portions of writing. One is a bound as a book, the other is a short stack of papers. They are a decade apart in the making. Lines by Emily Dickinson I first read in another country flicker and burn:

> *When that which is – and that which was –*
> *Apart – intrinsic – stand –*

When I was a child I would draw with a stick in the dirt. What did I draw? Rooms, seashores, even a pair of wings. After making the drawings I would run between them with my stick and join them in a ceaseless figure of eight. Then I would scuff it all up with my heels, or race through the markings to make them disappear. What I drew in the dirt, in the garden of my childhood survives only in memory. Now I draw on paper, syllables turned to words, lines, sentences. I need to make a figure of eight, stitch up the wound of time, close this book of days.

In 1998 as I was making the earliest notes for "Book of Childhood," after a long and painful illness that consumed him, my father died. As before, this work is dedicated to him and to my mother. To my sisters Anna in Tiruvella and Elsa in Chennai, my cousin Verghis Koshy in San Jose, my husband David Lelyveld and our children, Adam and Svati, my love and gratitude. To Adella Wasserstein, thank you for listening to me. And dear friends who helped me survive my days and nights, I couldn't have done it without you: Talal Asad, Gauri Viswanathan, Erika Duncan, Warren Neidich, Karen Malpede. And how can I forget my childhood friend Sarra Ibrahim Anis who on a hot day in June 2001, as we sat by the waters of the Potomac, drew a map of Khartoum for me, so I could learn to remember.

Thanks to students at the Graduate Center who, through our shared reflections on poetry, trauma and memory, have led me into new paths of reading and writing, especially Jennifer Griffiths, Sarah Claire Peacock Raymond, Ronaldo Wilson. And to my friends and colleagues Nancy Miller, Bella Brodzki, Louise DeSalvo.

At the Feminist Press my gratitude to Florence Howe, visionary editor and friend who more than a decade ago asked me to write the story of my life and then proceeded to guide me through the turbulent waves of memory. At the Feminist Press in its new incarnation, my thanks to Jean Casella, publisher, for her support of this project; and special thanks to Jocelyn Burrell, superb editor, unfazed by distances, who read my pages with care and understanding.

My thanks to the Centre for American Culture Studies at Columbia University where I was a writer in residence in 1988; to the PSC-CUNY Research Foundation for grants in 1989 and 1990. And closer in time, to the Fondation Ledig-Rowohlt for a 2001 residency at Château de Lavigny in Switzerland; to Hunter College for a 2002 Faculty Fellowship; to the Fulbright Foundation for a 2002–2003 senior scholar award allowing me to return to India; to Alastair Niven for his friendship and hospitality at Cumberland Lodge in the Great Park at Windsor, October 2002, where the last pages of this book were written.

Two chapters first appeared in somewhat different form in the following journals: "Home at the Edge of the World," *Connect*, inaugural issue, Fall 2000; "Lyric in a Time of Violence," *The Little Magazine*, 3:5–6, Winter 2002. The four short poems included in chapter 21 are an intrinsic portion of my book of poetry *Raw Silk* (Triquarterly Books/ Northwestern University Press, forthcoming 2004).

MA
New York City
July 4, 2003

MEMOIR AND AUTOBIOGRAPHY
from the Feminist Press at the City University of New York

Across Boundaries: The Journey of a South African Woman Leader by Mamphela Ramphele. $14.95 paper, $19.95 cloth.

Always from Somewhere Else: A Memoir of My Chilean Jewish Father by Marjorie Agosín. $11.95 paper. $18.95 cloth.

Among the White Moon Faces: An Asian-American Memoir of Homelands by Shirley Geok-lin Lim. $12.95 paper, $22.95 cloth.

Black and White Sat Down Together: Reminiscences of an NAACP Founder by Mary White Ovington. $10.95 paper, $19.95 cloth.

Cast Me Out If You Will: Stories and Memoir by Lalithambika Antherjanam. $11.95 paper, $28.00 cloth.

Changing Lives: Life Stories of Asian Pioneers in Women's Studies edited by the Committee on Women's Studies in Asia. $10.95 paper, $29.95 cloth.

Come Out the Wilderness: Memoir of a Black Woman Artist by Estella Conwill Májozo. $14.95 paper, $21.95 cloth.

A Cross and a Star: Memoirs of a Jewish Girl in Chile by Marjorie Agosín. $13.95 paper.

A Day at a Time: The Diary Literature of American Women Writers from 1764 to the Present edited by Marjo Culley. $16.95 paper.

Fault Lines by Meena Alexander. $16.95 paper.

Juggling: A Memoir of Work, Family, and Feminism by Jane S. Gould. $17.95 paper, $37.00 cloth.

Life Prints: A Memoir of Healing and Discovery by Mary Grimley Mason. $14.95 paper, $19.95 cloth.

A Lifetime of Labor: The Autobiography of Alice H. Cook. $15.95 paper, $29.95 cloth.

Lion Woman's Legacy: An Armenian-American Memoir by Arlene Voski Avakian. $14.95 paper, $35.00 cloth.

The Little Locksmith by Katharine Butler Hathaway. $16.95 paper.

Magda's Daughter: A Hidden Child's Journey Home by Evi Blaikie. $16.95 paper.

Memories: My Life as an International Leader in Health, Suffrage, and Peace by Aletta H. Jacobs. $18.95 paper. $45.00 cloth.

These Modern Women: Autobiographical Essays from the Twenties edited by Elaine Showalter. $8.95 paper.

I Dwell in Possibility by Toni McNaron. $15.95 paper.

Songs My Mother Taught Me: Stories, Plays, and Memoir by Wakako Yamauchi. $14.95 paper, $35.00 cloth.

The Seasons: Death and Transfiguration by Jo Sinclair. $12.95 paper, $35.00 cloth.

Still Alive: A Holocaust Girlhood Remembered by Ruth Kluger. $14.95 paper, $24.50 cloth.

Streets: A Memoir of the Lower East Side by Bella Spewack. $10.95 paper, $19.95 cloth.

Under the Rose: A Confession by Flavia Alaya. $15.95 paper, $29.95 cloth.

Vertigo by Louise DeSalvo. $15.95 paper.

Zulu Woman: The Life Story of Christina Sibiya by Rebecca Hourwich Reyer. $15.95 paper, $45.00 cloth.

To receive a free catalog of the Feminist Press's 200 titles, write or call the Feminist Press at the City University of New York, 365 Fifth Avenue, New York, NY 10016; phone: (212) 817-7920; fax: (212) 817-1593. Feminist Press books are available at bookstores or can be ordered directly at www.feministpress.org. Send check or money order (in U.S. dollars drawn on a U.S. bank) payable to the Feminist Press. Please add $4.00 shipping and handling for the first book and $1.00 for each additional book. VISA, MasterCard, and American Express are accepted for telephone and secure Internet orders. Prices subject to change.